THE DEAD SEA SCROLLS
REDISCOVERED

THE DEAD SEA SCROLLS REDISCOVERED

AN UPDATED LOOK AT ONE OF ARCHAEOLOGY'S GREATEST MYSTERIES

STEPHEN HODGE

Seastone

BERKELEY, CALIFORNIA

Published by: Seastone, an imprint of Ulysses Press
　　　　　　P.O. Box 3440
　　　　　　Berkeley, CA 94703
　　　　　　www.ulyssespress.com

First published as *The Dead Sea Scrolls: An Introductory Guide* in Great Britain in 2002 by Judy Piatkus Publishers Ltd.

All quotations from *The Dead Sea Scrolls Rediscovered* unless otherwise stated are taken from Geza Vermes' *The Complete Dead Sea Scrolls in English* courtesy of Penguin Books

Library of Congress Cataloging-in-Publication Data

Hodge, Stephen, 1947-
　　　The Dead Sea scrolls rediscovered : an updated look at one of archaeology's greatest mysteries / Stephen Hodge.
　　　　　　p. cm.
Includes index.
　　　ISBN 1-56975-333-4 (alk. paper)
　　　1. Dead Sea scrolls.　2. Qumran community.　I. Title.

BM487 .H58　2003
296.1'55--dc21

2003044769

Printed in Canada by Transcontinental Printing

10　9　8　7　6　5　4　3　2　1

Cover design: Sarah Levin
Interior design: Leslie Henriques
Editorial and production staff: Kate Allen, Laura Brancella,
　　Lily Chou, Claire Chun, Lisa Kester
Index: Sayre Van Young
Maps: Rodney Paull

Distributed in the United States by Publishers Group West and in Canada by Raincoast Books

TABLE OF CONTENTS

INTRODUCTION

The twentieth century saw the discovery of several major manuscript collections: the early Han dynasty Mawangdui silk scrolls from China, the enormous quantity of Buddhist material concealed in a sealed cave at Dun Huang, the Gnostic texts from Nag Hammadi in Egypt and the Dead Sea Scrolls from the caves at Qumran. The researches undertaken on these finds over the decades have revolutionized and often enriched incomparably our understanding of the culture and religion of the people who wrote and copied them.

Yet although most non-specialist readers have probably never heard of Mawangdui, Dun Huang or Nag Hammadi, a surprising number know something of the Dead Sea Scrolls, whether through books or television documentaries. While reading background material for this book as I traveled on public transport, I was approached several times by other passengers and asked about the scrolls. So what is it about them that has so captured people's imagination?

To my mind there are several reasons, some of which now turn out to be spurious. There was an ongoing scandal of secrecy and nepotism that lasted for many decades. While material was being withheld from both the academic world and the general public, during the 1980s and early 1990s a number of books appeared, such as *The Dead Sea Scrolls Deception* by Michael Baigent and Richard Leigh, who claimed that there was a conspiracy by high-ranking members of the Catholic Church to suppress material found in the scrolls—material that was potentially embarrassing for Christian orthodoxy. No doubt skillful publicity by the publishers ensured good sales, but now that all the material is securely in the public domain it seems that these fears were groundless and interest in the scrolls may well wane.

Nevertheless, I believe that this sensationalist interest derives from a valid curiosity about the content of the scrolls and its relevance to Christianity, for although belief in that faith has markedly declined in most Western countries, we are still very much shaped and challenged by Christian attitudes and concepts. It is therefore unfortunate that the true value of the Dead Sea Scrolls seems to have escaped the notice of ordinary readers.

As we shall see, the scrolls do indeed have much to tell us about Jewish Christianity and its origins, but the information that they reveal is far more subtle and complex than any conspiracy theorists might have imagined. This is connected with the range and type of material that is now available from the decades just before the time when Jesus and John the Baptist were active in Palestine.

From the time when many Jews returned from exile in Babylon during the fifth century B.C.E. and rebuilt the Jerusalem Temple, down to the catastrophic Jewish Revolt that began in 66 C.E. and culminated in the destruction of that Temple, Jewish society and religious attitudes underwent enormous changes. The world of Second Temple Judaism was very different from that depicted in the historical books of the Hebrew Bible, which tell us of events during the earlier Israelite period of the kings and prophets.

Change and conflict were brought about by the impact of the sophisticated cultural world of the Greeks and, later, the Romans upon a conservative Jewish society. This was also a time of proud nationalistic resurgence under the Maccabees, marred by vicious and frequently bloody internecine struggles among the Jews themselves. The previous confident belief in the special relationship with God that was the hallmark of the Israelite religion had been undermined by the misfortunes that befell the Jewish people. For these reasons, many Jewish people sought new answers to their plight—or at least new interpretations of their holy scriptures. It was a time of miracle workers, would-be messiahs and prophets, each attracting a large following of desperate people who sought security and the reassurance that all would be well for them, that God had not really abandoned them to the encroaching hordes of pagan wolves.

Although some of the earlier literature produced during this turbulent period had been available in translation since the late nineteenth century, in the form of the apocrypha and pseudepigrapha, very little had survived from the decades immediately before and after the birth of Jesus. The existing sources for an understanding of that time were extremely limited, and little was known of Jewish spiritual life beyond what could be gleaned from the Christian Gospels, the historian Josephus or the heavily Greek-influenced Jewish philosopher Philo of Alexandria. Indeed, given the lack of any other substantial spiritual material from that time apart from the Gospels themselves, people in the past can well be forgiven for viewing early Christianity as a unique historical phenomenon—there was nothing else with which to compare its teachings. But all this was to change with the discovery and gradual publication of the Dead Sea Scroll material.

In the halcyon days of the 1950s and 1960s, Father Roland de Vaux of the École Biblique in Jerusalem and his team were carried away by the vast range of material in their care from the caves at

Qumran by the Dead Sea, and they made numerous unwarranted assumptions about the origins and significance of the scrolls. Given that these researchers often had a monastic background themselves, they were happy to identify the entire collection as the library of the Essenes, a hitherto mysterious ascetic Jewish sect that apparently lived a reassuringly familiar monastic style of life at the Qumran settlement, even though some of their doctrines seemed extreme. However, this confident certainty has eroded over the years, and the trickle of doubts concerning those initial assumptions has turned into a flood now that all the scroll material has been made available to competent historians.

Whereas it was previously thought that the Qumran library represented a homogeneous collection of works written, or at least highly prized, by the Essenes, on-going reappraisal has led many scholars to recognize that the collection is really an invaluable cross-section of religious material that reveals for the first time just how rich and varied Jewish spiritual life was at that time. The scrolls offer an intellectual and devotional landscape into which Jesus and his movement can be placed. No longer does Jewish Christianity seem an inexplicable, isolated occurrence. We can now see that it was an attempt by one group of Jews to make sense of the desperate religious and social crises that they faced in those tumultuous years.

In other words, the true value of the Dead Sea Scrolls is that they help provide a genuine context for what was to become Christianity. For example, they tell us the widespread expectation and longing for a saving Messiah among Jews at that time, and that there were a number of competing theories about the expected role of this Messiah in the world of Judaism. The scrolls also reveal that the expectation found in the Gospels that the end of the world was imminent was a dominant belief in many quarters in Judaea.

As all the old certainties about the Dead Sea Scrolls are being challenged by a new generation of scholars, I believe general readers will welcome a compact summary of the new interpretations and theories being put forward. Although my own speciality is comparative religion, in particular Buddhism and Hinduism, for many years I have followed the unfolding story of the scrolls with keen interest. Although there are numerous books on the subject, the majority are partisan to some degree, presenting their particular interpretation as the definitive one and all others as mistaken. Vituperative and bitter rivalry between many of the leading Dead Sea Scroll scholars underlies these accounts. But I have been able to stand back from the mass of conflicting hypotheses and evaluate them without personal prejudice, for I have nothing to gain or lose if theory X is right and theory Y is wrong.

This book sets out to give a balanced overview of the field of Dead Sea Scroll studies as it now stands 50 years after their discovery and at the beginning of a new millennium. After telling the story of the finding of the scroll fragments and the people involved in the long saga that ultimately led to the release of the scrolls in their entirety, I shall summarize the contents of the whole library and show the important relationship between this material and the evolution of the texts we now have in the Bible. Central to an understanding of the nature of the scrolls is an account of how they were dated and how ideas about their origin are related to the archaeology of the ruins at Qumran and neighboring sites. In particular, there are a number of new facts that have come to light which have not yet been given the publicity they deserve, even though they have the potential to alter radically our concept of the scrolls themselves.

Another feature of this book that general readers should find helpful is a relatively detailed account of the political and cultural background of Jewish society from the advent of the Maccabees around 168 B.C.E. to the destruction of the Jerusalem Temple in 70 C.E. Without this background it is impossible to grasp the undercurrent of events that was pivotal in the emergence of the apocalyptic and messianic teachings that pervade so many of the scrolls—yet the history of this period is dismissed in a few pages by most books.

Readers will also find here a balanced summary of current thinking on the key theological concepts in the scrolls, especially in relationship to the group of texts that are linked with a self-styled community of the elect—whether this was actually a single identifiable sect, as often thought, or whether there were several different groups with a common ideology. The complex history and organization of this community is a topic of great interest, and much can be learned about it from the various rule books and unique explanatory commentaries found at Qumran. Associated with this community is their mysterious founder, the Teacher of Righteousness, and his opponents, including the Wicked Priest and the Spouter of Lies. Controversy reigns here, too, regarding the identity of these key players in Second Temple Judaism. Additionally, the writings of this group show that they shared certain terminological and conceptual features with the earliest Christians and so help us understand assumptions made in the Gospels and the writings of the apostle Paul that were not hitherto obvious. In connection with this relationship I provide a summary and evaluation of the controversial hypotheses of Dr. Robert Eisenman and Dr. Barbara Thiering, who believe that the so-called sectarian writings among the Dead Sea Scrolls were produced by authentic Jewish Christians.

Though no doubt my own preferences may become apparent at times, I have tried to provide sufficient information about the several key, yet conflicting, theories about the origins, meaning and value of the Dead Sea Scrolls to enable readers to evaluate for themselves the current academic views. Readers may also, perhaps, obtain one of the fine translations of the Dead Sea Scrolls, such as that by Geza Vermes, and be in a still better position to make up their own minds about the message these precious documents have for us some 2,000 years after they were written. Against all odds they have survived, albeit in a fragmentary state. They deserve our respect and sympathetic understanding, for indirectly they have helped shape the society in which we live today.

Because so many features of the late Second Temple period are known to us from the Gospels, we unconsciously tend to apply Christian attitudes and ideas to a religious world that was not yet Christianized and so we perhaps distort the true picture of Jewish religious life at that time. Whatever his later followers may have made of him, Jesus himself was above all else a pious Jew and would have been more at home in the intellectual world that produced the Dead Sea Scrolls than in anything produced in his name by his later Gentile followers. For this reason—without any disrespect intended to Christians—to make readers look afresh at the man in the context of his times I have used the original form of his name, Yeshua.

Part I

The Discovery of the Scrolls

one

DISCOVERY

I t is curious how many great discoveries in all areas of human
endeavor are made by chance—no more so than in the field
of archaeology. In late 1946 or early 1947, a Bedouin shepherd
named Jum'a Muhammed stumbled on something extraordinary
while scrambling among the rocky cliffs that rise just behind a
terrace of land on which stand a group of ancient ruins, known
as Khirbet Qumran, by the shores of the Dead Sea.

As the story goes, he was looking for a stray goat when he
noticed a couple of openings in the rocks. He peered down into
the darkness but could see nothing, so he threw in some stones.
Then, as they crashed down inside, he heard the sound of breaking pottery. As the day was coming to an end, Jum'a Muhammed
and his two cousins herded the rest of the flock down from the
escarpment, intending to return for a closer look at the cave to
discover whether they had found anything valuable.

A day or so later one of the cousins, the nimble Muhammad
edh-Dhib, nicknamed the Wolf, woke early and climbed back up
to the site. He cleared some rocks away and wriggled down into
the cave. Inside he found a number of ancient pottery jars, most
of which were empty, although a few contained musty old scrolls

of parchment wrapped in cloth that he and his companions removed over the next few days. Being poor illiterate shepherds, he and his companions must have been disappointed for they had not found anything they could recognize as valuable.

Apparently the scrolls were taken back to the shepherds' camp and left dangling from a tent pole, of no great interest to anybody. It has even been rumored that some of the parchment was used for kindling cooking fires—every archaeologist's nightmare. Such was the fate of several of the less well-known papyrus Gnostic manuscripts that were found around the same time at Nag Hammadi in Egypt. Whether that happened by the Dead Sea or not, by the time the Bedouin shepherds thought about selling them they had just seven crumbling scrolls.

Winter over, the two older cousins, Jum'a and Khalil, took the scrolls into nearby Bethlehem. Nobody they spoke to had any idea what these battered bits of parchment could be and probably cared even less. Somebody suggested taking them to a local cobbler, who might give the men a few pence and use the scrolls for shoe repairs. So off they went to the shop of Khalil Eskander Shahin, better known to his friends as Kando, who also happened to be a part-time antiques dealer. A little more sophisticated than his Bedouin clients, Kando realized the scrolls might be worth something: he paid the two Bedouin roughly $7 and agreed to share any profits from the eventual sale of the scrolls. Crucially for the saga that was about to unfold, he also agreed to become their agent for any subsequent finds.

As it happened, both Kando and a friend of his, George Shamoun, were Syrian Orthodox Christians. Acting on a hunch, during Holy Week of 1947 Shamoun mentioned the scrolls to Metropolitan Athanasius Yeshue Samuel of St. Mark's Syrian Orthodox church in Jerusalem. After various delays, amid fears for the authenticity of the items on offer, Metropolitan Samuel eventually bought four scrolls for a mere $34.

Meanwhile, the well-respected archaeologist Eleazar Sukenik (father of the better-known Yigael Yadin), who worked at the new Hebrew University in Jerusalem, had been offered two fairly complete ancient scrolls and some fragments by another antiques dealer, Feidi Salah. He immediately realized with astonishment that the scrolls were not only authentic but truly ancient, dating from the Second Temple period, judging by the similarity of their script to that on grave inscriptions he had studied. This was a discovery of immense importance because nothing similar had ever been found before—indeed, in the harsh dry climate it was assumed that manuscripts from this period could not possibly have survived. One can well imagine his hand-trembling excitement as he examined the two scrolls. He immediately purchased them and the fragments on behalf of the Hebrew University and then, a few months later, in December 1947, he obtained a further scroll from the same source.

We now know that what he had bought were the Book of Isaiah, the Thanksgiving Hymns, and the Scroll of the War of the Sons of Light Against the Sons of Darkness, or *War Scroll*. Though Sukenik had no idea that a huge quantity of material still lay undiscovered, these three scrolls were to give the world a glimpse of the strange world of sectarian Jewish life during the turbulent last centuries between the Old and New Testaments. Of course, he was familiar with the Book of Isaiah, though this newly acquired copy offered a slightly different version of the text in the Bible. We shall return to the significance of this in Chapter 6. The two other scrolls, however, were totally new and attracted considerable attention from biblical scholars.

The Thanksgiving Hymns were a collection of hymns full of striking images and beauty, obviously meant to be used as part of religious worship. Despite their superficial similarities in tone to some of the Psalms, they spoke from a very different perspective from anything known from other sources. The question was: Who had written them? Were they for use in the daily rituals carried out in the great Temple that stood in Jerusalem, or were they composed by some fringe group? As more material gradually came to light from Qumran, some of these questions were answered, although the answers themselves often led to still more questions.

But the most extraordinary document was the so-called *War Scroll*, which spoke in great detail of the preparations that were to be made by the faithful for an imminent apocalyptic struggle between the forces of good and evil. This war, it said, would result in the utter destruction of the evil ones and the establishment of God's rule over the world under the stewardship of his holy representative—a scenario strikingly similar to the beliefs attributed in early Christian writings to the Galilean rabbi Yeshua and his followers, who also taught that "the Kingdom of God was at hand."

Having by an incredible stroke of good fortune found these few precious scrolls, would Sukenik be able to obtain any more from the same source? Unfortunately, fate now intervened in the shape of political events that would have profound implications for the custodianship and eventual publication of the scroll material that came to light over the next ten years or so. In late 1947 the United Nations voted in favor of the partition of Palestine, to be followed by the declaration of the State of Israel. New borders were drawn up. The Dead Sea region, where the scrolls had come from, would now fall within Jordanian territory where Jews such as Sukenik were not welcome.

Yet he was to get a tantalizing glimpse of the other scrolls the Bedouin had found. As a recognized expert on ancient Hebrew, he was asked for his opinion on the authenticity of the other four scrolls by one Anton Kiraz, acting on behalf of the Metropolitan Athanasius Samuel. They consisted of yet another copy of the Book of Isaiah; the *Rule of the Community*, which described the stringent regulations that governed membership of a hitherto un-known Jewish sect whose views on heaven and hell seemed to be closely linked to those expressed in the *War Scroll*; the *Habakkuk Pesher*, with its curious interpretations of the prophet Habakkuk that it linked with contemporary events involving a mysterious Teacher of Righteousness and his enemies; and a *Genesis Apocryphon*, which contained a rewriting of the events described in the biblical Book of Genesis.

No doubt reluctantly, Sukenik returned the scrolls in February 1948 and expressed a keen interest in buying them for the State of Israel. He is said to have offered up to $1400 for them, but this must have alerted the Metropolitan to their true value and he began to investigate other possibilities. One of the Metropolitan's colleagues, a monk named Butros Sowmy, had contacts at the prestigious American School of Oriental Research—now known as the Albright Institute—in east Jerusalem and took them there for a second opinion. The director was on leave but a young stu-dent, John Trever, saw them and immediately guessed they were very old even though he had little knowledge of Hebrew. While they were at the Institute, Trever had the foresight to take, with the Metropolitan's permission, some excellent color and monochrome photographs of three of the scrolls. These photographs are now extremely important since over the years the scrolls in question have faded and deteriorated through exposure to excessive light and careless handling by those later charged with their care.

While the Metropolitan was still weighing up the possibilities for the disposing of the scrolls, the political upheaval in the region took a turn for the worse. After the declaration of the State of Israel in May 1948, war had broken out, with fighting taking place even in the streets of Jerusalem. The next phase of the story is not entirely clear, but it is known that the scrolls were "evacu-ated" for their own safety and ended up in the United States, where they were exhibited in various cities. At this stage, some of the scholars who saw them believed that they were either fakes or medieval manuscripts of no great value!

Ultimately, in June 1954, a small advertisement was placed in the columns of the *Wall Street Journal* offering them for sale on behalf of the Metropolitan, who needed to sell them speedily for his own financial reasons. After some negotiation, a certain Sidney Esteridge purchased them for $250,000—it later transpired that he was acting on behalf of the Israeli state—and soon afterwards the scrolls came home to Jerusalem. The purchase had in fact been covertly organized by Yigael Yadin, Sukenik's son, an extraordinary polymath and politician who was later to conduct several major archaeological digs in Israel, such as that at Masada, and to publish important studies and translations of several of the Dead Sea Scrolls.

Meanwhile, events around the site of the scroll discoveries and in east Jerusalem had moved along. At the time of the first discoveries of the scrolls, Khirbet Qumran and all that region around the Dead Sea had been part of the British Mandate of Palestine, established after the Turks (who had governed the region as part of the Ottoman Empire) were defeated in World War I. Now the area was part of Jordan and, until the transfer of the West Bank to Israeli control after the Six Day War in 1967, all the scrolls emanating from Khirbet Qumran, their purchase and the subsequent archaeological investigations of the site were in the hands of the Jordanian Antiquities Department and their appointees. This division continues to have profound effects in that region even today, but for the Dead Sea Scrolls the results can only be described as a tragi-comedy of epic proportions.

As word got around the foreign academic missions in east Jerusalem about these miraculously preserved ancient scrolls, the search for their source began. As early as 1949, the location of the first cave that the Bedouin shepherd had found had been identified. What came to be designated as Cave 1 was actually located, after a search of several days, by a detachment of British and Jordanian troops on patrol in the area. The cave was examined and excavated by G. Lankester Harding, then director of the Jordanian Antiquities Department, and his old friend, the Dominican biblical scholar Roland de Vaux of the École Biblique in Jerusalem. They found around seventy small fragments of scrolls, some of which turned out to have fallen from the crumbling edges of those that the Bedouin had earlier discovered but carelessly dropped. In the following years, the search continued for more caves that might contain scroll remains and these were indeed discovered—often, however, not by the plodding archaeologists but by the resourceful Bedouin, who knew the features of the area so well. By 1956 a total of 11 caves, each containing some literary remains, had been discovered and excavated. Additionally, after the excavation of Cave 1, Harding and de Vaux spent the archaeological season of 1951 partially excavating the ruins at Khirbet Qumran on the terrace overlooking the Dead Sea.

DE VAUX'S THEORIES

Although we shall return to the details of what de Vaux and his team found at Khirbet Qumran, a quick preview would not be out of place. As they excavated the site, pottery, coins and other evidence were found that, in their view, clearly linked the scrolls with the site and corroborated their age. Whether he was right or not is still a matter of great controversy among what have come to be called Qumranologists, but de Vaux very quickly determined that the site was a kind of monastic settlement used by an ascetic Jewish group called the Essenes, which had been written about by the historian Josephus and the philosopher Philo of Alexandria. De Vaux thought that many of the writings that had already been found in the caves at Qumran had clearly been produced by the Essenes, for they contained detailed instructions for the organization and administration of a religious community that had many parallels to the ancient accounts of this group. But what was really surprising was something that none of the ancient authors had hinted at: members of this community believed that they were living in the very End of Days that was to precede the Last Judgement, when they alone would be vindicated and all others would be destroyed.

Over the decades, de Vaux's identification of the Qumran group with the Essenes has become the consensus. However, nowhere in the scrolls themselves is the group referred to as Essene. The name they favor for themselves is simply the Community, and this is the name that I shall use throughout this book to refer to the group that produced the so-called sectarian elements of the Dead Sea Scrolls. In addition, a simplistic identification of the Essenes with the Qumran Community is not without its problems, which has fueled considerable debate among Qumranologists. This topic will be discussed in later chapters, but let us finish this one with a brief tour of the caves themselves and see what emerged from them.

THE CAVES

As already explained, the first cave was discovered by the Bedouin cousins late in 1946 or early in 1947. It became clear from the excavations that Cave 1 had not been opened by anybody since it was sealed, probably some time during the Jewish Revolt of 66–70 C.E. that culminated with the destruction of Jerusalem and its Temple by the Roman legions under Titus, the son of the Emperor Vespasian. Within the cave itself were found 56 jars, in a good state of preservation, as well as the remains of some 80 scrolls.

The seven items found by the Bedouin were among the best-preserved of all the scrolls that were ultimately to be found at Qumran, for over the past 2,000 years the further finds in this and most of the other caves had been extensively damaged through the action of time, moisture, insects and rodents. This fact is often obscured in some of the more sensational books and articles which claimed that key documents were being suppressed because of their explosive contents. The unsuspecting public has perhaps been left with a lingering impression that the caves yielded stacks of neatly rolled scrolls just waiting to be read. Nothing could be further from the truth. It is now known that the total fragments discovered represent the remains of around 850 scrolls, but in only ten cases has more than 50 percent of the original scroll survived and only one scroll—one of the two Isaiah scrolls—can be called complete. Of the remainder, much has decayed away over the centuries, leaving some 50,000 tantalizing scraps. Since many of these scraps are no more than a few centimeters in size, it would perhaps have been less misleading to the general public, though a trifle disrespectful, to refer to the finds as the Dead Sea Confetti!

Cave 2 was discovered by the archaeologists in 1952, but it would seem that they were not the first visitors. The entrance had been partially opened by somebody in the past—perhaps a treasure-hunting ancestor of the Bedouin who found Cave 1. The shards of four smashed jars were found scattered on the floor, together with the remains of about 40 scrolls. When they were examined and transcribed, it was found that the majority of these scraps were pieces from various books of the Bible such as Genesis, Exodus and Deuteronomy, as well as some apocryphal works. Though not as exciting as the material that clearly belonged to some long-lost Jewish sect, these fragments of the Jewish Bible are important in their own right since they have been used by biblical scholars to make small but sometimes significant corrections to the standard text that has been handed down over the centuries.

The large cave that came to be called Cave 3 was discovered in 1952 by the archaeological team. Excavations revealed that it had originally been used as a dwelling and may have been occupied as early as 4000 B.C.E. As far as scroll remains are concerned, the evidence was rather disappointing. This cave, too, had been disturbed at some time in the past—though it was clearly several centuries ago. What the archaeologists found were the broken shards of 35 jars, the same characteristic jars as they had found in Cave 1. Yet strange to say, virtually nothing had survived of

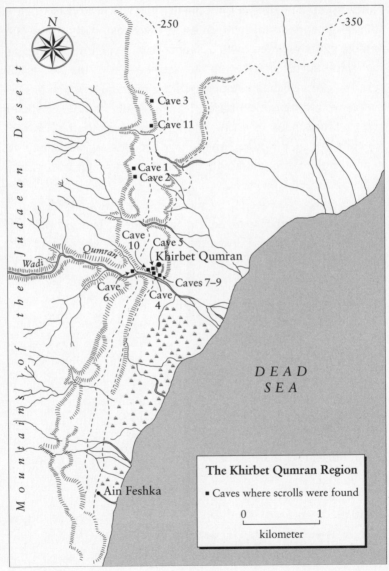

The Khirbet Qumran Region

■ Caves where scrolls were found

0   1
kilometer

their presumed contents—only a handful of very small fragments of around 24 scrolls. It is possible that not all of the 35 jars had contained scrolls—but again there is no reason to suppose that they had not. Based on the average size of ancient scrolls, traces of at least 70 to 140 small and medium scrolls would have been expected. Nevertheless, what the archaeologists did find was tantalizing and suggestive.

Most people today in the West are unfamiliar with books in a scroll format, but this was the normal way books were copied in the ancient world and still are in some circumstances in the Far East. In many respects a scroll-book is far less convenient to handle than the modern book, which was probably developed as a means of overcoming the inherent difficulties of the scroll. If we want to refer to a passage in the middle of a book, for instance, we can simply open it to the right page without any trouble. But when we try to do the same thing with a scroll, we have to unwind it from the beginning until we get to the right place. Because of this, considerable wear and tear occurs at the beginning of a scroll where it is repeatedly handled. To minimize damage to the contents, scrolls usually start with a blank sheet as a kind of safety buffer. Additionally, because scrolls do not have bookcovers as we understand them, they are often wrapped with some kind of cover sheet and even a cloth wrap. These numerous fragments of cover sheets were found littering the floor of the cave. It takes many centuries for parchment to become so brittle that pieces readily break off, while at the same time, as already stated, it seems very unlikely that anybody had entered Cave 3 in recent times. So what became of the presumably missing scrolls?

The well-respected German scholar Hartmut Stegemann believes he can explain the situation that confronted the archaeologists. He hypothesizes, quite reasonably, that somebody must have entered Cave 3 several hundred years after it was sealed off in ancient times. Indeed, he suggests that we can even identify when this occurred. Around 800 C.E. the Nestorian Patriarch Timotheus

I of Seleucia, who was based in Baghdad, wrote to a colleague, the Metropolitan of Elam, that he had received a reliable report some ten years earlier concerning a number of books found in a cave near Jericho. It was said that a hunter's dog had got into the cave, and this led to the discovery of the books in question. Timotheus also mentions that this discovery had been reported to the Jewish inhabitants of Jerusalem, who came in large numbers to look at the books. Apparently they found a number of books of the Bible and various other writings in Hebrew, and removed them all. The fragments of the cover sheets that the archaeologists found would have broken off unnoticed as the excited Jews unrolled the sacred scrolls in the cave. As Stegemann points out, there is a strong likelihood that this account relates to the caves above Khirbet Qumran since there are no other caves in the vicinity of Jericho. He also suggests that these scrolls and their contents must have re-entered the Jewish world and eventually ended up in the hands of a medieval Jewish sect known as the Karaites. We shall come back to this question and the reasons for Stegemann's theory in Chapter 8, when we look in detail at certain aspects of what are called the sectarian scrolls.

Yet despite the rather meager haul of scroll fragments found in Cave 3, something else lay concealed in the cave that was totally unexpected and quite different from anything that had been or was still to be found. Two corroded rolled pieces of copper were found by the archaeologists. Due to technical difficulties, several years were to pass before a way was found to open up this broken scroll and read the inscribed contents. What they had found was the so-called *Copper Scroll*, apparently a listing of over 60 sites where considerable amounts of treasure had been hidden, which has been the subject of animated debate and speculation. Some have dismissed its list of huge caches of gold and silver as the work of an ancient practical joker or lunatic, while others see it as the key piece of evidence that unlocks the mystery of the Dead Sea Scrolls themselves, as we shall find in Chapter 7.

Cave 4, one of the most important of the Qumran caves, was discovered in 1952 by the agile and tenacious Bedouin, who secretly removed many of the fragments until stopped by the archaeological team. The condition of the remains here was poor, yet from what can be read of the surviving fragments their contents are enormously important. When the fragments were eventually sorted and provisionally identified, it was found that the contents of this cave were very varied but represented the remains of about 566 scrolls.

Stegemann suggests that Cave 4 was the last of the 11 Qumran caves to have been filled with scrolls and sealed in ancient times. It would seem that the scrolls perceived to be of major importance were put into Cave 1, while those of secondary value were put into Caves 2, 5, 6 and 11—and perhaps Cave 3. On the other hand, Cave 4 seems to hold a wide range of material ranging from important sectarian works to odds and ends such as exercise books and receipts. As no jars were found, the bundles of scrolls must have been just stacked up on the floor or perhaps on shelves that have long since rotted away. The poor quality of the surviving fragments has led some to think that in earlier times an intruder had gotten into the cave and thoroughly rummaged through the stacks of scrolls. It has even been suggested that in the aftermath of the Jewish Revolt vindictive Roman soldiers found the scrolls and tore them up in a frenzy of destruction. Such may have been the case, but it is also quite likely that the guilty parties were just rats, mice, insects and the climate.

The discovery of these thousands of fragments was to be a body blow to the amateurish arrangements that de Vaux and his team had put in place for transcribing and publishing the Dead Sea Scrolls. Previously they had had a relatively small and manageable collection of manuscript remains, but now they were absolutely inundated with new fragments.

For decades afterwards, it was the contents of these fragments from Cave 4 in particular that were to become a bone of contention in the scholarly world because access to them was subjected to repeated delays and secrecy. Some popular books, and indeed not a few scholars, believed that the predominantly Christian team responsible for supervising publication of the scrolls had come across something that had devastating implications for our understanding of the development and early history of Christianity. This myth was fueled by the steps taken to ensure that all the fragments that the Bedouin had spirited away were acquired and kept together under the supervision of de Vaux's team, rather than being scattered worldwide in separate collections. As the Bedouin were by now well aware of the value of the fragments, special purchasing arrangements were deemed necessary to obtain them via our old friend Kando, who had continued to take a keen interest in the Dead Sea Scrolls for his "clients." It took de Vaux and his team six years to retrieve all the Cave 4 fragments!

On the understanding that all the fragments were initially to be kept together at the École Biblique, various organizations and institutions were asked by the Jordanian government to contribute funds to assist in the purchase both of the scroll fragments found in Cave 4 and of those found later in other caves nearby. Eventually a number of the archaeological institutes in east Jerusalem, several universities and, more controversially, the Vatican made money available to invest in the scroll fragments. The fragments were to be transcribed, edited and published along the same lines as earlier scroll remains had been, and would then be divided up among the contributors in proportion to their financial input. Obviously the precise amounts contributed by each organization were kept private, so some people suspected that the Vatican had contributed and secured rights over a large proportion of the elusive Cave 4 fragments. Sadly for most conspiracy theorists, the facts are rather more mundane. We now know that the Vatican only made a small contribution—insufficient for it to acquire any significant control over the release of the scroll fragments.

Before being sealed with scrolls inside, in ancient times Cave 4 had been used as a dwelling. Remains of objects used by the inhabitants were found, such as potsherds, and post-holes had been cut into the rock walls of the cave. Given that Cave 4 is the nearest of all the caves to the ruins at Khirbet Qumran, the way these holes are arranged has suggested to some scholars that the posts supported shelves and that the cave was originally used as a library by the supposed sectarian inhabitants of the settlement at Qumran. They postulate that, as the wood of the shelves rotted away, the scrolls that had lain upon them crashed to the floor and were reduced to shreds. This view may have some merit, but is rather dependent upon identifying the source of the scrolls themselves and the precise nature of the ruins at Khirbet Qumran. As we shall see later, this question has generated long and heated debates, highly charged with acrimony, accusations and counter-accusations.

The fifth cave was discovered by the archaeological team in 1952 during its investigations of the Qumran site. It, too, had originally been used as a dwelling before scrolls had been concealed in it. Here again it seems that the scrolls were rather hurriedly placed in the cave because no sign of protective jars was found and so they must have just been stacked on the floor. Cave 5 produced the badly decomposed remains of about 30 scrolls, mostly from books of the Bible such as Deuteronomy, Isaiah and the Psalms.

Playing their usual cat-and-mouse games with the archaeologists, the local Bedouin found Cave 6 and removed most of the fragments. The situation here seems very similar to that of Cave 5, with the decomposed remains of about 35 unprotected scrolls eventually being retrieved. These include yet further books from the Bible and several portions of apocryphal works and hymns.

Though described as caves, Caves 7, 8 and 9 are little more than recesses in the cliff face; however, given the friable nature of the rocks in this area, they might once have been more substantial. They were all discovered by the archaeological team in 1955, but virtually no scroll fragments were found in them.

Of the three, Cave 7 is the most interesting since the excavators found here for the first time scroll fragments that were not in Hebrew or Aramaic but in Greek, seemingly from several books of the Septuagint version of the Jewish Bible—the Greek translation of the Bible made in Alexandria during the second century B.C.E. Broken pieces of jars were found here as well, but very little of their contents had survived—just 23 minute fragments. Again, the nature of these fragments suggests that they were not the remains of scrolls that had otherwise decayed away but were pieces that had broken off the edges of the original scrolls. The same situation was found in Cave 8, where the fragments found were even more meager—just three in Hebrew; while in Cave 9 the excavators hit an all-time low with just one fragment in Hebrew.

However, judging from the traces that the excavators found in these three caves, it would seem that the scrolls that had originally been placed there for safe-keeping had already been discovered in ancient times. They probably remained undiscovered by the Romans in the immediate aftermath of the Jewish Revolt, since some of the broken pieces of pottery had legible ink imprints left on them by scrolls that have long since vanished. This would suggest that the concealed scrolls had lain in their jars for a while but were then discovered and removed long ago. Just as in the case of Cave 3, Stegemann proposes a feasible solution to the mystery.

Origen—one of the greatest early Church Fathers, those key figures in the formation of Christian doctrines during the first three centuries of the Christian era—was a rare and outstanding scholar who was extremely interested in establishing the best textual witness for both the Hebrew Bible and the Christian New Testament. Unlike many of his anti-Semitic fellow Christians, he had some respect for the Jewish tradition and what could be learned from it. During his work on the Jewish portion of the Bible, he compiled what is known as the *Hexapla*—an edition of all the books of the Bible with each of the six textual versions available at that time arranged in parallel columns. We know from the slightly later Church historian Eusebius that Origen had additionally used a further exemplar when editing the Book of Psalms, for he says that Origen used a text of the Psalms "which was found in a clay jar near Jericho in the time of Antoninus, son of Severus." Several decades later, in 392 C.E., another Church Father, Epiphanius, reported that "in the seventh year of Antoninus [217 C.E.], son of Severus, manuscripts of the Septuagint, together with other Hebrew and Greek writings, were found in clay jars near Jericho." So here again we have a possible link with the caves at Qumran because the same reasons we might link the separate discoveries described in the ninth-century report of Timotheus mentioned above. But even if Origen did use a manuscript of the Psalms from a cave at Qumran, we sadly have no idea what became of the remaining scrolls, which were no doubt discovered at the same time.

Caves 10 and 11 were the last two caves to be found. Cave 10 was probably never used as a hiding place for scrolls because not even the tiniest scrap of parchment was found there. It seems to have been used in ancient times as a dwelling, perhaps the lonely hideout of refugees fleeing the wrath of the Roman armies at the time of the Jewish Revolt or after the uprising of Bar-Kokhba a century later.

Cave 11 was discovered by the ever-active Bedouin in 1956. It seems clear from later examination that it had remained sealed since ancient times, but very little was found in the cave. By this time, the true value of the Dead Sea Scrolls was widely known among people directly connected with Qumran, whether Bedouin or archaeologists, and to the public, too. Though eventually around 20 severely damaged scroll fragments were retrieved, rumors have persisted that other, better-preserved scrolls were also found and have either been lost through neglect or ended up in the hands of private collectors.

This may well be the case. Long after all the caves had been found and cleared of their contents, the ubiquitous Kando re-emerged. He had made it known that he had a substantial scroll from Qumran in his possession, but again and again withdrew from negotiations for purchase at the last minute. Eventually matters were taken out of his hands when, during the occupation of Bethlehem by Israel in the course of the 1967 Six Day War, his shop was raided by Yigael Yadin acting on behalf of the Israeli authorities. Under the floorboards, rotting away in an old shoe box, was what has come to be called the *Temple Scroll*—a lengthy document that describes in considerable detail the construction of an ideal form of the Jerusalem Temple and that, as we shall see in Chapter 6, might even be seen as a hitherto lost addition or appendix to the Pentateuch. Even though it had evidently suffered while in the hands of Kando, this scroll is still relatively well preserved and was eventually translated and published by Yadin himself. It is universally accepted that it must have originally been found in Cave 11. The question of whether Kando had, or knew the whereabouts of, other material from this cave remains unknown, though rumors abound.

two

THE PUBLICATION SAGA

A fter seeing how the Dead Sea Scrolls were discovered, let us turn to the more controversial story of how they were edited and published. All went well in the few years immediately after the discovery of the first few scrolls. At that time, nobody seems to have realized that the seven scrolls found in Cave 1 were merely the tip of the iceberg.

The three scrolls that Sukenik had obtained in 1947 were edited and published fairly speedily, while the American School of Oriental Research (ASOR) published the photographs and transcriptions of the *Isaiah A Scroll* and the *Habakkuk Pesher* in 1950, followed a year later by the *Rule of the Community*. Overall, the manner in which these early publications were produced gave little cause for concern among scholars, while the general public remained mostly unaware that anything remarkable had emerged from the Judaean desert.

The heart of the eventual publication and research scandal lay with the team set up by the Jordanian Antiquities Department. In 1952 its director G. Lankester Harding appointed Roland de Vaux as editor-in-chief of the planned publication process, which was to be subsidized by the Palestine Archaeological Museum (PAM; now the Rockefeller Museum). A generous grant was secured from John D. Rockefeller himself to cover the costs of the scholars working on the scrolls in Jerusalem, their staff, as well as the photography and preservation of the fragments—work that was expected to last six years. As mentioned previously, the museum also provided funds to buy up manuscript fragments that had fallen into the hands of the Bedouin treasure-hunters. The aim was to enable Oxford University Press to publish edited versions of these fragments with accompanying annotated translations under the series title "Discoveries in the Judaean Desert."

During the first few months de Vaux assigned various portions of the material to Pierre Benoit, Jozef Milik and Maurice Baillet, his colleagues at the École Biblique in east Jerusalem. Conspiracy theorists hasten to point out, almost libelously, that all four scholars were Catholic priests and so would not be expected to treat anything controversial about Christian origins in an objective manner. Be that as it may, the Polish scholar Milik seems to have been the most industrious and his output is still highly respected today. It was he who later began the enormously difficult work of classifying the fragments from Cave 4 as well as editing the non-biblical items from Cave 1. The efforts of the French scholar Baillet eventually included editorial work on many of the fragments from Caves 2, 3 and 6–10 as well as the famous *War Scroll*.

However, with the discovery of Cave 4 and the steady influx of the enormous quantity of fragments retrieved from there, in the spring of 1953 de Vaux organized what was called the International Team. This was composed of a select group of representative scholars recruited from the various archaeological missions active in east Jerusalem, apart from Milik and Baillet.

The team initially had a further six members, for the most part relatively young and inexperienced. Despite the jaundiced views of those who see the whole operation as a front for Vatican-inspired manipulation, the religious allegiances of this group were evenly split: four Catholics and four Protestants.

Its new members included the American Frank Moore Cross, Jr., who was eventually responsible for publishing many of the biblical scrolls; the eccentric Englishman John Allegro, who edited a selection of the para-biblical work and commentaries; the American John Strugnell, later to become a Catholic convert, who took care of non-biblical texts as well as various liturgical works; the American Monsignor Patrick Skehan, who worked on parts of the biblical texts as well as some Greek material; and the Frenchman Abbé Jean Starcky, who specialized in the non-biblical texts in Aramaic. There was also a German, Claus Hunzinger, but he soon resigned. None of the team was Jewish, let alone Israeli. Since all the material found at Qumran was Jewish in origin, this seems bizarre, even if we discount the Vatican conspiracy theory, until we realize with sadness that many of the group were known to have held anti-Semitic or at least pro-Arab sentiments. It is quite outrageous that, though some Jewish scholars were later to be tangentially involved in the research work, they were not able to become heavily involved until 1990.

Moreover, in hindsight we can see that there were several other major causes for concern. It seems that de Vaux was not blessed with great organizational abilities because it is clear that he had adopted no long-term strategy for the distribution and publication of the fragments. The overall impression is that the work proceeded on an *ad hoc* basis. De Vaux seems to have believed with incredible arrogance that his small band of scholars would be capable of reassembling and editing the mountain of Cave 4 material within a mere ten or twelve years.

Worse still, the conditions under which the fragments were studied can only be described as primitive. Given the extreme age and consequent fragility of the material, it is astonishing that no serious attempts were made to conserve or preserve the fragments.

When piecing them together, the researchers used quite unsuit-able materials such as masking tape or even the edging from sheets of postage stamps. The fragments were often laid out in trays on desks exposed to the damaging effects of Middle Eastern sunshine streaming in through the windows, while the cups of coffee and cigarettes that fueled the tedious hours of identifying and match-ing the fragments must surely be the stuff of a conservationist's nightmare. Although good-quality photographs were made of the fragments, often using infra-red lighting to reveal the writing on the blackened pieces of parchment, it beggars belief that some members of the editorial team even painted illegible fragments with clove oil to bring out the writing a little more clearly!

Apart from damage that may have been caused by these con-ditions, worse was to come. During the Suez crisis in 1956 there were fears for the safety of the fragments from Cave 4. They were therefore transferred from east Jerusalem to the Ottoman Bank vaults in the Jordanian capital, Amman. When returned a year later they were found to have deteriorated markedly, perhaps because of inappropriate storage conditions—many of the fragments had patches of mildew on them.

Nevertheless, despite occasional internal friction and disagree-ments from some members of the team (in particular John Allegro, who eventually embarked on a private vendetta against the rest of the team and Christianity in general), the team worked reason-ably efficiently throughout the 1950s and 1960s with its Rock-efeller funding. As time went by, some of the original members left and other scholars were invited to join the group. Most notable of these was the American doyen of Qumran studies, J. Fitzmyer, who in 1957 began working on the concordance of words from all the manuscripts from Caves 2–10, which in 1991 would even-tually play an important though unintended role in breaking the scroll studies cartel that developed over the decades.

It was also in the late 1950s that the enigmatic *Copper Scroll* was finally opened in the United Kingdom at the Manchester Institute of Technology, using a special sawing machine that had been invented for the purpose by Professor Wright-Baker. However, by the late 1960s the work had slowed to a snail's pace. By 1967, only five volumes of "Discoveries in the Judaean Desert" had been published. Work on the scrolls during the following 20 years was marred by an extraordinary degree of chaos and delay— after 1967, only one further volume was to appear before the 1990s.

The Six Day War in 1967, which resulted in Israel occupying east Jerusalem and the West Bank, might have been expected to change the situation since, with the exception of the *Copper Scroll* and a few small fragments on exhibition in Amman, all the material was now under the jurisdiction of the Israeli authorities. Yet, curiously enough, they left de Vaux and his entirely non-Jewish team in complete control of the mass of scroll fragments from Cave 4 that had not yet been published. The small amount of material from Cave 11 was allocated to several Dutch and American scholars for editing and eventual publication.

However, between this time and his death in 1971, de Vaux seems to have completely switched off, perhaps understandably due to his antipathy to the Israeli state. In the following year his post as editor-in-chief was taken over by his old friend, the now elderly Pierre Benoit. Over the following years many of the members of the original team had either retired or left to take up posts at various universities. Monsignor Skehan died in 1980, followed by Starcky in 1986, without having published their assignments. With inadequate supervision, a culture of inefficiency, secrecy and nepotism set in. Two of the senior members, Strugnell and Cross, took it upon themselves to distribute portions of their allocated material to favored, though relatively inexperienced, Ph.D. students in their care.

By now any outside scholars who wanted access to the Dead Sea Scroll material were met with a point-blank refusal. Though the Cave 4 fragments had been largely identified and catalogued, not only were outsiders prevented from seeing anything, even the list of items was placed off-limits. It was this state of affairs that fueled a whole industry of sensational books claiming sinister reasons for this secrecy. As already mentioned, conspiracy theorists were quick to point the finger at the Vatican in the belief that something extremely embarrassing to the history of the Christian faith was being suppressed. Now that we have access to the entire material this seems far-fetched—the only slightly disquieting conclusion we may draw is that Christianity, in its sectarian Jewish origins, is a little less original than we have been led to believe, as will be explained in Chapter 11.

Benoit resigned in 1986 and died the following year, to be succeeded by John Strugnell. By all accounts Strugnell was a very talented scholar, but he seems to have operated on a totally different timescale from the rest of the world because he had not published a single text in 33 years! Then, in 1990, he gave a notorious interview to an Israeli newspaper, in the course of which his anti-Jewish and anti-Israeli sentiments became clear. Perhaps pressure was applied to him, but soon afterwards he resigned "on health grounds."

Now the Israeli authorities did what they should perhaps have done way back in 1967: in 1991 they placed the entire project in the capable hands of Emmanuel Tov. A noted professor of biblical studies at the Hebrew University in Jerusalem, Tov was the first Jew to be directly involved with any of the Dead Sea Scroll material apart from what Sukenik and Yadin had published years earlier. Almost immediately, Tov set up a new international editorial team that was far more balanced in its composition than anything that had preceded it. Yet, regrettably, even he was to maintain the old "secrecy rule" instituted by de Vaux, and so in his turn prohibited access to the texts to all but a select few. This gives the lie to the fantasies of some popular writers that portions of the Cave 4 material were being suppressed deliberately by the

Vatican because what possible motives would a Jew have in protecting Christianity from any embarrassing revelations?

Years of personal experience in the academic world suggest a far more simple explanation to me. Scholars can be extraordinarily possessive or proprietorial about "their" special area of research, wanting all the fame and glory for themselves. Additionally, many university departments are rife with nepotism: posts and projects are frequently allocated through a kind of academic "old boys' network" to favored scholars, while others are excluded. It seems to me that the secrecy and delays in publication of the Dead Sea Scroll material form no exception to this pattern.

However, the situation began to change rapidly in the early 1990s. When excluded scholars realized that Tov was going to maintain the secrecy rule, a barrage of international criticism was unleashed. Two young researchers with computer skills, Ben Zion Wacholder and Martin Abegg, made an astonishing breakthrough by reconstituting 17 of the Cave 4 scrolls from the so-called Preliminary Concordance started by Fitzmyer and compiled over the decades, and circulated by Strugnell in 1988 for private use. These hitherto unreleased texts were published in the journal of the reputable Biblical Archaeology Society in September 1991. The Huntington Library was one of the few places outside Israel that had obtained one of the complete sets of photographs prepared as a fail-safe measure in case the scroll fragments themselves were lost in some disaster. In September 1991, to everybody's amazement, it, too, opened its photographic archive to all qualified scholars.

Realizing that they had now lost effective control of the scroll fragments, the Israeli Antiquities Agency and Tov's group of "official editors" had little option but to lift all restrictions. Simultaneously, two other sets of scroll photographs, those held at the Oxford Centre for Postgraduate Hebrew Studies in the United Kingdom and at the Ancient Biblical Manuscript Center at Claremont in the United States, were made available. Not only were the scroll fragments and photographs of them now accessible to all interested parties but the Biblical Archaeology Society went on to publish a two-volume photographic edition of the bulk of the Qumran fragments. This edition was compiled by the hitherto excluded and somewhat controversial scrolls scholars Robert Eisenman and James Robinson, though the source of their photographs remains a mystery.

So, since the beginning of the 1990s the situation concerning access to the Dead Sea Scrolls has, happily, changed beyond recognition, though there is still much bitterness in some quarters. Not only is the raw material readily available for scrutiny by any competent scholar in several formats, but translations into English and other languages are available in reasonably priced editions for the public. At the same time, publication of further volumes of the "Discoveries in the Judaean Desert" series aimed at the academic market has continued apace, with eight new volumes appearing by 1998. A whole new industry has now come into being for both established and younger scholars, who at the turn of the millennium have generated an enormous number of studies on all aspects of the Dead Sea Scrolls.

Part II

The Historical Background

three

THE MACCABEAN REVOLT
AND HASMONEAN RULE

The scholars who have worked on the Dead Sea Scrolls almost universally accept that these precious fragments of early Jewish literature were copied, if not written, sometime between 170 B.C.E. and 68 C.E., even though heated debate continues about aspects such as their interpretation and provenance. This dating relies on findings from the sciences of archaeology and paleography, which will be examined later in this book. Before looking at the scrolls themselves in greater detail it might be helpful to take a brief look at this tragic period of Jewish history, known variously as the intertestamental, post-exilic or Second Temple period. In other words, since the scrolls are the product of an extremely turbulent period of history, it is safe to assume that the events which occurred during that time must have had a profound influence on their contents or may have actually prompted the authors to write what they did.

Like so many other small nations, the Israelite kingdom was often at the mercy of its powerful, numerically superior neighbors. The centuries that followed the glory of Solomon's achievements are a long story of the Jewish struggle to maintain their own unique identity and independence from foreign domination. By 928 B.C.E., the unified kingdom of Israel was split into two: the rump of the kingdom of Israel itself, centered on Samaria, and the new kingdom of Judah. Two hundred years later, in 722 B.C.E., the kingdom of Israel was defeated by the belligerent Assyrians from Mesopotamia and the country was left extensively depopulated through mass deportations and massacres. Though the kingdom of Judah, meanwhile, had become a vassal state to the Assyrians, it, too, eventually fell prey to invaders from the east in the form of the Babylonians in 587 B.C.E. Not only was Jerusalem laid waste, but the Temple of Solomon was destroyed. Thousands of people from Judah were taken to Babylon, where they remained in exile for more than 50 years. Then, so typically of events in the region, the whole situation changed suddenly: much of the region, including Judaea and Babylon, was conquered in 539 B.C.E. by the magnanimous Persian king Cyrus the Great, who soon afterwards granted the Jewish exiles permission to return home.

No doubt these years had not been an entirely happy time for many Jews, as we can discern from the poignant words of Psalm 137, but life was perhaps not too harsh in Babylon since the return from exile took place in waves over the next hundred years. Many Jews had therefore been exposed to the alien religious ideas of both their erstwhile Babylonian captors and those taught by the sophisticated Zoroastrian religion, many of which were to be adopted and eventually to have a profound influence on Jewish religious thinking. This foreign influence is especially marked among members of the various Jewish sects that developed in later centuries down to the time of the Dead Sea Scrolls.

However, after the Jews returned to Judah the Persians proved to be benign rulers and allowed them many civil and religious liberties. By 516 B.C.E., for instance, the Jerusalem Temple had been rebuilt and rededicated largely at Persian expense, ushering in the

Boundary of Judaea in 166 B.C.E.

Hasmonean Kingdom under
Alexander Jannaeus
(103–76 B.C.E.)

Kingdom of Herod the Great
(37–4 B.C.E.) at its largest extent

▲ Greek city (*polis*)   ■ Fortress

N

Sidon

ITURAEA

Tyre

Caesarea
Philippi

BATANAEA

Ptolemais▲   Capernaum

Bethsaida

GALILEE

*Lake
Gennesaret*

Tiberias

Gadara

Dor▲

Caesarea▲

Scythopolis▲

Pella

MEDITERRANEAN
SEA

SAMARIA

Samaria

Gerasa

Gerizim △▲   Shechem

Sebaste

River Jordan

Alexandrium ■

Joppa▲

Philadelphia
▲

Modein ●

Michmash

JUDAEA   Jericho   ● *John's place of baptism*

Jerusalem ●

■Qumran

PHILISTIA

Bethlehem ●   ■Herodium

■Hyrcania

Ascalon

Dead Sea

Gaza▲

En Gedi ●

■Machaerus

IDUMAEA

Masada ■

0   50

kilometers

The Hasmonean and Herodian Kingdoms

so-called Second Temple period that will be the focus of attention in the rest of this chapter.

The prophet Ezra led another wave of returnees back from Babylon around 458 B.C.E. and he is thought to have also been involved in the crucial task of editing and canonizing the five books, sometimes called the Pentateuch, that make up the Torah and which have been the bedrock of Jewish life ever since. Though Ezra seems to have adopted a fairly conciliatory attitude to those Jews who had remained in Judah throughout the period of exile, the prophet Nehemiah, who was active a few decades later, was far less tolerant of their religious and moral standards. He introduced many religious reforms aimed at purging the country of semi-paganized Jews, while also devoting his energies to strengthening the city of Jerusalem through a series of building projects that included the reconstruction of the great city walls.

Still nominally under Persian overlordship, the inhabitants of Judah were nevertheless allowed to organize themselves as a distinct religious and political community. Crucially for our story, the now hereditary office of High Priest was to become overwhelmingly important: all internal authority within Judah was concentrated in the hands of this figure, who was not only the supreme head of religious affairs but also the *de facto* head of state for life. This situation continued even when there was a change of masters after the Persian Empire fell to the armies of Alexander the Great.

Under the Greek invaders political autonomy for the inhabitants of the small land of Judaea, as the country was now called, became even greater, but their Jewish brethren who now formed a minority in other areas that had once formed part of the old Israelite kingdom were less well favored. Though differing from each other in many respects, the Persian and now the Greek overlords of Judaea had one thing in common: a vision of a vast empire held together by a unity of language, customs and culture. As Alexander marched across the Middle East on his journey to the borders of

India, caravans of settlers followed who founded and built many cities specifically designed to embody these Hellenic ideals.

Following his sudden death in 323 B.C.E., the territory Alexander had conquered was divided into several smaller kingdoms after a brief but bloody struggle among his leading generals. The Near East was split into two: Egypt and surrounding areas went to the Ptolemaic dynasty, while Syria with parts of Turkey and Persia went to the Seleucid dynasty. Not surprisingly, control of the land of Judaea, which lay uncomfortably between these two power blocs, was hotly disputed. At first Judaea was under the benign rule of Egypt, which allowed the Jews considerable religious freedom; but the aggressive campaigns of the eastern Seleucids eventually wrested Judaea from Ptolemaic control, and the wheels of Jewish revolt were gradually set in motion.

But throughout all this time, both the Ptolemies and the Seleucids vigorously fostered Alexander's vision of a Hellenic world. This process was so successful that by the time of the Maccabean Revolt, which began in 168 B.C.E., most of the Middle East had become thoroughly Hellenized, especially the nobility and aspiring middle class. Judaea itself, despite its unique religious and social status in the area, was no exception. It could be argued that a certain degree of Hellenic influence was inevitable since much of the commerce with neighboring lands would have been carried out in Greek—without some familiarity with that language, economic survival would have been difficult—and with the language came the culture and customs. If it had not been for the crass insensitivity of the Seleucid ruler Antiochus IV Epiphanes, it is quite likely that Judaea would have completely lost its Jewish identity and world history would have traveled down a very different path. Though most of the Jewish upper class in Judaea were quite happy to collaborate with the accelerated program of Hellenization inaugurated by this ruler, tensions lay festering between the liberal Jewish Hellenizers and the Hasidim, a group of pious conservative Jews who were highly respected by the ordinary people. These tensions were soon to erupt in a unique religious war of resistance.

The Seleucid ruler Antiochus IV Epiphanes possessed a contradictory personality: he was utterly despotic, ferocious and unpredictable, while at the same time he was given to acts of extravagant generosity and had a penchant for mixing with the common people. When he came to the throne in 175 B.C.E., the office of High Priest at the Temple was occupied by the pious Onias III. Onias had a younger brother who, as pro-Hellenic as his older brother was a conservative, preferred to be called Jason rather than his Jewish name of Yeshua or Jesus. Although the office of High Priest had customarily been held for life since the time of Nehemiah, Jason coveted the position and promised Antiochus large sums of money and cooperation in his Hellenization project in exchange for support. Onias was deposed and went into exile in Egypt, while Jason took over as he had hoped.

The pace of Hellenization began to pick up speed, though at first there was no interference with the Jewish religion. Nevertheless, during Jason's time in office a Greek-style gymnasium was constructed a mere stone's throw away from the Temple precincts where men would exercise naked, as was the Greek custom. This display of nudity would have been extremely shocking to conservative Jews, though it is said that many of the priests at the Temple would pause in their sacred duties and gaze down appreciatively upon the exertions of the naked young men exercising there. (Though not a uniquely Jewish custom in the Near East, circumcision was alien to the Greeks. Many Hellenized Jewish men were therefore acutely embarrassed by the display of their scarred genitals, which led many of them to attempt an artificial "correction" of their circumcision—a painful and hazardous procedure before the days of anesthesia and plastic surgery.)

Within a few years Jason in his turn was deposed by one Menelaus, who also bribed Antiochus Epiphanes for his support.

According to Jewish religious law, the position of High Priest could only be held by one of Aaronic descent from the days of Moses; Menelaus, however, was of the tribe of Benjamin. In the eyes of the conservative pious Jews the situation was scandalous, but things were to get far worse. While working hand in glove with his patron Antiochus, Menelaus ordered the murder of Onias III in 171 B.C.E.

Meanwhile, the deposed Jason had not relinquished his claims. While Antiochus was away fighting in Egypt in 170 B.C.E., Jason moved on Jerusalem and seized it by surprise. Fearing for his life, Menelaus hurriedly took refuge in the citadel. Antiochus was outraged, probably seeing Jason's actions as a direct challenge to his authority, and marched in person against Jerusalem. After the ensuing bloodbath Antiochus plundered the Temple of its immense treasures, assisted by the obsequious Menelaus.

The following year Antiochus again mounted a campaign against Ptolemaic Egypt, but his ambitions were thwarted by the vigilance of the Romans, who were probably worried both by the threat of interrupted grain supplies from Egypt and by the growing power of the Seleucid Empire. They ordered him to leave Egypt alone or face the consequences. In the best tradition of all bullies, Antiochus vented his frustrations upon the hapless inhabitants of Judaea.

He now decided to implement his Hellenization plans in the region even more cruelly. At his behest a program of massacre, pillage and destruction was carried out in Jerusalem and the rest of the country. All those who refused to cooperate were disposed of—the men slaughtered, the women and children sold into slavery. The city walls rebuilt by Nehemiah were destroyed, although the old Davidic city on the citadel was fortified and garrisoned by Seleucid troops.

The situation continued to deteriorate. Antiochus first ordered the abolition of the Temple cult and all observance of the Law. Pagan cults were to replace these and all Jewish observances were prohibited, especially Sabbath and circumcision, on pain of death. The final outrage occurred at the end of 167 B.C.E., when a pagan altar was built on top of the great altar of burnt offering in the Temple and then sacrifices, possibly of taboo pigs, were offered on it to Zeus.

This is the famous "abomination of desolation" that was to become a rallying cry for resistance over the years to come. Not only Jerusalem but all Judaean towns were now ordered to make pagan sacrifices to the gods, while mere possession of the Torah was punishable by death. Throughout this reign of terror, many Jews resisted with great courage and remained faithful to their religion and its practices. However, these brave acts of passive resistance could not have continued for long, and if it had not been for the actions of a humble priest and his sons in the town of Modein, Judaism would have disappeared from the land of its birth without a trace.

One day in 168 B.C.E., the banner of open revolt was raised. When ordered to make a pagan sacrifice by one of Antiochus' officers, a pious priest of Modein near Jerusalem named Mattathias refused and killed the officer. He and his five sons, John, Simon, Eleazar, Judas and Jonathan, then destroyed the altar and fled to the mountains. There they were joined by a number of sympathizers, but many of these were slaughtered by a pursuing detachment of Syrian soldiers from Jerusalem because they were so pious in their observance of the Torah that they offered no resistance when they were attacked on the Sabbath.

The fate of these devout martyrs strengthened Mattathias' resolve to resist the Seleucids and their collaborators—even if that meant fighting on the Sabbath if necessary. Mattathias was joined now by many pious Hasidim—"the Devout"—who had so far patiently endured events at considerable cost to themselves. His band began traveling around Judaea, opposing Antiochus'

enforced Hellenization by destroying pagan altars, killing apostate Jews, circumcising children and generally encouraging open
revolt on the Seleucids.

After the death of Mattathias in 165 B.C.E., two of his sons succeeded him: Simon became the religious adviser and Judas the
military commander. Judas had therefore become the leader of
the resistance movement and took on the *nom de guerre* "Maccabee," which many think means "hammer," perhaps in the sense
of his being a warrior who strikes hard and swiftly. It was said of
him: "In his deeds he was like a lion, and like a lion's whelp roar-
ing after prey."

Initially, Judas' actions with his small band of rebels went
unchecked, but Antiochus decided to adopt more stringent measures and sent a large army into Judaea. However, Judas had been
busy. He assembled his forces, which by now he had forged into
a well-organized army, at Mizpah. After preparing themselves
with prayers and fasting, they met the Syrian army at Emmaus.
Against all odds, the Jews won through the skillful use of tactics.
Never one to give up, Antiochus sent a further force up from
Idumaea in 164 B.C.E.; but again Judas' army defeated the superior
Seleucid forces at Beth-Zur near Jerusalem.

Soon afterwards Antiochus died on campaign in the east, so an
uneasy truce between Judas Maccabee and the Seleucids was
declared. Availing himself of this lull in the fighting, in 164 B.C.E.
Judas captured Jerusalem from the hands of the Seleucid sympathizers—although it still remained a divided city with a Seleucid
garrison in the citadel and the usurper High Priest Menelaus at
large. Nevertheless, Judas was able to have the Temple purified
and rededicated. The old altar, which had been defiled, was demolished and a new one constructed, and new ritual vessels were
provided. Whether by design or chance, the rededication of the
Temple took place on the anniversary of the day when, three years
earlier, the altar had been desecrated by Antiochus' pagan sacrifice.

These events marked the end of the first phase of the Maccabean Revolt. A semblance of normality returned to Judaea for a while: the Seleucids were busy elsewhere, allowing Judas to consolidate his hold on the country. To this end he fortified the Temple mount and a number of other places in Judaea. If the settlement at Khirbet Qumran was, as some think, a military installation, one might suspect that it was reconstructed and strengthened around this time. Additionally, Judas made several raids on neighboring territories to protect Jewish minorities living there, often getting them to resettle in Judaea.

Meanwhile in Seleucia the heir, Antiochus V Eupator, was still under-age so a general named Lysias made himself *de facto* ruler. Heeding calls for help from the now beleaguered garrison in the citadel of Jerusalem, he raised a powerful army and led it into battle with the Jewish army at Beth Zachariah near Jerusalem. Though it fought with great bravery, the Jewish force was routed and a complete reversal of fortunes seemed inevitable.

But fate intervened: Lysias was called back to Syria urgently to deal with domestic problems, and so was happy to agree to peace on lenient terms. Most important of these was that the Jews were to be allowed to practice their own religion as they wanted. Though conflict with the Seleucids was to drag on for decades, this concession was not rescinded by any of the later Seleucid kings who were still nominal overlords of Judaea. The real fight now focused on internecine struggle between the nationalist supporters of the Maccabees and the Hellenistic factions among the Jews themselves.

JUDAS MACCABEE VERSUS THE PRO-HELLENIC JEWS

All pro-Hellenic Jews had been removed from positions of influence by Judas Maccabee, but now they were itching to regain power by any means. They soon got their chance. A new ruler, Demetrius I Soter, had come to the Seleucid throne in 162 B.C.E.

He had been kept in Rome as a hostage to ensure his uncle Antiochus IV Epiphanes' good behavior, but managed to escape. Entering Syria, he quickly gathered enough supporters to take control and had both Antiochus Eupator and Lysias executed. Inevitably the leader of the pro-Hellenic faction of Jews, a priest named Alcimus, complained bitterly to Demetrius of their ill-treatment at the hands of Judas Maccabee. Swayed by their arguments and possibly their bribes, Demetrius appointed Alcimus High Priest and sent an army to Jerusalem to have him installed in office and to execute the usurper Menelaus.

Once Alcimus was in place there was not a great deal of opposition towards him on religious grounds, even by strict Jews such as the Scribes and the Hasidim. In fact, probably the only people who were not happy with him were Judas Maccabee and his followers. After the Seleucid army had returned home, power seems to have affected Alcimus' judgement, and he stupidly ordered the execution of some 60 men of the Hasidim party, which merely served to alienate many others. Almost immediately, open warfare broke out between Alcimus and the Maccabean party.

In panic, Alcimus called on Demetrius for help and an army was dispatched to Judaea under the Syrian general Nicanor. He seems to have been a rather inept commander, and his army was massacred by Judas Maccabee in 161 B.C.E. In order to ensure that the Maccabean party would remain in permanent control of the country, Judas now decided to sever Judaea from the Seleucids completely. Though he could not have imagined the ultimate consequences of his action, he turned to the Romans, who were already concerned about the power of the Seleucids, for help. Judas' embassy to Rome resulted in a treaty of friendship that committed both parties to mutual assistance in time of war. But sadly for Judas, Demetrius swiftly sent a strong army against Jerusalem in the autumn of 161 before any Roman help could arrive. In the face of vastly superior forces, Judas' forces panicked and many fled. Those who remained fought valiantly but fell on the battlefield along with Judas himself.

Judas Maccabee was survived by his two remaining brothers, Simon and Jonathan, and of these it was Jonathan who assumed leadership of the nationalist forces. In the immediate aftermath, the victorious pro-Hellenic faction with their Seleucid patrons wrought some degree of revenge upon the nationalist faction. Their numbers severely reduced, the Maccabeans fled from Jerusalem and other cities into the countryside, where they waited to regain their strength. For a while they were little better than bandits in their activities, waylaying rich victims.

Meanwhile the Seleucid representative, Bacchides, sought to strengthen control over Judaea by fortifying and garrisoning a number of towns, including Jericho, Emmaus, Beth-Zur and Jerusalem itself. Yet the High Priest Alcimus did not live to enjoy the fruits of victory. In mid-160 he had the walls of the inner court of the Temple demolished, and soon afterwards died of a stroke, which was seen by many as divine retribution for his impious deed. The name of the next High Priest is not known—but this coveted office is highly unlikely to have remained unoccupied, given the vital role played by its holder in Jewish civil and religious life. It may be that the anonymous successor to Alcimus was somebody of central importance to the sectarian group associated with Qumran and the scrolls, as we shall see in Chapter 10.

Since everything now seemed to have calmed down in Judaea, Bacchides decided to return to Syria. There followed a period of seven years (160 B.C.E.–153 B.C.E.) about which little is known. It can be assumed, however, that the Maccabean party under Jonathan was growing in strength all the while. There is some evidence that during this time Jonathan established a rival government in Michmash from where his influence extended across the whole of Judaea, for the largely aristocratic pro-Hellenic faction had no strong roots among the ordinary people. Seleucia itself was weakened by a bloody power struggle. By now Jonathan had become a power to be reckoned with, and his favor was sought by rival claimants to the Seleucid throne. The tables had turned, and now it was the Seleucids who had to act in a conciliatory manner towards the Jewish people in order to keep them quiet while matters were being sorted out at home.

One of the rival claimants to the Seleucid throne was Alexander Balas, who opposed Demetrius and made his bid for power in 152 B.C.E. Since Demetrius was unpopular, he tried desperately to retain Jewish support with a range of concessions such as granting Jonathan full military authority as well as releasing Jewish hostages being held in Jerusalem. Jonathan was able to enter Jerusalem and immediately took steps to fortify both the city and the Temple within it. Not to be outdone, Alexander Balas outbid Demetrius and, crucially for the Dead Sea Scrolls Community, according to many scholars, nominated Jonathan as High Priest and sent him tokens of princely rank. Despite the fact that Jonathan had no entitlement to become a priest under Jewish religious law, he donned the sacred vestments on the Feast of the Tabernacles and in so doing became the formal head of the Jewish people. As a result, the Jewish pro-Hellenic faction was driven from office permanently.

An impression of the measure of power now wielded by Jonathan can be gained from the fact that Demetrius immediately tried to win his support by outdoing the bribes offered by Alexander Balas. But his attempts were in vain. Shortly afterwards, in 150 B.C.E., Demetrius I Soter was killed in battle and Alexander Balas became ruler. In recognition of Jewish support, he bestowed many honors upon Jonathan.

But Seleucia had only just begun the drawn-out process of tearing itself apart. Alexander Balas seems to have been a weak and unpopular ruler and soon others were casting their eyes on the throne. Sitting comfortably in Jerusalem, Jonathan constantly exploited the Seleucid power struggle in order to strengthen the Judaean position, and was happy to allow his favors to be bought at the price of territory ceded to him.

In Seleucia, Demetrius II Nicator set himself up as a rival to Alexander Balas. Despite the continued support of a grateful Jonathan, Balas was defeated and fled to Arabia, where he was treacherously murdered. Naturally the new ruler was infuriated at Jonathan's support for his predecessor, though there was little he could do in retaliation because by now the power of Seleucia had been all but broken. On the contrary, in his weakness Demetrius was obliged to make still further concessions to Jonathan's demands, including the transfer of the three Jewish districts of south Samaria to Judaea.

The tedious round of struggles for the Seleucid throne now entered its next phase, although this time the results for Jonathan were not to be as he might have hoped. A Syrian general named Tryphon seized Antiochus, the son of Alexander Balas, and set him up as a rival to Demetrius, probably with the intention of using him as a pawn in his own bid for the throne. Jonathan, ever eager to strengthen the Judaean position, went to the aid of Demetrius, who had promised to hand over the disputed fortress in Jerusalem and other strongholds in Judaea in return for support. With the help of his ally, Demetrius was able to quell a revolt in the Seleucid capital at Antioch, but then stupidly failed to keep the promises he had made to Jonathan. Next Tryphon, with Antiochus in tow, managed to seize Antioch and in turn promised to give Jonathan all that Demetrius had failed to deliver.

Then Jonathan switched sides and began to play a dangerous game. With his brother Simon, Jonathan subjugated various Seleucid territories on behalf of Tryphon and Antiochus, but at the same time he cunningly garrisoned or strengthened a number of places in Judaea for his own ends. Even Tryphon began to get worried, and eventually turned against Jonathan. Since they were supposed to be allies. Tryphon marched into Palestine and met Jonathan at Scythopolis. Both were accompanied by large armies. Perhaps Jonathan was too sure of himself, but Tryphon succeeded in allaying his suspicions and had him disband his army. Jonathan and a small band of followers went with Tryphon to Ptolemais on the coast. There he was arrested and his men slaughtered.

Simon, the last remaining Maccabee brother, took over as leader in Jonathan's absence and put Judaea on a war footing. Since they were still nominally allies, Tryphon arrived in Judaea with an army and Jonathan as a prisoner. Tryphon sent a message to Simon explaining that he had merely arrested Jonathan because he owed him a large sum of money for past favors, and would be happy to release him if the money was paid and Jonathan's sons were sent to him as hostages. In good faith, Simon did all that he had been asked. But Tryphon did not release Jonathan and had him murdered soon afterwards.

With Jonathan dead, the Maccabean forces officially elected Simon as their leader. By now all the original religious aims of the Maccabean Revolt had been fulfilled and all that remained to be achieved was full independence from Seleucid rule. Meanwhile in Syria, the opportunist Tryphon showed his hand and had his young ward Antiochus IV murdered. Then he had himself crowned, but his struggle with Demetrius continued. Not surprisingly, Judaea under Simon switched sides once again and became allied with Demetrius on the condition that Jewish independence would be recognized. Desperate for support, Demetrius acceded to Simon's demands: in 142 B.C.E. he formally released Judaea from all tax arrears and granted it exemption from all future tribute. In effect, Demetrius had granted Judaea full independence or, as the biblical I Maccabees puts it, "the yoke of the Gentiles was taken from Israel."

Simon did not waste any time in consolidating his power in Judaea and succeeded his dead brother in the office of High Priest and as Prince of the Jews. The last token presence of foreign rule in Jerusalem was eliminated in mid-141 B.C.E., when the Seleucid garrison in Jerusalem was captured. After so many years of bloodshed a well-earned period of peace and prosperity followed in Judaea, during which Simon is reputed to have cared for both the material and spiritual well-being of the land. Finally, late in 140 B.C.E., in recognition of the Maccabean achievements, a great assembly of priests and people declared that Simon and his descendants should hold the office of High Priest, military commander and ethnarch of Judaea, "for ever until a trustworthy prophet should arise" (I Maccabees 14:41). This event marks the founding of the Hasmonean dynasty.

But history in the Middle East never seems to have a happy ending. Although all seemed to be going well, with international recognition from Rome and elsewhere, Simon once again became embroiled in Seleucid affairs. While away on campaign against the Parthians, Demetrius II was taken prisoner. Taking advantage of this situation, his brother had himself crowned as Antiochus VII Sidetes. At this time Tryphon was still stubbornly trying to establish a kingdom for himself and so Antiochus VII sought to gain Simon's help by confirming all privileges hitherto granted and offering still more. With assistance from his ally, Antiochus was quickly able to defeat and kill Tryphon. Then, with typical Seleucid ingratitude, Antiochus went back on his promises and cancelled all the concessions previously granted to Judaea. To make his point plainer Antiochus moved his forces against Judaea but, failing to make any headway, he soon returned to Syria.

But Simon was not to have any peace. He had a treacherously ambitious son-in-law, Ptolemy, who was commander of the forces on the Jericho plain. On the pretext of holding a splendid celebratory banquet early in 135 B.C.E. for Simon and two of his three sons, Judas and Mattathias, he waited until his guests were suitably drunk and then had them slain.

Simon's sole surviving son, John Hyrcanus, inherited the titles of High Priest and Prince of the Jews. First he successfully dealt with the troublesome pretender Ptolemy, who was defeated and fled into exile. But then the Seleucids reappeared on the scene. In 135 B.C.E. Antiochus VII once again invaded Judaea, devastating the country and besieging Jerusalem. Having demonstrated who was in charge, he returned to Syria after concluding a peace treaty with John Hyrcanus, who had to pay tribute, give hostages and demilitarize certain towns. Though the Romans warned the Seleucids to back off, Judaea had once again become dependent on Seleucid Syria. With reluctance, Hyrcanus even had to participate in Seleucid action against the powerful Parthians who now ruled Persia in the east.

As luck would have it, Antiochus himself died on this campaign in 129 B.C.E., and the pressure on Judaea was relieved. Since it suited their own ends, the Parthians released the weak Demetrius II, who then reoccupied the Seleucid throne. In effect, Judaea was once again entirely free of Seleucid control. John Hyrcanus was able to benefit from this change of fortune and aggressively began to incorporate sizeable chunks of neighboring territory into Judaea. Most notably, he invaded Idumaea to the south and forcibly Judaicized its inhabitants, as well as subjugating the Samaritans and destroying their temple at Mount Gerizim. By now Judaean territory had expanded enormously. These conquests, however, had little to do with the religious fervor that had originally motivated the Maccabees but were inspired by dreams of political power.

During his long reign of 30 prosperous years, John Hyrcanus filled the post of High Priest as might be expected, but in secular matters he seems to have regarded himself as more of a president than an autocratic prince because the legend on his coins states: "John the High Priest and the Congregation of the Jews." This implies that he ruled in collaboration with some kind of national assembly, perhaps a prototype of the Sanhedrin. Of possible relevance to the contents of some of the sectarian Dead Sea Scrolls, it is recorded by the historian Josephus that John incurred the hostility of the Pharisee party, who resisted him, and so had to turn to the Sadducees for support. This is the first time that these two factions are mentioned by name together, although Josephus speaks of the Pharisees themselves during his account of the time of Jonathan.

After the death of John Hyrcanus in 104 B.C.E., Aristobulus, his eldest son, took over as High Priest. John had intended his widow Alexandra to become the secular leader—female rulers not being unheard of in the ancient Near East. However, defying his late father's wishes, Aristobulus had her imprisoned and starved to death. Under his short reign some degree of Hellenization was allowed to continue in Judaea, although clearly Jewish culture and customs were encouraged for he is also thought to have conquered Galilee and begun the process of Judaicizing that region. Then, after a reign of just one year, Aristobulus died in great pain of some disease, which many would have seen as divine punishment for the murder of his mother.

After the demise of Aristobulus in 103 B.C.E., his widow Alexandra Salome released his imprisoned brothers and made the eldest of them, Alexander Yannai (or Alexander Jannaeus, as he is generally known), High Priest while also offering him her hand in marriage. He was a belligerent and bloodthirsty ruler whose reign was characterized by continual wars, usually of his own making. He was not always successful, and one disastrous conflict almost resulted in Judaea becoming incorporated into Egypt.

Hasmonean rule was becoming increasingly despotic and a long way from the original pious aims of the Maccabean Revolt. This had not gone unnoticed by various religious factions in Judaea, and particular disquiet was felt among the populist Pharisees who even dared to question Alexander's credentials to be High Priest. On one occasion in the Temple when he was sacrificing for the important Feast of the Tabernacles, he was pelted with lemons and jeered at by the participants. Enraged, he ordered his mercenaries to attack the crowds; 6,000 are reported to have been slaughtered. This was to be an ominous portent.

Later, while away on yet another campaign of aggression against neighboring countries, Alexander was ambushed and barely escaped with his life. Though he eventually made his way back to Jerusalem, he was at that time little better than a fugitive. By now, hostility towards him had reached breaking point and open conflict erupted. The Pharisees and other opponents raised an army to fight him and unleashed a bloody conflict that was to last for six years. In 88 B.C.E., the anti-Alexander faction did what seemed to come naturally in those days and called on the Seleucid Demetrius III for help. With the help of forces from Syria, Alexander Jannaeus was utterly defeated and barely escaped with his life.

Then, suddenly, his fortunes changed. It must have occurred to the Jews who had wanted to get rid of him that they would now be under Seleucid control once again. They decided, it seems, that it would be preferable to live free in a Jewish state under a Hasmonean ruler, even one like Alexander Jannaeus. Most of Alexander's opponents now switched sides and Demetrius had no alternative but to go back home to Syria. Alexander swiftly defeated the remaining rebels and took the prisoners back to Jerusalem after the last battle. Here he inflicted a terrible revenge upon his enemies, for, according to Josephus, he had about 800 of them crucified in the center of the city while he caroused with his concubines. Moreover, the victims are said to have been forced to watch the slaughter of their wives and children before they themselves died. Significantly for allusions made in the Dead Sea Scroll material, it is believed that many of these victims of Alexander's retribution were Pharisees.

The remainder of his reign was marked by peace within the country because most of his opponents fled in terror into exile where they remained until his death. But outside Judaea, it was business as usual. Taking advantage of the dying Seleucid Empire, Alexander went on various campaigns against the Nabateans and areas east of the river Jordan. Perhaps not before time, he eventually died of illness on one of these campaigns in 76 B.C.E.

By the end of his reign, Judaea had reached its maximum extent, running from Lake Merom in the north down to Idumaea in the south. In the course of these conquests, many Hellenic cities along the Mediterranean coast and to the east of the Jordan were subjugated by him. Once captured, the inhabitants were usually Judaicized by force and those cities that refused to comply were destroyed—an ironic reversal of the Hellenizing policies of Antiochus IV 100 years earlier.

After Alexander Jannaeus' death, the twice-widowed Alexandra Salome became secular ruler and she nominated her eldest son, Hyrcanus II, as the High Priest. In contrast to her late husband's support of the aristocratic Sadducees, Alexandra was well disposed to the Pharisees and got them involved in the government. For this reason, Pharisee accounts view her reign as a kind of golden age. In fact, according to Josephus they were in effect the rulers of the country and were quick to settle old scores with their enemies. But overall Alexandra's reign was peaceful both at home and abroad and seems to have been a time of prosperity.

After the death of Alexandra Salome in 67 B.C.E., Hasmonean fortunes gradually took a turn for the worse and dragged the whole country down into misery. She had intended that her eldest son, John Hyrcanus II, who was already High Priest, would take over but, typically of the Hasmoneans, his younger brother Judas Aristobulus had ambitions of his own. He was supported in his scheming by the disaffected members of the Sadducean faction.

Aristobulus defeated John Hyrcanus II in battle after many of the latter's unreliable men switched sides. Hyrcanus II surrendered and seems to have happily renounced his titles while being left with all the revenues due to him. Josephus gives us the impression that he was a weak and indolent man, so the terms of this agreement may well have suited him.

But although Judas Aristobulus II had seized the pontificate and rulership, this was not the end of the matter; other opportunists appeared like vultures gathering over a dying animal. The then military commander of Idumaea was Antipater, father of the future Herod the Great, and he realized that it would be in his best interests to have the weak Hyrcanus II as his overlord rather than the more active Aristobulus. Inevitably he began plotting with Hyrcanus II to bring Aristobulus down. To boost his Idumaean army, Antipater promised the Nabatean king, Aretas, that he would return some territory to him in exchange for military help. Aristobulus was defeated in battle. Many of his troops and most of the populace switched sides, while Aristobulus himself took refuge in the Temple, where he was besieged. Things might have remained thus, in a stalemate reminiscent of the time of Menelaus—but this was not to be, for another powerful player was set to enter the stage of Judaean politics.

four

JUDAEA UNDER THE ROMAN YOKE

G radually over the past decades the power of late republican Rome had grown, with the rapid expansion of its territory through the conquests of Julius Caesar and his rival Pompey the Great. As fate would have it, while Aristobulus and Hyrcanus were slogging it out, the great general Pompey was in the area. He had just achieved a major victory over Mithradates of Pergamum, securing much of Anatolia and parts of Syrian territory for Rome. Scarus, a representative of Pompey who was based in Syria, entered Judaea in an attempt to take advantage of the situation in true Roman style.

Without much hesitation, both Aristobulus and Hyrcanus II each attempted to gain Roman support for their cause. To begin with, Pompey supported Aristobulus, who was gaining the upper hand. But it then seemed to the Roman general, thinking along the same lines as Antipater of Idumaea previously, that it would be more to his advantage to support the weaker Hyrcanus II. After some resistance Aristobulus surrendered to Pompey, but not surprisingly his supporters in Jerusalem did not want peace. In 63 B.C.E. they installed themselves on the fortified Temple mount and held out there, while the rest of the city opened the gates to the invader. Pompey had to lay siege to the Temple for more than three months, so strong did the massive walls prove against the Roman siege engines brought in specially for the task.

What followed when the Roman troops broke through was a terrible foretaste of what was to happen just over a hundred years later. Josephus estimates that in the mass slaughter over 12,000 died, and even the priests in the Temple were cut down as they attended to the sacred duties of the daily sacrifices. In the aftermath Pompey himself went into the Holy of Holies, but showed remarkable restraint for that age: He left everything untouched. There was no looting of Temple property, and the sacrifices were thereafter allowed to continue undisturbed. Many of Aristobulus' war party were beheaded and their property confiscated, though Hyrcanus II was reinstated as High Priest. However, Judaean territory was considerably reduced and the confiscated towns placed under direct Roman rule, even though Pompey himself did little to interfere in internal Judaean affairs This spelled the virtual end of the once proud Hasmonean dynasty, for Judaea was now little more than a Roman client or vassal state supervised by the governors of Syria.

It is hardly surprising that the years of John Hyrcanus II's pontificate saw a further decline in Judaean and Jewish fortunes. Gabinius, the Roman pro-consul of Syria, had to deal with trouble caused by Alexander, one of Aristobulus' sons, and defeated him. Furthermore, the Romans instigated important administrative changes within Judaea: John Hyrcanus II's status was reduced to High Priest in Jerusalem, while for a period the rest of the country was divided into five districts ruled by separate aristocratic councils. A series of fresh insurrections, led by Aristobulus or his other son Antigonus, were put down swiftly by the Romans. For a time Roman rule became oppressive: Gabinius' successor, the greedy Crassus, confiscated more than 200 talents' worth of gold and 8,000 talents' worth of precious objects from the Temple.

But things took a turn for the better in the aftermath of the Roman civil war that led to Julius Caesar's rise to power. Hyrcanus II had shrewdly supported Julius Caesar against Pompey and was well rewarded: his titles of Judaean ethnarch and High Priest were confirmed and made hereditary by decree of Caesar, and considerable concessions and rights were granted to the Jews. Nevertheless Hyrcanus II was ruler only in name because by now Antipater of Idumaea, who had also supported Caesar, was the real power in the land.

Aristobulus' son Antigonus took advantage of the disorder in the Roman world caused by the assassination of Julius Caesar and in 40 B.C.E. encouraged an invasion of Judaea by the Parthians, who were in league with him. They swept in and captured John Hyrcanus II, installing Antigonus in his place. For a brief period (40 B.C.E.–37 B.C.E.), with their support the usurper was able to style himself High Priest and king of Judaea. Poor Hyrcanus II had his ears bitten off by Antigonus himself, which barred him from ever taking up the post of High Priest again—Jewish religious law required all priests to be physically unblemished.

Predictably, Antigonus soon came into conflict with Herod, son of the now murdered Antipater, who harbored ambitious plans of his own. A few years earlier Herod had been nominated tetrarch of Judaea by Mark Antony, and he certainly intended to retain that status. Even after the death of his patron in Egypt following the fateful battle of Actium, Herod went to Rome and pleaded for help from Mark Antony's enemy Augustus Caesar. Not surprisingly, both Caesar and the Senate declared him king of Judaea, seeing in him a useful ally or pawn, though it was to be a few years before he could install himself on the throne in Jerusalem. After a bloody campaign through Judaea, in 37 B.C.E. Herod was eventually able to wrest control of the country from Antigonus and his Parthian supporters. Antigonus was captured and swiftly beheaded by the Romans at the behest of Herod, the first time that the Romans had executed the ruler of a foreign country. So died the last of the once mighty Hasmoneans.

HEROD THE GREAT: PARANOIA AND EXECUTIONS

Once he had taken control of Judaea, Herod quickly took steps to eliminate all remaining opposition to his rule. As an Idumaean of mixed parentage he was not a true Jew in the eyes of the pious population of Judaea, and so had to make considerable efforts to control them through a judicious use of terror and concessions. Herod must have suffered from chronic paranoia since he did not trust anybody who might challenge his authority, even members of his own family. With sickening regularity he had people executed without any compunction.

The first to go in his immediate circle was the deposed Aristobulus II, who was murdered in 34 B.C.E.; Joseph, the husband of his sister Salome, was executed later that year. In the following decade he executed the hapless John Hyrcanus II (30 B.C.E.), his second wife Mariamne (29 B.C.E.) and Costobar, the second husband of Salome (27 B.C.E.), to name but a few. If close relatives were not safe, what protection could lesser mortals have had from his notoriously ruthless measures? Though the story of the massacre of the innocents that is associated with the birth of Jesus is not historically true, such a deed would have been quite typical of Herod.

Perhaps inspired by Augustus Caesar, who was busy rebuilding Rome into a splendid city of marble temples and palaces, Herod embarked on a series of grand architectural projects. In the first years of his reign he organized the rebuilding of Jerusalem, which had suffered greatly through the ravages of war. Apart from having a splendid palace constructed for himself, in 20 B.C.E. he initiated a major refurbishment of the Temple to win favor with the Jewish population—though this project was only completed long after his death, in 63 C.E. He took care not to offend Jewish sensibilities, but also promoted Hellenistic culture and customs wherever he could by building theaters, amphitheaters and hippodromes for the Gentiles throughout Judaea.

Ever conscious of the debt he owed the Romans, he carefully cultivated the patronage of Augustus Caesar. Caesar in return granted him extensive additions to the Judaean territory with which he had started. To protect the Judaean frontier against Arab incursions he built or rehabilitated a chain of fortresses that were later to prove of great value to the Jews in their insurrection against Rome. It is during this time that the settlement at Qumran may have been reoccupied, especially if we accept the hypothesis that it functioned as a military base rather than as a religious institution.

As his reign drew to its end, he was plagued by ceaseless and complicated political intrigues within his palace. Another round of executions followed, during which Alexander and Aristobulus, sons of his first marriage, were strangled in 7 B.C.E. In the last months of his life Herod was wracked with disease and verging on insanity—he had one son, Antipater, executed days before his own death, and changed his will to name his successor three times.

In his *Jewish War*, Josephus graphically describes the torments of Herod's last days and his unrelenting cruelty. Knowing that he was unlikely to be mourned by the people, he had the leading men from every town and village in the land locked up and gave orders that they were all to be killed the moment he died, so that the country would have something to bewail. Fortunately, his more compassionate sister Salome was able to avert this tragedy by releasing these hostages before Herod's death became known to the military who were to carry out his horrific orders.

Herod finally died miserably at Jericho in the spring of 4 B.C.E. His kingdom was divided among three of his sons: Herod Antipas, Archelaus and Herod Philip, who were appointed tetrarchs of their respective territories.

The three sons who inherited various parts of Herod's kingdom by Roman appointment were a mixed bunch with quite different personalities. The least offensive of the three was Philip (4 B.C.E.–34 C.E.) who was allocated the area northwest of Galilee known as Trachonitis. Later rabbinical accounts describe him as a mild and peaceful man who was both pious and well loved by his people. His uneventful reign lies outside the scope of Judaean history as it relates to the Dead Sea Scrolls.

Herod Antipas (4 B.C.E.–39 C.E.), who was made tetrarch of Galilee and Peraea, shared some of his late father's characteristics though in a less extreme form. Though less able politically than Herod the Great, he was still an astute and ambitious ruler. He was also an extravagant builder of cities, most notably constructing his capital, Tiberias, on the west bank of Lake Gennesaret in the Hellenistic style.

Antipas is well known to readers of the Gospels as the ruler who had John the Baptist beheaded, supposedly at the request of his daughter Salome, prompted by her mother Herodias. This may indeed have been the immediate cause of John's death, since Herodias was known to be a vindictive troublemaker. The fact underlying this legend is that Antipas probably feared outbreaks of unrest due to John's popularity among the ordinary people, incited into action by John's scathing criticisms of him. We also know from the Gospels that Antipas is said to have taken part in the trial of Jesus but refused to get involved—probably killing John the Baptist had already undermined his popularity in Galilee. Some years later he was in Italy with Herodias, trying to better himself at her instigation, when he was confronted by the Emperor Caligula, who accused him of disloyalty. Given Caligula's reputation, Antipas was lucky to escape with his life—although he lost his lands and was exiled to Lyons in Gaul. His former territory was taken over by Agrippa, a brother of Herodias, who had already been granted the territory of Philip, who had recently died.

The last of the three brothers was Archelaus (4 B.C.E.–6 C.E.), who was named ethnarch of the largest portion of Herod's old kingdom, which included Judaea, Samaria and Idumaea. Archelaus was a true son to his father, for he was just as brutal and tyrannical and spent vast sums of money on extravagant and unnecessary building projects. His reign was cut short when a deputation of the aristocracy from Samaria and Judaea went to Rome and complained about his outrageous behavior and misrule. He was deposed and the Romans placed his territory under their direct rule as an annex of the province of Syria, though with its own governor, the prefectus or, as he was later known, the procurator.

The Romans established a large garrison of troops in Jerusalem in the huge Antonia fort, which was specifically located next to the Temple so that the enormous crowds of pilgrims coming to Jerusalem for the Passover each year could be policed effectively. From 6 C.E. to 41 C.E. the key office of High Priest was entirely in the control of the governors, who appointed the most pliable and cooperative candidates—though this right reverted briefly to the last Judaean ruler, Agrippa I. This 35-year period of direct Roman rule was basically tolerant of Jewish customs and culture, though rumblings of dissatisfaction occasionally made themselves felt, such as during the time the thuggish Pontius Pilate was governor. In hindsight one could almost believe that all would have been well if these general principles had been observed, but for stupid, insensitive and greedy governors appointed by Rome in the last decades before the Jewish revolt erupted.

Agrippa I, already ruler of the territory previously assigned to Philip and Herod Antipas, was eventually made a vassal king by Caligula over the entire kingdom that Herod the Great had ruled. For the brief period (41–44 C.E.) that he controlled Judaea and Samaria, it must have seemed as though there was some hope for the future. Those few years were a short final golden age, especially for the Pharisees, whose power in Judaea had gone from strength to strength. Agrippa himself was regarded as a pious man who meticulously observed Jewish religious law, although some viewed this as a cynical way of gaining popularity since he behaved in non-Jewish ways outside Palestine. To be more charitable, he might just have been trying to make compromises in what was undoubtedly a difficult situation. But whatever the truth may have been, he died suddenly without having had much time to make his mark on history for good or bad.

Agrippa's heir, inconveniently also called Agrippa, was only 17 at the time of his father's death so the Roman Emperor Claudius decided to have Palestine revert to a Roman procuratorship. Perhaps Claudius thought that in this way he would be able to avoid political unrest or war in the region, but in the event it was a disastrous decision. Many of the Roman governors in that era who were appointed to office overseas clearly regarded the job as an opportunity to enrich themselves and wield great power with little control from distant Rome. So it was that from 44 C.E. a whole series of thoroughly unsuitable governors seem to have deliberately gone out of their way to provoke the Jews into rebellion.

The last 20 years before the outbreak of the Jewish Revolt were marked by growing tensions within the Jewish community itself. As always there were those, especially among the rich and aristocratic members of society, who were only too happy to collaborate with the Roman administration, but they had their enemies. This was a time of fanaticism, both political and religious, though often the two can hardly be distinguished. The ultra-nationalistic xenophobic movement known as the Zealots had come into being, and they used terrorism to punish those who cooperated with the Romans. The Zealots employed urban guerrillas known as *sicarii*, or "dagger-men"—judging from his name, Judas Iscariot is thought to have been involved with them—who murdered their victims in public with knives concealed under their cloaks.

According to Josephus, there was a corresponding rise in religious fanaticism fueled by self-styled visionaries and messianic prophets. He tells us that some led their desperate though gullible followers into the desert, promising them redemption through repentance, while others incessantly preached against Rome and urged the people to take up arms against their overlords. Even the priesthood was not free from discord: many of the richer, powerful priests seized the tithes due to the poorer ones and left them destitute. Josephus even relates that once a street brawl broke out between a reluctant ex-High Priest and his successor. Throughout the land robbery and extortion were commonplace, often with the connivance of the Roman governors, who made sure that they took their cut from the proceeds.

Finally, in 66 C.E., the whole explosive mixture ignited and the calamitous Jewish Revolt erupted. The precise cause of the revolt is unclear but it involved two distinct elements: a burning hatred of the privileged aristocratic members of Jewish society that turned poor against rich, and a nationalistic desire to be rid of the oppressive and corrupt rule of Rome.

Most areas of Judaea took up arms and went on the rampage. The Romans were quick to react and poured troops into the country. The unstoppable war machine of the legions under Vespasian and later his son Titus swept through the land, gradually overcoming resistance and then, in early 70 C.E., moving on Jerusalem itself, which was the main Zealot stronghold. The ensuing siege lasted for months, during which the citizens fell prey to rival feuding Zealot gangs, starvation and disease. Thousands had died even before the Romans finally broke through into the city and fought their way street by street. The Temple, the pride of the Jewish nation and the focal point of their religion, was torched.

The end came within a month when the last Zealot strongholds were crushed and survivors were flushed out of their hiding places in the sewers and underground passages to face slavery and crucifixion. Much of the city was burned to the ground and the great defensive walls were all demolished. The cost in Jewish lives was enormous: several hundred thousand must have died in Jerusalem alone, quite apart from the thousands more who were slaughtered indiscriminately in the mopping-up operations that culminated in the siege and capture of the Masada fortress in 73 C.E. This brief outline of those terrible events can hardly do justice to what happened, though the Jewish historian Josephus describes the entire cataclysmic period in graphic detail in his *Jewish War*.

The aftermath of the destruction of Jerusalem and the slaughter or enslavement of hundreds of thousands of Jews must have left deep wounds in the country. Many would have struggled on with their lives in a state of shock, their religious bearings completely awry with the loss of the Temple. Yet slowly as the years went by, some kind of normality returned to the country.

One would have thought that the lessons of the Jewish Revolt would have been learned and everybody would have realized the futility of taking up arms against imperial Rome. But this was not so. A second brief uprising in 132–135 C.E. was led by Simeon bar-Kosiba, better known as bar-Kokhba. He had been acclaimed as the expected Messiah by some rabbis, including the famous Rabbi Akiba, but did not enjoy universal support—though this is unlikely to have affected the inevitable outcome. Of interest in connection with the Dead Sea Scrolls is the fact that Bar-Kokhba is known to have operated in that area, and some caves in the Qumran region and elsewhere are known to have been used by his followers since rebel administrative documents have been found in a number of them.

But though he initially made some headway in his struggle for liberation, he, too, was ultimately defeated and the former Judaea was once again devastated by the vengeful Romans. This time, Jerusalem was razed to the ground and rebuilt as a purely Roman city called Aelia Capitolina, which Jews were forbidden even to enter.

CONCLUSION

For some readers this account of the history of Judaea may have seemed unnecessarily long, even though I have just summarized the highlights of the period. However, these basic facts should enable readers to get a feel for those times—essential if we are to make any sense of the contents of the Dead Sea Scrolls, for they, too, are a product of that age. Later we shall look at some of the sectarian scrolls and see if they give any hints as to how they might be related to the events of this 200-year period. In the meantime, as food for thought, let me ask readers to imagine how they would have coped with life if they had lived during those terrible years so filled with dashed hopes and misery.

Part III

The Contents of the Scrolls

five

DATING THE SCROLLS

A s the thousands of manuscript fragments were gradually accumulated by Roland de Vaux's small team, the enormously complex task of sorting and identifying them began. The work was simplified when many of the fragments were found to contain passages that could be identified as portions of known Hebrew biblical texts, sometimes with interesting variations from the established text. Additionally, there was considerable excitement when it was realized that there were also fragments from a number of texts already known to scholars but not included in the Bible—texts belonging to a group of writings known as Apocrypha and Pseudepigrapha. In most cases these texts had been passed down through the ages in languages such as Greek, Ethiopian Ge'ez or Slavonic, rather than the original Hebrew or Aramaic; nevertheless they, too, could be identified fairly speedily. Yet though we now know that over 40 percent of the texts from the caves at Qumran are biblical or quasi-biblical in origin, the remaining 60 percent were entirely unknown beyond a single important exception, the *Damascus Document*, to which we shall return in Chapters 6 and 10.

Certain deductions had been made about the date of the scrolls based upon the archaeology of the Qumran site and, to a lesser degree, upon the contents of certain texts, but establishing the age of the fragments beyond doubt was of crucial importance to determining the nature and import of the hitherto unknown texts. At first some scholars could not believe that writing materials could possibly have survived in the inhospitable climate, and claimed that the scrolls were either medieval in origin or else cunning forgeries. These extreme views have now been discarded unanimously and it is accepted that the scroll fragments come from material written some time during the late Second Temple period—perhaps between 200 B.C.E. and 68 C.E. or a little later. However, early in the study of the scroll fragments certain very specific conclusions about their dates were reached by de Vaux's team that have continued to provoke controversy in the academic world.

To understand these controversies we need to look at how they arrived at these dates. When dealing with ancient manuscripts, there are two indispensable tools for dating: paleography and radiocarbon dating. We shall consider each of these in turn, together with the dates they yield for the scroll material and objections to these dates that have been raised in some quarters.

The study of ancient scripts and their relationship to each other, known as paleography, is still an art rather than a science and depends to a considerable degree on the skill and experience of the paleographer. When people write a language over a period of centuries, various changes can be detected in the style of script and in the way in which words are spelled. For example, various peculiarities can be detected in the formation of the individual letters, the thickness of the strokes that make up each letter, or even the amount of space allowed between each line.

To understand how paleography is used to date manuscripts, let us take an example nearer home. If we look at a selection of documents written in English over the centuries, many of us will recognize the so-called Gothic black-letter style of medieval writing, the decorative italic hand popular in the seventeenth century and the copperplate script of Victorian times. Many of us would, or that basis, be able to sort the documents into a rough relative chronology. If we were experts we would also know that, for example, medieval black-letter script gradually evolved in recognizable ways over the centuries in which it was used. Many surviving medieval documents contain some kind of date. This allows us to say that such-and-such a style of writing is associated with a certain period of history. The more dated manuscripts that are assembled, the easier it becomes to slot any undated manuscript into the overall chronology by comparing its script style with examples having known dates.

So in general terms the theory of paleographical dating is to compare the handwriting of undated documents with that of dated ones, and this is what Solomon Birnbaum and Frank Cross, two of the researchers connected with the Dead Sea Scrolls, attempted to do during the 1950s. But there was one major problem: there were very few known samples of writing in Hebrew or Aramaic script that were contemporaneous with the assumed date of the Qumran library. All that they had at their disposal were one tiny manuscript known as the Nash Papyrus and some inscriptions from ossuaries, so they were virtually working in a vacuum.

Nevertheless, with the great assurance characteristic of the early Qumranologists they divided the texts into three categories based on general characteristics and arrived at the following plausible periods: Archaic c.250 B.C.E.–150 B.C.E., Hasmonean c.150 B.C.E.–30 B.C.E., and Herodian c.30 B.C.E.–70 C.E. Then, incredibly, they proceeded to date manuscript fragments within each of these periods according to a very narrow system of dating that usually allows a margin of just 25 years—for example, the Book of Isaiah was deemed to have been copied between 125 B.C.E. and 100 B.C.E.

While the broad categorization might be acceptable as a rough guide to the relative chronology or age of the material, it is truly surprising that these two paleographers should have been so confident in their skills—based on such little corroborative evidence—to go on to date the material so precisely. As the dating of the various sectarian texts in particular is crucial for a reconstruction of the history of the community that produced them, it is small wonder that a number of scholars have objected vehemently to these findings. They point out that the variants which Cross and Birnbaum discerned in the scripts and which allowed them to arrive at these rather exact dates may be misleading for a number of reasons that preclude their being used as a basis for constructing a very specific chronology.

Robert Eisenman gives a useful example. Let us imagine an 80-year-old scribe sitting writing a manuscript next to a 20-year-old scribe. The younger scribe has not yet fully mastered his art and so may well produce a copy that contains a number of unintentional but confusing variant features in the script, although he basically tries to write in a "modern" hand. The older scribe was taught 60 years earlier and still writes in the "old-fashioned" way he learned as a youth. When a paleographer compares the two manuscripts he will almost certainly conclude that the old man's is up to 60 years older than the younger man's, while the mistakes in the latter's version might be interpreted as modern innovations. Now imagine further that the old scribe was himself taught by a very old conservative scribe who learned his script when he in turn was still young. In this scenario, the paleographer's error may well be compounded and lead him to believe that the manuscript copied by the old scribe is more than a hundred years older than the young scribe's version, though they were actually both written on the same day!

Apart from this problem, there is also the question of scribes deliberately using or reviving old scripts. We saw earlier that a black-letter script was characteristic of the medieval period, but what will paleographers in 2,000 years' time make of the Victorian revival of the various Gothic scripts? Without any internal dating evidence, they may well misdate a document from the 1870s to the 1470s.

This could well be the situation with one of the handwriting styles found among the Qumran material, the so-called paleo-Hebrew or round-hand script that is known to have been supplanted by the later Aramaic-influenced square-hand in which Hebrew is still written today. The sectarian Community associated with the Qumran manuscript fragments were undoubtedly extremely conservative in many respects, so it would not be out of character for some of their scribes to have purposely archaicized their texts. This is quite possible, given that the daily language of the Jews during the Second Temple period was the Aramaic they had picked up during the exile in Babylon. Hebrew had faded from general use, but later, during the nationalistic Maccabean era, it is believed that there was a marked revival in its use, which can be seen in the language of the texts from the Qumran caves. What could be more natural in such circumstances than for a scribe deliberately to use an older Hebrew script for such texts rather than the more "modern" one based on Aramaic?

Whatever the validity of their results, the paleographers made certain important assertions about the so-called sectarian texts from Qumran. First, they claimed that none of the manuscripts that are linked by reason of contents and style with the sectarian Community date from the Archaic period (c.250 B.C.E.–150 B.C.E.), implying that the Community was not creating or at least copying manuscripts before 150 B.C.E. They then placed the oldest sectarian documents at around 100 B.C.E.–75 B.C.E.—especially the group consisting of the *Community Rule* fragments from Cave 1 and the *Testimonia* from Cave 4, which, judging from the handwriting, were all copied by the same person. The equally important *Damascus Document* they dated slightly later, to 75 B.C.E.–50 B.C.E.

We shall return to this question of dating the individual manuscripts later, but suffice to say it is vital to get the dates right for the sectarian texts because some of them seem to contain veiled hints about the history of the Community. If the dates are wrong, any conclusions that might be drawn from their contents may also be erroneous.

There is one final problem concerned with dating the scrolls. Apart from a few inconsequential legal documents such as receipts and accounts there are no autograph manuscripts, only scribal copies. What this means is that none of the important texts is an original in the handwriting of the person who composed it—they are all later copies.

Obviously a copy of a particular document may be made at any time after it was first written, so we must distinguish the hypothetical date when a text was first composed and when it was copied. We know that some of the biblical texts, such as Leviticus or Deuteronomy, found at Qumran must have been composed or compiled several hundred years before the surviving copies of them were made, and this can be ascertained indirectly in various ways so no problem arises with them. However, in the case of non-biblical texts difficulties are encountered when trying to reconstruct the history of the sectarian Community if we lose sight of this fact. Even if we accept a relatively early date on paleographic grounds for such texts as the *Community Rule* or the *Damascus Document*, we must remember that these dates only relate to the time when the manuscript itself was copied and not to when it was composed, which could have been decades or even, though unlikely, centuries earlier.

RADIOCARBON DATING

Since the 1950s another more scientific method than paleography has been used for determining the age of organic remains—radiocarbon dating. The principle is simple. Carbon atoms are a component of all living things such as plants or animals, but there are three types of these atoms and each type has a different atomic weight. Two of these, ^{12}C and ^{13}C, are stable and undergo no change, whereas ^{14}C is unstable and subject to continuous formation and decay. ^{14}C is constantly being absorbed by living organisms from the atmosphere where it is formed, although it is only found in them in minute proportions in comparison with the stable carbon atoms—roughly one part in a million million.

When an organism dies, this process of absorption ceases and any ^{14}C present begins to decay. What is interesting for archaeologists is that under ideal conditions it decays at a fairly constant rate. Over time, the presence of any radioactive material halves over a set period of time—approximately 5730 years in the case of ^{14}C—and so a measurement of the ratio of ^{14}C to the stable forms of carbon atoms remaining in dead organic matter can theoretically establish how much time has elapsed since it died. This is popularly known as carbon-14 dating.

However, it was soon realized that the concentration of ^{14}C in the atmosphere where it is formed is not always constant, and that its rate of uptake by living organisms varies. The result is significant distortions in estimated ages. There is no easy way to resolve this problem, but the most reliable method involves calibrating the radiocarbon dates with those known from dendrochronology—literally, "tree timing."

Each year a growing tree forms a new ring that can readily be seen on a cross-section of its trunk, and each of these annual growth rings is slightly different from the others due to climatic factors such as the amount of rainfall and the temperature. By overlapping older and older samples of Californian bristle-cone pines, a complete sequence of dated tree rings has been built up that stretches back over the past 8,000 years. It can provide data for general climatic changes in the northern hemisphere. Other more specific local tree ring sequences have been compiled for parts of northern Europe and elsewhere, though they are still lacking for arid Middle Eastern areas like Egypt, which have few trees. But generally speaking, tree rings can provide a fairly accurate method of dating ancient wood from much of Eurasia and North America if a suitably large cross-section is available.

From this it is a simple process to perform carbon-14 tests on pieces of wood with dates derived from dendrochronology and to adjust the initial dates derived from ^{14}C readings accordingly. In other words, if a piece of wood known by dendrochronology to be exactly 2,000 years old is subjected to carbon-14 testing and the results show a discrepancy of 200 years, the carbon-14 derived date can be adjusted or calibrated to take this degree of variation into account. So when the age of a piece of bone or textile is estimated by carbon-14 testing, that date can be corrected by a known degree of variation.

This is the basic principle behind modern carbon-14 dating methods, although obviously there will always be an element of uncertainty. Readings are usually expressed by a pair of dates, one higher and one lower, within which the true age of the object is assumed to fall, but even these, for technical reasons, only have a probability of around 68 percent. Also, in some cases the material will generate two sets of paired dates, as in the list of dated manuscripts given below. Nevertheless, it is important to note two things here: the true age can be anywhere between the two dates, and there is no current consensus on how carbon-14 dates are to be calibrated with precision. This means that any carbon-14 derived date is at best an approximation.

Early carbon-14 testing was rather crude and required a fairly large sample of the material under investigation. This meant that many small or precious objects could not be dated in this way without irreparably damaging or even destroying them. Fortunately, at the close of the twentieth century a more efficient method of measuring the presence of ^{14}C was developed. AMS—

accelerator mass spectrometry—is a very expensive and complex process, but it has two advantages. It only requires very small samples of material and it is much more sensitive than the older method and can therefore give narrower date ranges. Over the years both of these methods have been used on the material found at Qumran, with some success.

In 1952, some of the linen used to wrap the scrolls in Cave 1 was subjected to carbon-14 testing and the range of dates established was 167 B.C.E.–233 C.E., with the actual age guesstimated as 33 C.E. Because of the size of sample needed at that time, none of the precious scrolls was tested in this way. However, with the introduction of AMS eight manuscript fragments from Qumran, together with some from Masada and elsewhere, were tested in Zurich in 1990. The resulting calibrated dates for the Qumran parchment fragments are as follows, with the dates derived from previous paleographical estimates by Birnbaum and Cross for comparison:

Scroll Fragment	Calibrated ^{14}C	Paleography
Testament of Qahar	388–353 B.C.E.	100–75 B.C.E.
Pentateuch Paraphrase	339–324 B.C.E.	125–100 B.C.E.
	209–117 B.C.E.	
Book of Isaiah	335–327 B.C.E.	125–100 B.C.E.
	202–107 B.C.E.	
Testament of Levi	191–155 B.C.E.	Late 2nd/early
	146–12 B.C.E.	1st century B.C.E.
Book of Samuel	192–63 B.C.E.	100–75 B.C.E.
Temple Scroll	97 B.C.E.–1 C.E.	Late 1st century B.C.E./early 1st century C.E.
Genesis Apocryphon	73–14 B.C.E.	Late 1st century B.C.E./early 1st century C.E.
Thanksgiving Hymns	21 B.C.E.–61 C.E.	50 B.C.E.–70 C.E.

Further tests on another 13 fragments were carried out in 1994–95 at the AMS Laboratory at the University of Arizona. The results confirmed the general paleographic dating but we should be cautious about this for, as can be seen from the above table, the correspondence between the paleographic dates and the radiocarbon dates is often not very close.

Supporters of the consensus view that all the Dead Sea Scroll material predates the Christian era were delighted with these results as they interpreted them. Dr. Geza Vermes stated on the day that the 1991 results were announced that "most of the Scrolls date to the last two centuries B.C.," and it was reported that he "and his fellow paleographers are gratified that in almost all cases their estimated dates have been corroborated by science."

On the other hand, scholars such as Dr. Robert Eisenman and Dr. Norman Golb have questioned this triumphant claim of certainty. They point out that the correlation between the radiocarbon dates and the paleographic dates is not as watertight as some might wish and that in most cases they overlap only marginally, so the use of paleography to date the remainder of the scroll fragments which have not been radiocarbon dated is at best speculative. Eisenman and Golb also remind us that even AMS calibrated radiocarbon dates can have a wider margin of error than is apparent, since the quantity of ^{14}C atoms present in a sample can be affected by a variety of reasons such as annual variations of atmospheric ^{14}C due to sun-spot activity or contamination of the material through handling in modern times.

Furthermore, it must be remembered that carbon-14 results only indicate the estimated period within which the *source* of the sample died. Parchment such as was used for the scrolls is usually prepared from the skins of sheep, so the radiocarbon dates indicate when the sheep was killed and not when the parchment itself was used. This is important because parchment is not suitable for immediate use but must be matured like wine for several years before it is fit to be used for a manuscript. Additionally, it can be stored for many decades before it is finally used by a scribe. It is not unlikely that some sheets of prepared but unused parchment may have lain in storage for over 50 years. This was actually the explanation given by the consensus scholars for the great discrepancy between the radiocarbon dates and the estimated paleographic dates in some of the items in the list above.

In consideration of these factors, Golb, Eisenman and others maintain that these tests have merely shown that the scrolls were originally written at some time between the third century B.C.E. and the first century C.E. This is no great surprise, and does not help much in determining the history or origins of the scrolls except to demonstrate conclusively that the scrolls were neither medieval nor modern forgeries.

Reviewing the situation regarding the derivation of dates for the Dead Sea Scrolls from both carbon-14 tests and paleography, my overall impression is that scholars tend to play up or down the various difficulties arising from the dating methods in order to confirm their own hypotheses about the scrolls and who wrote or copied them. As one scholar has said, those dates that confirm one's theories are emphasized, those that diverge a little are relegated to footnotes, and those that are totally contradictory are discarded!

DNA MATCHING

There is one final technique that science has recently placed at the disposal of the Dead Sea Scroll scholars—the use of DNA matching. This, naturally, cannot be used for dating the scrolls, but may well prove valuable for piecing together some of the many unidentified fragments or linking them with larger known portions of the scrolls. It has even been suggested that an in-depth DNA analysis of all the scroll fragments would help to group the documents on the basis of family relationships between the sheep whose skins were used to make the parchment.

This could well be a very useful way to settle some of the arguments that rage in the academic world about the provenance of the scrolls. If a family tree could be constructed showing the relationship between the various sheep, it might be possible to determine which scrolls are genetically connected and come from the same flock of sheep. One scholar jokingly commented that we could end up knowing more about the genealogy of the sheep at Qumran than about their contemporary human owners!

This is an exciting development because though many scholars believe that the scrolls were largely copied at Qumran, others such as Dr. Norman Golb claim, as we shall see later, that they come from elsewhere with a diverse range of sources. If the proposed research goes ahead, this vexed question may be finally settled.

six

THE BIBLICAL WORKS

I t is now time to look at the contents of the scroll collection in detail. This chapter is concerned with the most important biblical writings found at Qumran, while Chapter 7 will deal with the works thought to have been produced by the sectarian Community often identified as the Essenes.

Since all the texts found at Qumran have now been made available to scholars and several complete translations have been prepared, we can finally understand the overall composition of the collection. To begin with, it is now known that just under 80 percent of the texts were written in Hebrew, as may be expected, with most of the rest in Aramaic and a few in Greek. The precise number of individual works found is a little more difficult to estimate, since there are many unidentified loose ends that may or may not belong with other more complete fragments. The general view at present is that we have the remnants of around 840 works, though the total number of items is higher since there are multiple copies of some texts—the greatest number being the Psalms, with at least 39 copies identified. It is likely that those texts which exist in multiple copies were of particular significance at that time and therefore in greater demand. The Psalms, for example, are known to have been important liturgically for many Jewish groups and would have been widely copied, while others, such as Isaiah, were popular for their religious message.

Based on his understanding of the contents of the various texts, in the early 1990s, the leading German scholar Hartmut Stegemann put the scrolls into four groups: 33 percent sectarian texts (249 manuscripts), 29 percent biblical texts (223 manuscripts), 25 percent non-sectarian texts (192 manuscripts) and 13 percent unidentified items (96 manuscripts). There is little disagreement about the percentage he gave for the biblical material since this can be easily identified, and naturally little can be said about the unidentified items. However, the respective percentages given by him for sectarian and non-sectarian texts are currently open to debate.

In the early stages of Qumranology, almost everything that was not biblical was deemed to be sectarian in origin. But in recent years researchers have begun a close re-examination of the contents, language and style of these supposed sectarian scrolls and have sometimes concluded that works hitherto thought to belong to the Community should not in fact be linked with them directly. For example, there are differing views about the status of the important *Temple Scroll*—some believe it is a sectarian work, while others think it is not. Additionally, although the sectarian texts were all thought at one time to have been composed by the Qumran Community, it is now possible that they represent the writings of not one but several, possibly related, groups with slightly different agendas.

Let us now look at the three main categories of documents found at Qumran. It will be easiest and least controversial if we look first at the range of biblical material, though even these texts were to provide some surprises for scholars. Nowadays, whether they are Jewish or Christian, readers are accustomed to using one of the modern translations of the Hebrew Bible based on a standardized Hebrew text, though the actual translations themselves may vary a little—some parts of the Christian version, known as the Old Testament, may be slanted to conform with various passages quoted in the books of the New Testament. Additionally, there are discrepancies between the number of books included in the Hebrew Bible, according to differing Christian and Jewish ideas of what constitutes the canon, and even the various Christian Churches are not unanimous on what should be recognized.

To understand this situation we should first consider what is meant by the term "canon." This term derives from the Greek word for a straight rod, hence a rule or standard. Applied to scriptural texts, it implies a fixed selection of works that are considered authentic, divinely inspired and authoritative. The word was first used in connection with the scriptures by the early Christian Church Fathers, although the notion, even if not clearly expressed, is found in many other religions.

Given that the early Christian Church developed a large body of literature expressing a wide range of views, there was much disagreement about what should and should not be considered canonical. Once a particular faction within the Church had secured a dominant position for itself and considered itself the arbiter of orthodox teachings and writings, a number of scriptural works were deemed heretical and unworthy of inclusion in the canon. Others excluded were texts that, though not deemed heretical, were still considered to be of a dubious nature in some sense or other. These texts are generally termed "apocrypha" or "pseudepigrapha."

The apocrypha were texts that, as the original Greek meaning implies, were to be hidden away—not suitable to be used as part of the liturgy. In the case of the Christian Old Testament, such apocryphal works include the Wisdom of Solomon, the two Maccabee books and Tobit. Pseudepigrapha, literally "false writings," are works ascribed to a particular author for prestige but clearly not written by that person. One famous and popular set of works in this category are the three Books of Enoch—they are unlikely to have been written by Enoch, who was a legendary descendant of Adam. Some of these secondary texts are of pre-Christian Jewish origin, while others are products of the early Christian Church or at least modified by them. Nevertheless, since many of the apocrypha and pseudepigrapha were considered valuable even though they were thought to be less authoritative than the "official" scriptures, a number of them were included in the Bibles of the different Christian Churches.

THE TANAKH

As we are not concerned with the Christian New Testament in this book, we should consider how the Jewish collection of books known as the Old Testament evolved. Since we are also considering Jewish views about this collection of books, it will be helpful to note the Jewish term for the Old Testament.

The standard Jewish view, as early as the Second Temple period, is that this collection of books can be divided into three categories: the Torah or "Instructions," the Nevi 'im or "Prophets" and the Kethuvim or "Writings." They are known collectively as the Tanakh, from the first letters of each category. Of these, the Torah was so basic to the Jewish way of life that it was accepted as authoritative at an early date. It comprises five books—Genesis, Exodus, Leviticus, Deuteronomy and Numbers—and for this reason is known in Christian circles as the Pentateuch, derived from the Greek word for five. Though based on a number of earlier sources, it is believed that these books took on their final basic form under the direction of the prophet Ezra when the Jews returned from the exile in Babylon. The make-up of the second section, the books of the Prophets, seems to have been determined by Herodian times, but it was the third section, the Writings, that remained in a state of flux for some time without any agreement about what should be included or excluded. The present body of books that make up the Tanakh was probably not finalized until some time in the second century C.E., when it was felt necessary to exclude books with Christian leanings or inspiration.

When the content of a canon has become permanently fixed it is known as a closed canon, while one that permits the inclusion of other additional works is known as an open canon. Importantly, it seems probable that the canon of Jewish scriptures was still open at the time the sectarian Community linked with the Qumran finds was active.

Yet although much of the contents of the Tanakh had achieved canonical status by the time the Jewish Revolt began in 68 C.E., one other factor had to be determined before the actual text of the books was standardized. The version we now have was finalized only around the fourth century C.E. by a group of scholars and scribes known as the Masoretes—the "transmitters." Choosing the best copies of the texts that they could obtain, these scholars edited the books, invented a system for representing the vowels that Hebrew had not previously shown in writing, and divided the text into paragraphs and verse divisions. This became the standard text of the Tanakh that is still used by Jews today, although the earliest surviving manuscripts only date from the early eleventh century C.E.

Some time prior to the Masoretes' work—certainly at the time of the Dead Sea Scrolls—there had been a number of what are called recensions in circulation, even though the overall contents had basically been fixed. The term "recension" is used to indicate any version of a text that has been passed down which differs from others. There are several reasons that recensions come into being. For example, particular religious groups sometimes add or delete material to reflect their understanding of the meaning of the text better or to promote a particular doctrinal position.

Another cause of deviations lies in the fact that, before the age of printing, all books were in manuscript form. Once a book had been composed and written down, it would be copied by scribes repeatedly as often as necessary. Because the scribes were only human, they would sometimes make mistakes due to tiredness, carelessness, poor eyesight and the like. The more a text was copied, the greater the number of errors it might contain. A later scribe might notice a mistake and try to correct it as best he could—without any guarantee that he was restoring the text to its original form. If he was unsure of the original form, he would often just copy the garbled text in front of him.

With the discovery of the Qumran collection of biblical material, the manuscript horizon of the Tanakh can be pushed back by more than a thousand years. One of the exciting insights gained from the Qumran biblical books concerns the range of recensions of the books of the Tanakh that were still in circulation at that time. Around 60 percent of the manuscripts are very close to the final standard or Masoretic recension, though they sometimes preserve better readings than are currently available. So new translations of the Tanakh have, where possible, made use of the Qumran scrolls to suggest corrections, for example in the case of Isaiah. Readers will usually see a reference to Qumran manuscripts in the footnotes, as in the new version produced by the American Jewish Association.

But apart from the Masoretic style of recension, the presence of four other versions was discovered. Some of the scroll fragments represent a hitherto unknown "Qumran-style" recension, with its own unique readings which must have been transmitted through the Community that is linked to the other sectarian material found at Qumran. Then there were versions of texts that are representative of the Samaritan Torah.

The Samaritans were the descendants of those inhabitants of the northern kingdom of Israel centered on Samaria who remained there after the conquest and depopulation of the country by the Assyrians in the eighth century B.C.E. Though they followed the Mosaic law as prescribed by the Torah, they split from the Judaean Jews late in the Second Temple period and had their own rival temple at Mount Gerizim as well as their own Torah, which differs in some respects from the Masoretic version. The Samaritan Torah is still used by the few hundred Samaritans who live in Israel today, and so has always been known to scholars. Though it had been thought that any divergences in the Samaritan Torah from the traditional Masoretic text were the result of deliberate ideological alteration, it now seems that there are far fewer such cases than originally believed. On the contrary, it seems that the version of the Torah preserved by the Samaritans not only predates their schism from Judaean Judaism but was also widely used and acceptable to Jews throughout Palestine up until the time the scrolls were concealed in the Qumran caves.

The discovery of a fourth type of recension of the Tanakh, the Septuagint edition, in its original Hebrew caused the greatest surprise among biblical scholars. During the Second Temple period there were many Jews living in Egypt, especially around Alexandria. The everyday use of Hebrew in Judaea had given way to Aramaic after the exile period, and since many Jews were unable to read the Hebrew texts, interpretative translations in Aramaic known as *targums* were created. On the other hand, the Alexandrian Jews used Greek almost exclusively at that time since that area of Egypt had become strongly Hellenized after it was conquered by Alexander the Great. Although in reality it is more likely to have been the product of several centuries' translation work, there is a legend that in the third century B.C.E. one of the late Egyptian pharaohs wanted a copy of the Jewish scriptures in Greek for the official archives, and invited 70 (or 72) scholars from Palestine to translate them.

Named after these 70 scholars, the Greek Septuagint version of the Tanakh has survived until the present since this was the version of the Hebrew scriptures initially favored by those Christians who used Greek as their scriptural language. The Septuagint has several noteworthy features that make it a valuable adjunct to the study of the Hebrew Tanakh. For one thing, it preserves a number of books that were not considered canonical by the Masoretes or their rabbinical predecessors and so had not survived in Hebrew. Additionally, even in the case of the books that both recensions have in common, there are many variations in the Septuagint text that were traditionally thought unreliable by scholars—the result of a loose or free style of translation. However, the Qumran caves yielded a number of fragments of biblical books in Hebrew that are clearly linked to the Septuagint Greek version. In other words, what scholars had thought were inaccuracies in the Septuagint text turn out to have a respectable Hebrew parentage and therefore derive from yet another recension of the Tanakh that was in circulation in Judaea in ancient times.

Apart from these four recensions of the Hebrew scriptures whose existence is now proved by the Qumran finds, there are also traces of what may be a fifth recension that exhibits random features from the other ones. However, little can be said at present about the origins of this version and how it has been handed down. But despite the discovery of these five versions of biblical books, many existing side by side, the majority of examples are linked to the recension associated with the later Masoretic tradition.

It is not known for certain how the people who preserved the Qumran material viewed the range of biblical books found there—whether they had a closed canon or not—but these included fragments from all the books now included in the Tanakh, with the possible exception of the Book of Esther. The number of examples of each biblical book is quite revealing and gives some indication about the preferences and doctrinal leanings of those who concealed the scrolls. The following table shows the number of each biblical book found at Qumran, and we can also surmise which were of significance to the sectarian Community because they composed commentaries on them. For comparison, I have included the number of times each biblical book of the Tanakh was quoted or alluded to in the Christian New Testament, whose writers shared a number of ideological concerns with the Qumran Community.

Book	Category	Number of Copies	Commentary	New Testament
Psalms	Writings	39 + 2?	2	94
Deuteronomy	Torah	31 + 3?		57
Isaiah	Latter Prophets	22	2	107
Genesis	Torah	18 + 3?		42
Exodus	Torah	18		45
Leviticus	Torah	17		24
Numbers	Torah	12		8
Twelve minor prophets	Latter Prophets	10 + 1?	6	57
Daniel	Writings	8 + 1?		15
Ezekiel	Latter Prophets	7		27
Jeremiah	Latter Prophets	6		17
I–II Samuel	Former Prophets	4		7
Job	Writings	4		3
Song of Songs	Writings	4		
Ruth	Writings	4		
Lamentations	Writings	4		
Judges	Former Prophets	3		1
I–II Kings	Former Prophets	3		6
Joshua	Former Prophets	2		1
Proverbs	Writings	2		15
Ecclesiastes	Writings	2		1

Ezra–Nehemiah	Writings	1	
I–II Chronicles	Writings	1	2
Esther	Writings	0	1

Knowing that the sectarian Community thought to be associated with Qumran was extremely zealous in its attention to details of Mosaic law, it comes as no surprise that the five books of the Torah are well represented. The large number of copies of the Psalms may not be especially significant since this book was well loved and widely used among all Jews both in the Temple and for private prayer. But the apparent popularity of the books of Isaiah, the Twelve Minor Prophets and Daniel was undoubtedly linked to the eschatological or apocalyptic content of the world view of the sectarian Community, a view that seems, as we shall see, to have been shared in some respects by the early Christians.

PARA-CANONICAL WORKS

As we have seen, there are a number of scriptural works known as apocrypha and pseudepigrapha, which we may call para-biblical, that have an ambivalent status and are dealt with differently by Jews and Christians. The final canon of the Jewish Tanakh was the most conservative and omits them all, whereas some are included in Christian Bibles—though not consistently.

Generally speaking, all the modern Christian Bibles omit the pseudepigrapha but usually include the apocrypha somewhere. Protestant Bibles do not include these works in their Old Testament but relegate them to a separate appendix-like section, the Apocrypha, often found sandwiched between the Old Testament and the New Testament. Catholic Bibles are slightly different in that they accept these works within the Old Testament, although they are termed "deuterocanonical" instead of apocrypha. The Eastern Orthodox Churches accept still more works into their Old Testament, since they follow more closely the arrangement of the Septuagint, while the smaller Ethiopic and Coptic Churches include even more.

Not a great number of apocrypha texts were found at Qumran, but among them were two important ones. The first was the anthology of wise sayings collected in the work known as the Book of Ben Sira, or Ecclesiasticus as it is called in Christian circles. Though it had been transmitted in Greek as part of the Septuagint, over the centuries there had been much debate about the original language in which it had been written. The Greek version had a prologue which states that it was first written in Hebrew by Joshua ben Sira around 180 B.C.E. and translated into Greek 50 years later by his grandson, Jesus ben Sira, but some people doubted the authenticity of this statement.

Around the beginning of the twentieth century, a huge horde of Jewish manuscripts was found in a Cairo synagogue; they included several damaged manuscript copies of the Ben Sira work in Hebrew. Since the bulk of this manuscript collection was medieval in origin, many scholars thought they were merely translations made from the Greek some time in the Middle Ages when there was a renewed interest in the book. This view has conclusively been disproved by the discovery of several portions of the book in Hebrew at both Qumran and Masada.

The Book of Ben Sira belongs to a popular class of Jewish writing known as sapiential or wisdom literature—compilations produced by groups of sages organized into "wisdom schools." These schools seem to have been a common feature of Middle Eastern cultures from Mesopotamia to Egypt. They were not overtly religious but emphasized practical wisdom, perhaps for the training of bureaucrats and scribes. Apart from the work by Joshua ben Sira, the Tanakh includes several similar books such as Proverbs and Ecclesiastes, but there must have been many other books of this kind that have not survived. Some scholars believe that in the

Jewish cultural sphere these wisdom schools were the forerunners of the rabbinical schools that emerged in the late Second Temple period. That such works were then popular is highlighted by the discovery at Qumran of many other fragments from over a dozen sapiential books that bear witness to the vibrancy of Jewish intellectual life at that time.

Another work formerly only known from its Greek translation, the short Book of Tobit was also discovered in fragmentary Aramaic manuscripts. The fact that it was written in Aramaic would seem to indicate that it is a fairly late composition, post-dating the return from exile but before the Maccabean Revolt. Its message would have had a wide appeal to many groups of Jews in general as well as to zealous sectarian groups, and it is also mentioned in the New Testament.

It tells the story of a charitable and pious Jew named Tobit who was devoted to the charitable deed of burying the unclaimed bodies of deceased Jews. One day, while having a nap, Tobit was blinded by some bird-droppings falling into his eyes. His son Tobias later went to Ecbatana, where he married a Jewish woman who had been plagued by a demon who had killed all her previous seven husbands on the wedding night. Through his piety he was able to enlist the help of Raphael, the angel of healing, and dispose of the demon. When Tobias and his wife returned to the home of his father Tobit, he was able to cure him of his blindness.

The story declares that pious people will eventually overcome adversities and have the ability to cure others. This idea of the suffering righteous ones who are ultimately vindicated as a reward for their pious adherence to the Mosaic law would have appealed to the sectarian group associated with the Qumran collection, which may account for the presence of this text there.

Apart from these apocryphal books, many examples of influential pseudepigrapha were found at Qumran that had only been known previously from translations. Undoubtedly these works were preserved there because they were important to the sectarian Community, but they must also have been widely known and appreciated in the greater Jewish world and were inherited by the Christians, who were largely responsible for preserving them in other languages. The Book of Enoch is classed as pseudepigrapha because its contents are attributed to this legendary descendant of Adam, even though their contents and concerns are clearly late in origin.

There are actually three works associated with Enoch, referred to as I Enoch, II Enoch and III Enoch. We are only concerned with I Enoch because II Enoch is a later derivative work while III Enoch is medieval. I Enoch was previously known only from a few Greek fragments found in Egypt and a fairly complete Ge'ez Ethiopian version, but the discovery of numerous fragments at Qumran was an extremely important development in the study of this neglected text. One can say that it is neglected because, despite the fact that eight references are made to it in the New Testament, very few Christians are aware of its existence and relevance to the origins of their beliefs since it never achieved canonical status in most Christian Churches.

I Enoch itself was formerly known to comprise five parts: the *Book of the Watchers*, the *Book of Parables*, the *Book of Astronomical Writings*, the *Book of Dreams* and the *Epistle of Enoch*. As a result of the Qumran finds, it is now recognized that I Enoch is a composite work that brings together texts that were originally independent of each other and were written in post-exile Aramaic, rather than Hebrew, at different times during the Second Temple period. The themes of this work—the origins and ultimate destruction of evil, the role of angels and demons in the human world, and the coming new age—must have had popular appeal for many pious Jewish groups at this time since, apart from passages in the New Testament, various allusions and echoes are found in many of the writings of the Qumran sectarian Community.

The oldest section of I Enoch is believed to be the *Book of Astronomical Writings*, which, judging from the fragments found at Qumran, seems to have initially been an independent work dating from before 200 B.C.E. It is also now obvious that this section, as we have it in the Ethiopic version of I Enoch, is an abridgement of a considerably more extensive work which presents a detailed system based on a solar calendar of 364 days. In the post-exile period, the vital question of what calendar should be used to regulate holy days and religious festivals was the subject of much debate. Some groups wanted to retain the old short lunar calendar, while others wanted to adopt the more accurate solar version or even an amalgam of the two. The sectarian Community associated with the Qumran manuscripts was especially vocal in advocating the use of the solar calendar, which seems to have been one of the chief reasons that they evolved as an independent sect and separated themselves from the religious establishment at the Temple during the early Maccabean period.

Slightly younger than the *Book of Astronomical Writings*, but still pre-Maccabean in origin, is the *Book of the Watchers*. This section of I Enoch expands some material from Genesis and presents doctrinal themes concerned with the End of Days and the Last Judgement that must have had poignant implications for Jews living in the Second Temple period. Surrounded as they were by hostile or alien cultures that implicitly sought to undermine Jewish religious and social identity, the Second Temple period Jews were troubled by the problem of evil in the world. Wherein lay the responsibility for evil—were humans inherently evil, was God ultimately responsible, or did its source lie elsewhere?

The answer provided by the *Book of the Watchers* marks a new phase in Jewish religious thought and may have been inspired by concepts that the Jews encountered during the exile in Babylon. Most religions are not happy about identifying God as the author of evil in the human realm, so they usually lay the blame on humanity itself. However, taking a cue from the enigmatic passage in Genesis 6:1–4 concerning the Sons of God who took wives from the daughters of men and gave rise to a breed of giants known as the nephilim, the Book of the Watchers identifies these beings as the cause of evil that resulted in God sending the Flood to destroy much of humanity.

We are told that God appointed 200 angels to watch over his newly created human progeny. As time passed by, the allegiances of these angelic Watchers gradually shifted and they became enamored of their erstwhile charges. In effect, they had become rebellious or fallen angels. Not only did they take human wives for themselves but they also divulged secret knowledge such as the ability to work metals and other skills. These deeds began to have repercussions in the human world, which resulted in the emergence of widescale sin and evil. The offspring borne by the human wives of these fallen angels, the gigantic beings known as nephilim, shared many of the attributes of their angelic fathers. Given that this section of I Enoch is thought to have been composed during the late third century B.C.E., it may well be an allegory for the impact of Hellenic culture on traditional Jewish society that began to be felt after Alexander the Great and his successors occupied Palestine.

As the outcry against the irresponsible evil wrought by these Watchers increased, they incurred the wrath of God who was minded to destroy them. They came to Enoch, asking him to intercede on their behalf with God. Enoch agreed to do so, so presenting the author of the Book of the Watchers with an opportunity to describe various apocalyptic visions seen by him in heaven. This probably takes its cue from an old legend associated with Genesis 5:24: "Enoch walked with God; then he was no more, for God took him," since it implies that Enoch was taken up to heaven by God while he still lived. While in heaven Enoch has visions concerning the unfolding of history, the eventual destruction of evil and the regeneration of the world in a new age of righteousness.

These visions are expanded in the *Book of Dreams*, which describes the future world as seen from Enoch's perspective, encompassing the Flood and subsequent events down to the coming of a Messiah and the End of Days. Within this book we also find the so-called Animal Apocalypse, which symbolically describes various groups of people and events that may be identified with the early Maccabean period. This form of visionary animal symbolism was also adopted by the author of the Book of Daniel— which, based on internal evidence, would similarly have been written a little after 168 B.C.E.—and must have been a popular medium for commenting on the state of the world at that time. One noteworthy feature of this Animal Apocalypse is that it speaks of a group of "sheep" and their offspring "lambs" which emerge in the run-up to the destruction of the wicked at the End of Days. Using this imagery, the account foretells the emergence of an elect group of righteous Jews who would be instrumental in punishing the wicked ones of the world and, as we shall see, the sectarian groups associated with many of the writings from Qumran were inspired by identical ideas.

The *Epistle of Enoch*, which combines themes from both the *Book of the Watchers* and the *Book of Dreams*, is written in the form of an exhortatory testament attributed, like all the previous works, to Enoch. Here again the history of the world is described, but this time it is divided into a sequence of ten consecutive "weeks," each with its special features, from the time of Enoch until the Last Judgement. This so-called Apocalypse of Weeks would have been important for sectarian groups, since it outlines a repetitive pattern in historical events where wicked people rise to power only to be overthrown or destroyed in some way.

However, despite its inclusion in the Book of Enoch the *Epistle of Enoch* is not entirely consistent with the rest of the work, for it disagrees in certain respects with the sections concerning the origin of evil and lays the blame less with the fallen angelic Watchers than with mankind itself. Yet in each of the cyclical "weeks" a certain group of righteous, pious people are chosen or predestined for salvation. So, for example, Noah is chosen for salvation when God decides to rid the earth of evil people who have been corrupted by the fallen angels. Yet, as already mentioned, this idea of an elect group emerging just before Judgement would have been attractive to the Qumran Community.

Another key feature of the *Epistle* is its teachings about an afterlife spent in the company of the angelic hosts in heaven, for earlier biblical material is remarkably silent about the possibility and nature of an afterlife. Here again we can see strong parallels with the ideology of the Qumran sectarian groups, for they, too, are thought to have had a strong belief in an afterlife, perhaps even associated with a physical resurrection.

Included among the five sections of I Enoch known from its Ethiopic translation is the *Book of Parables*, but no trace of this work has been found at Qumran. As well as dealing with now familiar themes such as the coming End of Days, the punishment of the fallen angels and resurrection, it was of considerable interest to Christians because it contains several passages referring to a "Son of Man" figure who is conceived as being the agent of God's salvation of the righteous and punishment of the wicked. Given that this section has not been found at Qumran, some scholars suggest that it is a relatively late composition, perhaps dating from the early decades of the Christian era, which might even have been written in the circles from which Christianity eventually emerged as a distinct movement with its belief in a Messiah.

Where the *Book of Parables* is located in the Ethiopic I Enoch, the Qumran versions of the work preserve an entirely different work—the *Book of Giants*. Like the other elements of the Book of Enoch, the *Book of Giants*, too, was once an independent work.

Versions of it had long been known but nobody suspected a Jewish origin since it was always assumed to form part of the Manichaean canon, with copies being found in various languages across Asia as far as China. Manichaeism, named after its third-century C.E. Persian founder Mani, combined elements from Judaism, Christianity, Zoroastrianism and even Buddhism and was for several centuries extremely influential in various regions of the East—it was even the state religion of the Turkic Uighurs for a while. The discovery of portions of the *Book of Giants* among the Qumran scroll fragments suddenly made it clear that it was actually composed in Aramaic in Jewish circles in Judaea, rather than having been composed by Mani himself as hitherto believed.

This work covers some of the same ground as the *Book of the Watchers* because it deals with the *nephilim*, the demonic giant offspring of the fallen angels and their human wives. It describes these giants as having wings that enable them to fly swiftly around the world. Since they share many attributes with their angelic fathers, they, too, were thought to be invisible and immortal—at least until the end of creation and the Last Judgement, when they will be destroyed by fire. They are representative of the demons whose task is to tempt humans into sin, preying especially on women, and to cause disease. The text details the names of their leaders, a vital piece of information since knowledge of the names of demons was believed to result in power over them for the purpose of exorcism and healing. This association of disease with demons must have been a common belief in the Second Temple period, as Yeshua is mentioned as curing sick people by casting out demons in the New Testament.

Fragments from another major though neglected apocalyptic text, the Book of Jubilees, previously only known indirectly through translations, were also found at Qumran. Like the Book of Enoch, upon which it depends in part, the Book of Jubilees is

View of Qumran caves on the steep descent to Wadi Qumran where the Dead Sea Scrolls were discovered (© *AKG London/Jean-Louis Nou*)

Westerly view toward Cave 4, from the edge of the outcrop on which Khirbet Qumran lies (© AKG London/Erich Lessing)

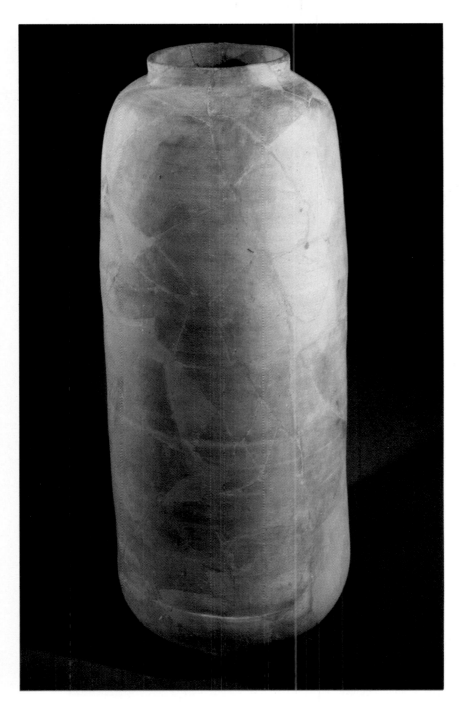

Example of a jar in which the Dead Sea Scrolls were found
(© AKG London/Erich Lessing)

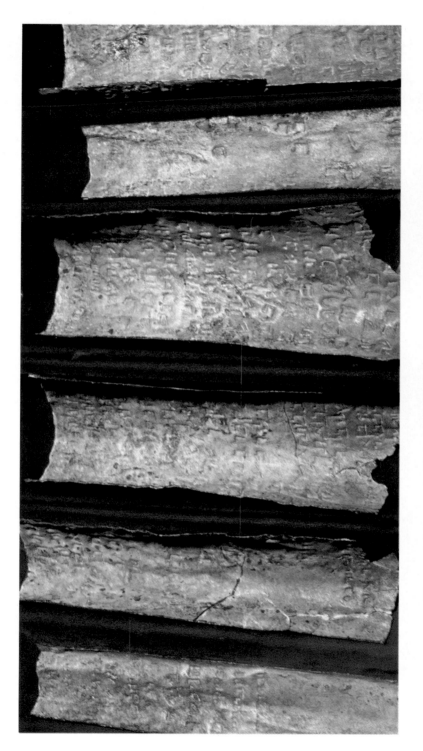

The opened *Copper Scroll* describing hidden treasures (© *AKG London/Jean-Louis Nou*)

Text from one of the two Isaiah Scrolls found at Qumran
(© AKG London/Erich Lessing)

A typical Hellenic city—Ephesus street scene
(© AKG London/Erich Lessing)

a late work produced during the Second Temple period, probably during the middle of the second century B.C.E. at the latest, but it purports to relate a revelation given by an angel to Moses on Mount Sinai. On the basis of the fragments found at Qumran, it seems that the Book of Jubilees was originally composed in Hebrew in contrast to the Aramaic of the Book of Enoch. Nevertheless, like the Book of Enoch, it must have been a much-studied text in the late Second Temple period because not only is the New Testament familiar with it but a significantly large number of individual scrolls—14 in all—have been identified from Qumran.

It seems that various Jewish groups of this period were engaged in rewriting, reworking or reinterpreting much of the contents of the Torah to suit their own ideological leanings, often as a reaction to the pressures that Hellenism was exerting upon their society at that time. Though some Jewish intellectuals such as Philo of Alexandria were keen to introduce Greek philosophical approaches to their study of the Torah, many within Judaea were inclined in the opposite direction. These people, many of whom would have been linked with the hasidim, were characterized by attitudes that were often more hard-line conservative than those taught in the Torah itself. The Book of Jubilees is an extensive rewriting of Genesis and parts of Exodus and presents itself as a kind of alternative, more accurate Torah. Some parts of the Torah are quoted verbatim in it, while others are expanded to allow the author to insert many innovative additions to Jewish law. For example, it contains very harsh condemnation of marriages between Jews and non-Jews, whereas the Torah itself is less damning. This prohibition of intermarriage should, of course, be understood in the context of the rising tide of Hellenism that was being promoted in Judaea both peaceably and violently.

Like Enoch and Daniel, the Book of Jubilees displays strong eschatological and apocalyptic tendencies. Also like these works, it displays a distinct interest in the cyclical nature of history and overlays the events of Jewish history with a chronological scheme based on Sabbatical and Jubilee cycles of seven and fifty years from which it derives a lengthier title, the "Book of the Divisions of the Periods according to their Jubilees and their Weeks," that is found in the *Damascus Document*. And like the Book of Enoch it asserts the primacy of a solar calendar for determining the dates of rituals and festivals, which may be an additional reason it appealed to the sectarian Community.

Apart from being a kind of reworked Torah, the Book of Jubilees is concerned with the presence of evil in the world and the manner in which it will be overcome. Like Enoch, Jubilees maintains that evil was introduced into the midst of humanity by the demonic offspring of the fallen angels, although it does offer some innovations of its own. Jubilees is particularly interested in charting the decline of mankind into wickedness. Addressing the people of its own Hellenistic era, it speaks of the "evil generation" that has forgotten "the commandments and covenant and feasts and months and sabbaths and jubilees and all of the judgements" (23:11–21). The author of Jubilees evidently believed that the stringent instructions on religious law which the text promulgates were vital for the salvation of the pious, for it is by obedience to these laws that the End of Days will be set in motion. It states that a transformation for the better will begin in society when "the children will begin to study the law and to search the commandments and to return to the way of righteousness" (23:26).

As with many other apocalyptic works, the culmination of the End of Days is the Last Judgement, when the wicked will be eliminated from the face of the earth and a new, more perfect creation will follow. Such teachings are reminiscent of the concept of an elect who will emerge in society that is described in the Enochian Apocalypse of the Weeks and the Animal Apocalypse. Afterlife is mentioned, but probably no physical resurrection was envisaged. As we shall see later, such beliefs formed a key element in the eschatology of the sectarian Community.

Another quasi-biblical work that has survived in sizeable fragments found in Caves 1 and 4 is the *Genesis Apocryphon*, written in Aramaic. Because the ink used to write this scroll has corroded the parchment, many lines are virtually illegible, although recent attempts using spectral imaging have now allowed further words to be read. The larger portion was one of the four scrolls purchased by Yigael Yadin in 1954 from the Metropolitan Athanasius Samuel. As its title suggests, this work is a paraphrase of the main events described in Genesis, rewritten as a popular work for a more general audience. The portions that survive tell of the miraculous birth of Noah, various incidents in his life and then the beginning of an account of Abraham's life. It is quite likely that the scroll originally covered most of the material in Genesis as far as the life of Moses. Judging from the portions that have survived, it is thought that this version of Genesis included many additional prescriptions for Jewish religious law interwoven with the stories that we also see in the Book of Jubilees. This has led scholars to associate the *Genesis Apocryphon* with the same doctrinal milieu that produced Jubilees and Enoch, which would probably account for its preservation at Qumran.

Finally, a number of fragmentary testaments have been identified among the Qumran material. Some, like the testaments of Levi and Naphtali, were known previously from a larger collection known as the Testaments of the Twelve Patriarchs, which is available in a Christianized Greek form. During the later Second Temple period such testaments, purporting to be the last words of people such as the Jewish patriarchs, were a popular literary genre. They are usually set into a framing story and consist of exhortatory words as well as the almost obligatory predictions and revelations about the future of the Jewish people.

Too little survives of these testaments for us to draw definitive conclusions about their doctrinal leanings, but the *Testament of Naphtali*, for example, contains a passage foretelling the End of Days with its subsequent destruction of the wicked and the vindication of the righteous in terms that are echoed throughout the literature directly linked with the sectarian Community. It is also noteworthy that the writer implies that the righteous who are to be saved were predestined for this end before they were created— a view also characteristic of the Community.

That ends this survey of the range of biblical and para-biblical material found in the caves of Qumran, though even this brief account emphasizes the complexity of the process by which the later canons of the Tanakh and the Christian Old Testament were determined. It is regrettable that so many of the scrolls have only survived in a very fragmentary and mutilated form because what they tell about the origins of the standard Hebrew Bible is tantalizing: so much more might have been revealed had complete scrolls been found.

seven

THE NON-SECTARIAN WORKS

A part from masses of biblical and para-biblical works, a large number of other writings have been identified among the scroll fragments from Qumran. These can be divided into two main categories: general non-sectarian and sectarian works. However, the boundaries between these two groups are fluid and scholars are far from unanimous on the classification of several texts.

It now seems obvious that there was a wide range of Jewish religious thought during the Second Temple period. Just as with the biblical material, we should take account of the historical dimension of the remaining literature found at Qumran as well as its broad sectarian connections. A number of the scrolls would have been composed earlier in the post-exile period before the distinct groups of Pharisees, Sadducees, Essenes and others emerged, but represent trends around which such religious groups later coalesced during the Hasmonean period. Even within these groups there must have been a continual process of conceptual refinement as circumstances changed, so even those texts that can be associated with particular groups often show a pattern of development.

One such text, which most scholars believe was composed as early as the fourth century B.C.E., is the *Temple Scroll*. Although not a direct product of the sectarian Community, it incorporates a few features that would have been attractive to them even if not central to their ideology. Important though the *Temple Scroll* is in general terms, only two examples were found at Qumran—the well-preserved scroll, 27 feet (9 meters) in length, from Cave 11 that Yigael Yadin retrieved during the Six Day War, and a few small fragments of another scroll from the same cave. This suggests that it was not regarded as an essential work by the sectarian Community.

So what is the *Temple Scroll*? Judging from its contents, which are largely concerned with the construction and regulation of a vast ideal temple and the sacrifices to be performed there, its authors viewed it as a supplement or even an addition to the five canonical books of the Torah. Since its concerns are almost entirely focused on matters associated with this temple, it is natural to assume that it was compiled by a group of proto-Sadducean priests in Jerusalem soon after the return of the first exiles from Babylon, perhaps in the late sixth or early fifth century B.C.E., although some authorities date its final form to the early years of the Hasmonean dynasty several centuries later.

Hartmut Stegemann hypothesizes that, prior to the final editing and closing of the Torah canon that Ezra carried out around this time, copies of the Torah in use in Jerusalem contained additional material that was not found in the version that he believes had been compiled and edited in Babylon by the exiles. When Ezra returned to Jerusalem he made known publicly the "authorized" version of the Torah, which resulted in the extra material in the earlier Jerusalem-based Torah being pruned away.

A careful analysis, such as that done by Andrew Wilson and Lawrence Wills, reveals that the *Temple Scroll* is really a composite work that draws on material from at least five different sources. Stegemann suggests that the editors of the *Temple Scroll* wanted to preserve the supplementary material that had been removed by Ezra's reform of the Torah and so combined the various pieces into one work. This view is corroborated by the traditional style and language of the *Temple Scroll*, which is close to that of the standard Torah and does not show any signs of the special conceptual terminology associated with sectarian groups such as the Qumran Community. For the priests who produced the *Temple Scroll* it would have functioned as an indispensable addition to the Torah, a sixth book that, unlike later works such as the Book of Jubilees, does not claim to supersede or be a substitute for the other five books. But they did view it as authoritative in the highest degree since, in the process of editing the material, they attempted to eliminate the intermediary role of Moses and to suggest that the various instructions contained in the *Temple Scroll* were given directly by God to the entire Israelite nation assembled at Mount Sinai.

Though some of the beginning of the scroll is missing or badly mutilated, the scene is set by God speaking of His covenant with the Hebrews. The basic terms of this agreement were that the land of Israel would be given to the Hebrews on condition that they separated themselves from their idolatrous neighbors and worshipped Him alone. This concept derives, of course, from Exodus 34:10–16, where the idolaters to be shunned were the Canaanites, the original inhabitants of the land invaded by the Hebrews. However, the Babylonian exile and the return of the Jews can be viewed as an event that parallels the sojourn in Egypt, the exodus and entry into Israel. As God in His mercy had allowed the Jews to return to Judaea from Babylon, any continued tenure of the land would have seemed to the authors of the *Temple Scroll* to be contingent upon a strict observance of the terms of the original covenant in the face of the new idolaters—the various Hellenizing groups in and around Judaea.

From this opening portion of the scroll, the discourse moves smoothly on to God's instructions for the building of a special sanctuary or temple in which He might be present among the Jews and be worshipped by them as He specifies. Naturally, this temple is to be more splendid and perfect than the old Solomonic one destroyed by the Babylonians. The *Temple Scroll* describes in considerable detail the architecture of the temple, together with its furnishings and equipment. Yet despite all the detail one wonders whether the group behind the writing of the *Temple Scroll* seriously envisaged it being built—unlike the actual Temple constructed when the exiles returned from Babylon, which had just two surrounding courtyards, this idealized temple has a third courtyard of such enormous dimensions that it would have engulfed most of Jerusalem. Moreover, even if this ideal temple had been built in Jerusalem, it was not expected to be permanent. The scroll also mentions that after the End of Days God would replace it with a divinely created temple that would miraculously appear on earth.

After describing the temple itself, the *Temple Scroll* stipulates the religious laws governing sacrifices, the initiation of priests and the tithes due to them. The scroll goes on to discuss a ritual calendar for determining the festivals, based on a solar calendar just as we saw with Enoch and Jubilees. The *Temple Scroll* inserts several additional festivals throughout the year, such as a second New Year in spring and first-fruits festivals for oil and wine in addition to the normal ones for barley and wheat.

In connection with the annual cycle of sacrifices, the scroll exhibits special concern with matters related to ritual purity so as to safeguard the holiness of the sanctuary. This became a topic of vital significance for Jews living in Judaea prior to the Maccabean Revolt and later, since the continued purity of the inner sanctum, where God was thought to be literally present, was essential for the well-being of the Jewish nation. If it was not retained, disaster for the whole nation could be expected—Jewish tenancy of the land of Israel was conditional on the strict observance of God's laws. Those who suggest a late date for the composition of the *Temple Scroll*, such as Lawrence Schiffman, detect veiled criticism here against the later Hasmonean High Priest rulers of Judaea. This is a possibility, since the scroll goes on to stipulate laws relating to the king who should rule over the Jews. As we have seen, the offices of High Priest and ruler were combined during the Hasmonean period, whereas the authors of the *Temple Scroll* wanted the two roles to be separated; this may be a covert attack on the legitimacy of the Hasmonean High Priests. It is also possible that the restrictions which the scroll places on the military activities of this king may be aimed at the excessive aggression and rapaciousness of Hasmonean rulers like John Hyrcanus I.

Many of the non-sectarian works found at Qumran relate to practical matters connected with Jewish religious laws and their application. Some deal with everyday matters that would have been of interest to the ordinary pious Jew of the period, while others seem to relate more to the duties and concerns of the priests servicing the Jerusalem Temple. Given the great significance of the various religious festivals throughout the year for all practicing Jews, the question of correctly determining when they were to be celebrated was a matter of considerable debate during the Second Temple period. Should the calendar used be lunar or solar? For this reason we should not be surprised that a number of calendrical tables and related works were discovered at Qumran.

Scholarly opinion is divided over the question of whether a solar calendar was traditionally used in the First Temple because the evidence is ambiguous, but after the exile the picture is clearer. The Sadducees who formed the Temple priesthood used a solar calendar to fix the days of festivals based on indications given in Leviticus (23:9–14) concerning the timing of the barley firstfruits offering. Late post-exile para-canonical works such as Jubilees and Enoch clearly recommend the use of a solar calendar, so we may assume that their authors were connected in some way with the Jerusalem priesthood. Opposed to the use of the solar calendar were the Pharisees, who interpreted the key passages of Leviticus differently and advocated the use of a lunar calendar to determine the all-important dates of the festivals. The material from Qumran is interesting in this context because though the solar calendar was definitely used by the sectarian Community, some calendrical works were found that attempt to merge the solar and lunar calendars, just as was done in the Egypt of the pharaohs.

As the term suggests, a solar calendar is based on the annual cycle of the sun rather than that of the moon, which results in a shorter year of 354 days. The Jewish solar calendar was based on a year of 364 days, divided up into 12 months that each have 30 days, with the proviso that one extra day was to be added to solstice and equinox months. The figure of 364 is, however, only an approximation of the solar year, since it falls short by one and a quarter days. If this shortfall is not dealt with, the start of each year gradually falls out of synchronization and some kind of adjustment, known as intercalation, needs to be employed.

Whether or how this was actually done by those using the solar calendar remains a mystery because the calendrical tables found at Qumran are silent on the topic. Indeed, scholars such as Lawrence Schiffman are of the opinion that the solar calendar was never widely used, despite being advocated during the Second Temple period in a number of sources. He suggests that these calendars were either ideal calendars that were never used, or else were only in use for such a short time that the one-and-a-quarter-day annual discrepancy never had time to accumulate and become pronounced.

Yet there is clear evidence that the sectarian Community adhered to the solar calendar for determining their annual cycle of festivals because the scrolls contain several attacks on their religious opponents which castigate them for using the wrong calendar. For example, the sectarian commentary on Habakkuk mentions an enemy of the Community, the Wicked Priest, paying them a sudden and unwelcome visit, 'at the time appointed for rest, for the Day of Atonement, he appeared before them to confuse them, and to cause them to stumble on the Day of Fasting, their Sabbath of repose." This clearly indicates that the Community was following a different calendar from its enemy, for the simple reason that the Day of Atonement, a major Jewish festival to this day, was so sacred that no pious Jew would even set out on a journey then. If the Wicked Priest was following a different, presumably lunar calendar, he would not have considered himself to be at fault if he happened to travel on the day that, according to the solar calendar, was the Day of Atonement.

Apart from large numbers of fragments dealing with religious law, there are also many concerning liturgical aspects of worship. The best and most complete non-sectarian example in this category is the *Songs of the Sabbath Sacrifice*, known more descriptively as the *Angelic Liturgy*.

It is a matter of debate how widely used this work was among pious observant Jews, but the discovery of nine manuscripts at Qumran as well as others from Masada suggest it was important for some sections of the population. It was formerly thought that the presence of this liturgy at Masada implied that refugees from Qumran had brought it with them, but most scholars no longer believe this. The general opinion now is that it was popular throughout Judaea and that its composition may predate the bulk of the Qumran sectarian material, though the earliest examples are dated paleographically to around 75 B.C.E. There is a distinct possibility that it formed part of the regular liturgy associated with the Temple and used at Sabbaths throughout the year. An alternative view is that this angelic liturgy was used by the sectarian Community as a substitute for normal Sabbath offerings in the Temple, since they had withdrawn from activities there for reasons of conscience.

As its alternative titles indicate, it is a set of liturgical hymns for the Sabbath sacrifices purporting to be the praises offered by the angels to God. Hymns for only 13 Sabbaths appear to be included, but it is possible that they were intended to be repeated as a cycle throughout the year or that they form part of a larger compilation now lost. Each hymn begins with a short indication of when it was to be used, for instance: "To the Master. Song of the sacrifice of the first Sabbath, on the fourth of the first month." The text for each Sabbath urges the various ranks of angels to utter praises and psalms of exaltation to God, as well as providing examples of the actual praises. Features of the heavenly Temple are described, together with details of its angelic priesthood.

This idea of a heavenly Temple is of considerable significance for it figures in a number of other post-exile works, some of which have survived at Qumran. According to this view, the Temple on earth is mirrored by a more splendid and perfect one in heaven. When humans engage in worship and other religious acts, their deeds were thought to be accompanied simultaneously by similar acts on the part of the invisible angels. This concept of angels acting in concert with pious Jews on earth was expanded in a number of the writings linked to the sectarian Community, forming, for example, a key element in the eschatological beliefs expressed in the *War Scroll*.

In contrast to the negligible presence of angels in the older books of the Hebrew Bible, a marked role for named angels is a noteworthy feature of many works from the Second Temple period. It is generally accepted that a Jewish interest in angels derives from the role played by angelic beings in Mesopotamian and Persian beliefs, where they acted as intermediaries between the human realm and God. In contrast to ancient Israel, a small country whose rulers would have been quite visible and accessible to many, the great empires of the Middle East had rulers who resided in cities far distant from most of their subjects. Post-exile Jewish ideas about God viewed Him as a great emperor, so the feeling that He was remote from human affairs would have corresponded to ordinary people's experience of earthly emperors. This situation would have encouraged a feeling that intermediary beings were necessary to communicate with God himself, and the role of angels came to the fore during the Second Temple period.

Another important feature of the *Angelic Liturgy* is its descriptions of the divine throne, the *merkabah*, surrounded by an angelic retinue. Such imagery ultimately derives from the visions ascribed to Ezekiel and other late Jewish prophets who were transported to heaven and shown its splendors. This idea of a visionary ascent to heaven later formed a central element of Jewish mysticism that is known to have been flourishing by Herodian times, if not earlier—we know from the writings of the apostle Paul that he himself engaged in such practices. However, the descriptions in the *Angelic Liturgy* of the divine throne in its celestial setting do not necessarily imply structured mystical practices because the hymns themselves do not speak in terms of a mystical ascent or a guided tour of heaven but relate the details from the static perspective of the angels. Nevertheless such descriptions help us understand the origins of later Jewish mysticism since they indicate a movement away from exterior public worship associated with the Temple to the interiorization of religious devotion that gained in momentum as the integrity of Temple worship noticeably declined in Herodian times and culminated in the physical destruction of the Temple.

One final scroll must be considered before we move on to the specifically sectarian writings found at Qumran. This scroll differs in so many respects from everything else found there that it has provoked the most intense debate and controversy. It is known as the *Copper Scroll* for the simple reason that the contents were inscribed on to a sheet of copper, unlike all the other manuscripts that were written on parchment or papyrus. The fact that it was a roll of brittle copper, broken into two portions, delayed its opening for a number of years until a suitable technique for cutting it into strips was developed. When the contents were finally read, edited and translated, Roland de Vaux's team realized that the *Copper Scroll* had profound implications for the history of the Qumran cache of scrolls and the nature of the ascetic Community they believed had lived there.

Unlike most of the other scrolls, the *Copper Scroll* was written, or rather inscribed, in a late style of Hebrew—in terms of both the writing itself and the language. It contains a catalogue of 64 items, mostly precious metals and Temple artifacts, with the locations where they were apparently concealed.

In view of the contents, those who believe that the *Copper Scroll* describes actual treasures feel that it represents material smuggled out of Jerusalem just before the siege or in its early, less restrictive days, and hidden for safe-keeping in the Judaean desert and other places. Unfortunately, many of the locations cannot be identified today and those that have been found show no trace of treasure.

On the other hand, so much treasure was listed that at one time many scholars dismissed the whole scroll as an ancient hoax or fantasy. However, a new edition and study of the *Copper Scroll* by Judah Lefkovits suggests that the amount of precious metal listed was greatly exaggerated by earlier researchers. Based on a more accurate measurement of the talent, the unit of weight used to quantify precious metals, he suggests that the real amount of precious metal listed is not around 200 tons, as previously thought, but just 60 tons. Furthermore, much of the hoard was not gold, which he states made up 17 percent of the total, but mainly silver and copper; this represents a much more realistic quantity of precious metal.

Yet it is not so much the contents of the *Copper Scroll* that have proven so challenging but what is implied by the very existence of the scroll at Qumran—what was its connection, if any, with the rest of the manuscripts found there? Although the *Copper Scroll* was found in Cave 3, there is a marked discrepancy between accounts of its precise location when discovered. Several sources state that it was found buried at the back of the cave—in other words, it would have been located behind parchment scrolls that were deposited in front of it and was therefore placed there at the same time or beforehand. On the other hand, Hartmut Stegemann states that it was found at the mouth of the cave under a pile of stones in front of the still sealed rear of the cave, and so has no connection with the people who deposited the library of scrolls there. Perhaps this is another example of scholars bending the facts to fit their own pet theories about the nature and origins of the sectarian Community!

If we accept the list of treasures in the *Copper Scroll* as factual, a serious problem arises for the older consensus view of the Dead Sea Scroll manuscripts. De Vaux's team and their successors maintain that all the manuscripts found there formed a sectarian library based at Qumran itself and were hidden for safety during the Jewish Revolt, perhaps as early as 68 C.E. Since these sectarian Jews were known from their own writings to be ascetic, would they have possessed such a huge amount of wealth if the *Copper Scroll* originated with them?

The consensus view recognizes this problem but still has difficulties explaining where the treasure came from originally. Looking at the kind of sacred artifacts that are also listed, however, the Temple in Jerusalem seems to be the most likely source because it not only had great wealth of its own but also acted as a kind of safety deposit for others. But as we know from the sectarian scrolls, the Community, wherever it was based, had broken off all ties with the Temple and its establishment. So if they had actually lived at Qumran, as suggested, would they have been likely to accept this hoard of treasure from the Temple or even be entrusted with it in the first place? This means that we have to either reconsider the nature of the Community or come up with another hypothesis.

Norman Golb and those who follow his line of thinking take the latter course and maintain that the consensus view about Qumran and the origins of the scroll collection is mistaken. According to them, the scrolls found at Qumran have no connection with the settlement there because they believe it was never home to a sectarian Community. Instead, they suggest that there was a general evacuation of valuables from Jerusalem in the early years of the Jewish Revolt, and that the *Copper Scroll* was composed as a catalogue of the items and their locations. The scrolls found at Qumran would therefore have come from Jerusalem, some perhaps from the Temple and some from private libraries.

This view is plausible because there is another piece of information in the *Copper Scroll* that is played down in some quarters—the mention of a total of eight locations where books are stated to be hidden. When we acknowledge this fact, the perceived unique nature of the Qumran collection becomes less plausible and we might see it merely as one hoard of manuscripts from Jerusalem that had, by chance, largely escaped discovery or retrieval until modern times. The alternative is to believe that the sectarian Community hid its scroll holdings in the caves above Qumran while separately, but at the same time, somebody with Zealot affiliations from Jerusalem was allowed to hide his *Copper Scroll* in Cave 3. I leave it to readers to decide which alternative is more reasonable.

eight

THE SECTARIAN WORKS

We can now turn to the main works that are almost universally thought to be sectarian in origin. As with the other scrolls, all that has survived in most cases are small fragments that are difficult to piece together. Nevertheless, there are clearly three main categories that give a fascinating insight into the life and beliefs of the Community: the various rule books, the biblical *pesher* commentaries and the thanksgiving hymns known as *hodayot*. These works are also important since they contain a number of obscure allusions to the origins of the Community and certain key events in its history.

Throughout the Community's history, its members seem to have felt it was necessary to update or even replace their rule books in the face of changes in society from their perspective, especially with regard to the uncertainty surrounding the exact beginning and culmination of the End of Days. One large, reasonably well-preserved scroll was found in Cave 1, which contains several sets of rules governing the Community. A further ten fragments were found in Cave 4 and two in Cave 5, which testifies to the importance of these documents. The scroll from Cave 1 encompasses several works each of which can be dealt with separately, as they seem to have originally been independent compositions. Stegemann maintains there are four of these but other scholars, such as Geza Vermes, count only three items. Of these, the longest and most important is the *Rule of the Community*, which has been dated on paleographical grounds to c.75 B.C.E.–50 B.C.E.; but, since it is a composite work that also contains scribal corrections, it may well date from 150 B.C.E.–100 B.C.E. in its present form, with even older elements.

The hierarchically structured Community was led by a Master or Overseer, for whom the *Rule of the Community* was a handbook regulating entry into the Community and stipulating the statutes governing the lives of the members. The work opens with a general statement of the aims and purpose of the Community—to enable members to live a righteous life that is pleasing to God, so that His vengeance will not fall upon them during the Last Days. Those who are willing to live strictly according to God's precepts should be encouraged to enter the Community of their own free will. The text then details how new members are to be admitted into the Community and older members are to renew their commitment and be promoted in rank at the annual festival of the Renewal of the Covenant. This important feast-day, celebrated on the fifteenth day of the third month, is equivalent to the Christian Pentecost. As part of this rite, the priests and their assistants, the Levites, are to recite praises of God, invoking his blessings upon the righteous, known in the Community as the Sons of Light, and his curses upon the sinful Sons of Darkness, those Jews and pagans who have sided with Belial, the evil angel or spirit who leads them.

At this point in the *Rule of the Community* a short treatise known as the *Teaching on the Two Spirits* is inserted. Though probably an independent work, it fits quite well at this juncture since it presents the Community's views on the nature of creation and humanity. It teaches that when God created the world, the elements of light and darkness were present in equal proportions in the entirety of creation but in varying proportions in its individual elements. On a moral level, the light represents goodness or righteousness and the darkness evil or sin.

This dualistic understanding of creation does not seem to have been a conspicuous feature of First Temple Israelite beliefs, but is a central teaching of Persian Zoroastrianism. According to early Zoroastrian teaching, the creator God Ahura Mazda generated a pair of twin spirit children—the good Spenta Mainyu and the evil Angra Mainyu, or Ahriman as he later came to be known. The world is a battlefield between these two evenly matched spirits, and the final outcome is only determined by the intervention of Ahura Mazda at the end of time. Jews living in Babylon during the period of the exile and later would have been exposed to this Zoroastrian belief, and clear traces of it can be seen in the biblical books produced during the Second Temple period.

The members of the Community seem to have gone one step further with this concept, for they maintained that God predetermines the moral quality of each individual before birth. This predetermined quality was thought to be immutable, so those with a preponderance of negativity can never improve themselves no matter how much they strive. Only the righteous elect have the potential to be saved, though even they may be damned if they fail to live up to God's commandments.

This idea of an elect gradually evolved throughout Jewish history, from the simple idea that the Israelites were a special race set apart by their covenant with God through to the teachings about a pious or righteous group that are found in the Book of Jubilees and Enoch. Its final expression appears in the doctrines of the Community, but such ideas must have been fairly common in late Second Temple Judaism since they are also found in Christian teachings. A modified version of this theory of predestination is a tenet of Calvinism and of many of today's fundamentalist or evangelical Christian Churches, which are apparently content to consign the greater part of humanity to eternal perdition in the fire of hell.

It was therefore very important for the overseeing Master to be able to distinguish the potential of each prospective candidate according to the contents of this short treatise. To assist him in this task, it seems that the Community believed that each individual is made up of nine parts of good and evil in different ratios, ranging from eight parts of good to one of evil through to eight parts of evil and just one of good. Fragments were found at Qumran of a kind of divination text combining astrology and physiognomy, which would have been used as a way of determining the moral nature of individual candidates for entry into the Community.

Following the *Teaching on the Two Spirits*, the *Rule of the Community* continues with a more detailed disciplinary code, the *Manual of Discipline*. As mentioned above, most scholars view this as an integral part of the *Rule of the Community* but Hartmut Stegemann maintains that it is a separate work. Careful analysis shows that the *Rule of the Community* and the *Damascus Document*, described below, are both composite works that incorporate several literary layers produced over many decades. This can also be seen from the differences that have been noted between the scroll pieces found in Cave 1 and the fragments from Cave 4, which present a less evolved version of the work. For this reason, Stegemann may be correct in assuming that the *Manual of Discipline* is a separate work, although the Community itself may have seen it as an authentic part of the *Rule of the Community* as a whole.

The introduction to the *Manual of Discipline* recapitulates the aims and purpose of the Community. It then briefly stipulates the process for admittance into the Community and subsequent progress within it before detailing the regulations deemed to govern all aspects of a member's life. In addition to the precepts laid down in the Torah, which were naturally binding for the members, further statutes and rules are given that are exclusive to the Community. These statutes would have governed all aspects of the life that members shared in the Community under the leadership of the priests, called here typically the "Sons of Zadok." Other rules govern council meetings to deal with entry into the Community and the ensuing period of probation. The work concludes with a detailed listing of these statutes and the stern penalties for infringing them, from temporary or permanent exclusion from communal life to reduction of rations and other penances. It is stated that these rules are to remain in force with the Community until the emergence of a new prophet and the two Messiahs of Israel and Aaron—a concept to which we shall return in Chapter 11.

The *Rule of the Community* is followed by two shorter appendices that exhibit all the signs of having been independent works at some time. The first of these is the *Congregational Rule*, sometimes called the *Messianic Rule*. Here again scholars are not unanimous about the role or history of this Rule. Vermes regards it as a proscriptive or ideal rule to be adopted by the Community when the Messiah finally appears, while Stegemann points out that the Community regarded itself as already living in the End of Days and would therefore have viewed this *Congregational Rule* as valid and binding during the lifetime of its author. Since the Rule talks about various classes of people with physical or mental imperfections, it would seem that Stegemann is right in saying that it deals not with a future ideal time after the elect have been saved but with the current situation according to the beliefs of the Community.

As already mentioned, the Community believed in two Messiahs, one priestly and one princely, who would be preceded or accompanied by a prophet. Whatever its exact status within the Community, this Rule lays down regulations for the entire "congregation of Israel" in the last few years before the imminent appearance of these Messiahs. The whole congregation includes women and children, not just the men mentioned in the other Rules. This Rule therefore includes precepts governing the whole life of the individual from childhood to marriage, as well as adult participation in the life of the greater Community.

Importantly, the *Congregational Rule* alludes to the Community's militia and its participation in war. Stegemann believes that it was the earliest rule book of the Community, but on the contrary the evidence suggests a later period of the Community's history. The ever-deteriorating spiritual and politico-social atmosphere in Judaea must have led the Community members to believe that the End of Days was truly upon them. The prophet-like founder of the Community, the Teacher of Righteousness, had already died and the Messiahs would have been expected to arrive at any moment. The mention of war and need for warriors hints at the period of turmoil that precedes the final destruction of the evil Sons of Darkness, a theme expanded in the *War Scroll*. The Community may therefore have been far less pacifist than is often assumed, and this may account for the fortress-like features of the Qumran settlement if we allow that the Community actually lived there, as the consensus view maintains.

The second appendix comprises a set of liturgical blessings, probably designed to be used for recitation by the Master. They complement the *Congregational Rule*, for they, too, assume that the Community was actually living in the End of Days before the imminent arrival of the two Messiahs. The blessings fall into four groups relating to four elements of the whole Community at this time. First, the Master is to bless all the members of the Covenant; then the High Priest, whom some see as a reference to the Aaronic Messiah priest; then the Zadokite priests, who were the leaders of the Community; and finally a person who is termed the Prince of the Congregation, who is usually identified with the princely or Davidic Messiah of Israel.

Although Stegemann characteristically inverts the historical place of the *Damascus Document* and regards it as the final definitive code of discipline used in the Community, most scholars disagree and believe that it represents the oldest code that the Community composed. The fact that only a few, though lengthy, fragments were found in Caves 4, 5 and 6, in contrast to the relatively well-preserved *Rule of the Community* found in Cave 1, supports the latter view, since it is generally thought that the scrolls from Cave 1 represent the most treasured current works of the Community, given that they were each carefully wrapped in linen and placed in jars for safety, unlike the lack of care shown towards the works placed in Cave 4.

Like the other rule books, the *Damascus Document* is a composite work with several layers, the oldest of which may date back many decades before the final version we have now, completed some time during the first half of the second century B.C.E. Internal evidence suggests that much of the *Damascus Document* had been written before the *Rule of the Community* because certain features of the latter work are dependent on, and derivative of, the former.

The *Damascus Document* itself has a strange history in modern times because although only small fragments were found at Qumran, the work had been known to the academic world for many years. Like followers of many other religions, Jewish people consider it sacrilegious to throw away worn-out copies of sacred writings and so prefer to burn or bury them. Before they are respectfully disposed of, such old manuscripts are stored in a special place known as a *genizah*. In 1896, the renowned Jewish scholar Solomon Schechter followed up rumors of a very large quantity of medieval Jewish manuscripts that had accumulated in the *genizah* of an old Cairo synagogue for centuries rather than being destroyed. Among the hundreds of thousands of documents he found there were two incomplete manuscripts of the

Damascus Document, or the *Zadokite Fragments* as they were once called. These were published in 1910, and many scholars speculated that they were a work associated with the Essenes.

Since fragments from the same work have been identified among the scrolls from Qumran, there has been considerable debate about how the *Damascus Document* had found its way to the Cairo *genizah*. One hypothesis suggests that copies of the *Damascus Document* may have been included among the manuscripts discovered in the Judaean desert near Jericho that were mentioned by the Nestorian Patriarch Timotheus I of Baghdad in the early ninth century. Some scholars speculate that these manuscripts came from the Qumran caves themselves, which is a possibility, although it should be noted that the Qumran fragments found in the 1950s indicate that the version from the Cairo *genizah* is shorter or abridged and omits important details.

After these manuscripts returned to circulation, some may have come into the hands of the Jewish sect known as the Karaites. Founded around the 750s C.E. in Mesopotamia, the Karaite movement, which has a few members today, was at one time a very influential movement with adherents throughout the Middle East. Their basic tenets involve a complete rejection of the standard explanatory material added by the rabbis to the Torah, that was embodied in the Mishnah and Talmud and still forms the basis of orthodox Judaism, in favor of reliance solely on the Torah. In fact, many of their views are so similar to those found in the sectarian works from Qumran that at first some scholars thought the Qumran cache was Karaite in origin. There may indeed be a historical link of some kind between the two movements. Nevertheless, the presence of the *Damascus Document* in the Cairo *genizah* remains a mystery, since the synagogue in question is not Karaite—although it is frequently stated to be so in books on the Dead Sea Scrolls.

The *Damascus Document* opens with a short account of the origin of the Community, which we shall look at in detail in Chapter 10, and alludes to further events in its history. It refers to a new covenant that God made with certain pious Jews, priests and the Sons of Zadok, who are termed the elect, when they had departed from the land of Judah and sojourned in the land of Damascus. A lengthy theological interpretation of various aspects of the history of Israel is given to exhort the followers of the sons of Zadok to remain faithful to the new covenant and to reassure them that they will be rewarded for their righteousness by God after the End of Days. This portion of the text is characterized by many elliptical allusions to contemporary people and events, which would have been obvious to members of the Community but now tax the ingenuity of scholars who try to make sense of them.

The second section deals, like the rule books, with the various statutes that govern the lives of Community members. These statutes are arranged according to subject matter and cover such topics as vows and oaths, the working of the Community's tribunal, witnesses to infractions, the judges who are to deal with these infractions, purification by water, the observances of the Sabbath, and ritual purity. Many of the statutes are sectarian interpretations of traditional biblical laws, but others are innovative rules that concern the organization of the Community. In common with the *Rule of the Community*, the *Damascus Document* appends a penal code that agrees in principle with those found elsewhere in the sectarian rule books. Finally, the *Damascus Document* was intended to govern whole groups of Community members because many of the rules relate to women and children, which means it does not pertain to a celibate Community of men alone.

Linked to the events expected to unfold during the End of Days is the *War Scroll* and the fragments of the associated *War Rule*. The fact that the main copy of this large text was found in Cave 1 indicates that it was a work highly valued by whoever hid it there, though sadly it has suffered considerably from the ravages of time. Half a dozen related fragments found in Cave 4 reveal numerous differences from the more complete version of Cave 1.

As with many sectarian manuscripts found at Qumran, no firm date can be ascribed to the *War Scroll*, but there are certain indications that help us narrow things down. The author was undoubtedly inspired by the events described in Daniel 11:40–12:3 and, since it is generally accepted that the Book of Daniel was written just after the "abomination of desolation," the outrages in the Temple perpetrated by Antiochus IV Epiphanes in 167 B.C.E., the *War Scroll* must have been composed after this date. Other evidence for its date may be found in the descriptions of weapons and tactics, depending on whether they are modeled on Greek or Roman practice. If they are Roman, as many believe, the *War Scroll* would post-date the earliest direct contact between the Roman legions and the Jews that the conquest of Palestine by Pompey the Great in 63 B.C.E. The final composition of the *War Scroll* may in fact be even later, since it mentions the "king" of the Kittim, usually understood as a reference to a ruler of the post-republican imperial Roman era inaugurated by Augustus Caesar. As this work also shows signs of several stages of development, it was possibly started just after 167 B.C.E. and then revised at a later date when the Romans had entered the Judaean political arena.

The *War Scroll* is a curious text since it concerns the eschatological war to be waged in the final 40 years of the Last Days but describes the struggle in unrealistic terms. Though some scholars such as Schiffman view the work as a kind of military manual that stipulates the regulations for this final conflict, many others, including Vermes and Stegemann, consider it to be a symbolic presentation of the culmination of the struggle between good and evil.

According to Vermes, the battle is placed in an imaginary historical context with the forces of good and evil on earth being matched by their respective counterparts, the angels and the demons. The human component is made up of the Sons of Light, represented by the tribes of Levi, Judah and Benjamin, on one hand, and of the evil Sons of Darkness, who are represented by the Gentiles headed by the Kittim. In earlier Jewish literature the

Kittim often denoted the Greeks, especially the Seleucids, but by the time the *War Scroll* took on its final form the Romans are usually indicated.

My personal feeling is that the events described in the *War Scroll* are meant literally, since we know from other texts that members of the Community organized military units in preparation for the struggle that was to take place in the End of Days. The *Angelic Liturgy* shows that they believed their actions on earth to be paralleled by angelic activities on a higher plane, and this concept may well have been extended to the eschatological war that was foretold. The members of the Community would prepare themselves through their righteous lives and, when they had fulfilled their part of the bargain, God would intervene and send the angels to assist them. This idea may have had wider currency in the late Second Temple period, for this may also have been the intention and belief of Yeshua as he gathered a number of his followers on the Mount of Olives just before he was arrested for treason and crucified.

According to the *War Scroll*, six years of war would end with the reconquest of Jerusalem and worship in the Temple would then be restored. This stage of the war was to be followed by a further 33 years of conflict that would ultimately result in the defeat and destruction of all foreign nations. The scroll goes on to describe at length the various trumpets, the standards of the regiments, the array of men and their weapons, and the liturgy that was to be used before battle by the priests. In many respects, these descriptions resemble the preparations made by the Israelites under the command of Joshua outside Jericho, which was also destroyed by divine intervention.

One curious feature of the battle array concerns the ages and roles of those taking part. We are told that the warriors themselves should be men in their forties or fifties, with the auxiliaries and rearguard made up of the young. While engaged in active military duty in the war camps, these men were to observe strict ritual purity and the presence of women or children was forbidden. This last regulation may have been conceived in terms of the preparations for a real military battle, or as a figurative allusion to the rule of celibacy that was to be observed by some members of the Community while awaiting the End of Days—bearing in mind that many scholars maintain that the occupants of Qumran were celibate ascetics.

SOME LEGAL RULINGS PERTAINING TO THE TORAH

One other work that deals with legal matters has attracted a great deal of attention since it was belatedly published in the 1990s: the letter usually entitled *Some Legal Rulings Pertaining to the Torah* but also known as 4QMMT. It is not a letter in the handwriting of the original author, but six fragments of copies made at some later time.

The largest fragment starts with part of a calendar of Sabbaths, presumably based on the solar calendar used by the Community, and may not form part of the original letter. The beginning of the letter proper that would tell us to whom it was addressed is missing, much to the frustration of Qumranologists. The main topics are several disputed points of Jewish law, or *halakhah*, involving aspects of ritual purity and rules for marriage.

There are three parties mentioned in this letter, a "we," a "you" and a "they." If this letter originates with the Community, as most scholars think likely, the "we" may refer to the Teacher of Righteousness and his Community. However, Vermes and a number of other scholars reject this view and suggest that it was written by a member of a breakaway group of lesser Sadducean priests before the Teacher of Righteousness came on the scene. In that case, this breakaway group might be seen as the precursors of the later fully fledged sectarian Community.

Since the letter is couched as a piece of advice to somebody, most likely a temple High Priest, it is often assumed that the "you" refers to the person who ultimately became known by the so-briquet of the "Wicked Priest." Even if this is true, and the letter was actually written by the Teacher of Righteousness, it may represent a very early phase in the dispute between the Teacher and the Wicked Priest since the writer speaks in a conciliatory tone: "We have also written to you concerning some of the observances of the Law which we think are beneficial to you and your people, for we have noticed that prudence and knowledge of the Law are with you. Understand these [matters] and ask Him to straighten your counsel and put you far away from thoughts of evil and the counsel of Belial." However, even at this stage the writer and his associates signal that they have withdrawn from communion with the Jewish world at large with the words, "we have separated from the mass of the people and from mingling with them in these matters." This may even imply that they had already broken their ties with the activities of the Jerusalem Temple, as we know the Community did at some stage in their history.

As the letter seems by its contents to be addressed to the High Priest or somebody of importance at the Temple, this would suggest that the recipient "you" would have belonged to the Sadducean priesthood. There remains the question of who is intended by "they," who are criticized as "those who expound false laws."

This is fairly easy to answer if we look at the Hebrew words for that epithet—*doreshe halaqot*. One feature of much Hebrew literature—and that from Qumran is no exception—is a love of punning, to which the Hebrew language readily lends itself. It would have been obvious to the recipient of the letter which group was termed "expounders of false laws" in view of the similarity of the words to *doreshe halakhot*, "expounders of religious law" (*halakha*), who were none other than the Pharisees.

In Second Temple times the Pharisees were the great experts on matters of Jewish religious law and were noted for drawing up many extra, non-canonical laws to supplement those given in the

Torah. This propensity was heavily criticized by the Sadducees, who only recognized the validity of laws laid down in the Torah. Since the contents of this letter are often used by certain scholars as a means of identifying the origins and identity of the Qumran Community, we shall return to the matters it raises in Chapter 10.

THE *PESHER* COMMENTARIES

Apart from the various kinds of works mentioned above that concentrate on legal and organizational matters, the sectarian Community also produced a radically new and virtually unique type of literature known as *pesher*. The term itself derives from a Hebrew verb meaning to explain or to expound, and is found in biblical narratives in connection with the interpretation of dreams such as the stories of Joseph and Pharaoh or Daniel and Nebuchadnezzar.

An unusual feature of ancient Middle Eastern dream interpretation was the belief that it was not just sufficient to have an omen-filled dream—it had to be accurately interpreted in order for the events to come about. This aspect of *pesher* interpretation is likely to have formed one element of its use by the Community. However, the members of the Community added a totally new feature when they used this technique for expounding the meaning of earlier, typically prophetic, biblical writings.

At times of crisis in Israelite or Jewish history, prophets such as Isaiah or Jeremiah came forth and spoke to the people of their generation, often to warn them of impending disasters that would be inflicted upon them unless they mended their ways and adhered to the Covenant that their ancestors had made with God. The Community took these ancient utterances and explained them solely in terms of contemporary events. In other words, they believed that the prophets of the past were unwittingly making predictions that related not to their own times but to the distant future. The only other religious group at that time who employed the words of the prophets in a similar manner were the writers of the Christian New Testament, who used, for example, the prophecies of Isaiah to prove that Yeshua was the Messiah and the Son of God. Even today, some fundamentalist Christian groups interpret the Book of Daniel to explain contemporary events.

A number of such *pesher* commentaries were found at Qumran and although very fragmentary, they potentially provide a key source of information about the history of the Community. However, where early Christianity presents prophetic material in a transparent manner, the identity of the people and events mentioned in the Community's *peshers* is obscured by the use of a range of coded designations such as the Teacher of Righteousness, the Wicked Priest, the Spouter of Lies, the Seekers after Smooth Things, the Men of Truth and so forth. The members of the Community would have known who was intended by these sobriquets, but such veiled allusions have made it virtually impossible for modern scholars to arrive at any unanimous conclusions about the *dramatis personae* of these texts. For example, they have not even been able to agree whether the Priest is an alternative name for the Teacher of Righteousness, or whether the Wicked Priest and the Spouter of Lies are two individuals or one. Since the question of who was intended by these and other designations is intimately connected with the identity and history of the sectarian Community, this problem will be examined in detail in Chapter 10.

Most of the *pesher* texts are line-by-line commentaries on the various books of the Prophets which contained material that supported the Community's concerns and view of contemporary events. Typically, they quote a short passage and then comment on its significance, as for example these passages from the *peshers* on Micah and Nahum:

> And what is the high place of Judah? Is it not Jerusalem?
> Interpreted, this concerns the Teacher of Righteousness
> who expounded the Law to his Council and to all who

freely pledged themselves to join the elect of God to
keep the Law in the Council of the Community, who
shall be saved on the Day of Judgement.
Woe to the city of blood; it is full of lies and rapine.
Interpreted, this is the city of Ephraim, those who seek
smooth things during the last days, who walk in lies
and falsehood.

We see here typical use of coded language—the "Teacher of Righteousness," the "city of Ephraim" and "those who seek smooth
things." It is possible to identify some of these terms, but others
are elusive.

The most important *peshers* that have survived are those on
Habakkuk, Nahum, Isaiah and the Psalms, which are described
below. Only a few pieces of the *peshers* on Hosea, Zephaniah and
Micah remain.

The *Habakkuk Pesher*, the most extensively preserved *pesher*,
concerns events in the early history of the Community and is
viewed as the most important source for reconstructing that history. It describes a conflict between the Teacher of Righteousness
and his opponent or opponents, who include the Wicked Priest
and the Spouter of Lies. This Spouter of Lies seems to have been
some kind of religious leader who quarreled with the Teacher of
Righteousness over matters of religious law. The *pesher* also speaks
of the Wicked Priest, who began his term of office righteously but
later fell from grace in the view of the *pesher's* author. This Wicked
Priest went on to persecute the Teacher of Righteousness, although
he did not succeed in his intention to do away with the Teacher.
The work also mentions the arrival of the Kittim, an aggressive
people who would come from beyond the seas and punish the
priests of the Jerusalem Temple.

A single fragment from Cave 4 preserves part of the *Nahum
Pesher*. It is unusual since it gives actual names of historical indi-

viduals—an Antiochus and a Demetrius—but which of the Seleucid rulers are intended is not certain. Demetrius is said to be
allied with the "seekers after smooth things," who are normally
thought to be the Pharisees. Another person is mentioned who is
designated the "furious young lion," a bloodthirsty ruler who
"executes revenge on those who seek smooth things and hangs
men alive." Many identify this figure with Alexander Jannaeus,
who wrought such terrible revenge upon his Pharisee enemies
whom the writer often calls the "seekers after smooth things."
The *Nahum Pesher* also refers to two politico-religious groups
active in Judaea of that period by the code-names Manasseh and
Ephraim, and talks of events involving their interaction with the
Community. According to many scholars these groups are most
likely to be the Pharisees and the Sadducees.

The fact that many copies of the Book of Isaiah were found at
Qumran with associated *pesher* texts, and that it was used by
early Christians to prove that Yeshua was truly the expected
Messiah, indicates that it was an extremely popular book of the
Bible in Second Temple Judaism. Since the surviving *pesher* texts
dealing with selected passages from Isaiah are fragmentary, it is
not clear whether they comprise pieces of a single work or as
many as four separate *peshers*. However, the material covered
deals with familiar topics that were of great concern to the
Community.

One fragment foretells the eventual defeat and overthrow of
the Kittim who had crushed Israel—here, as usual in the coded
language of the Community, the Kittim are the Romans. Another
section of the same fragment looks forward to the imminent
arrival of the princely or Davidic Messiah who was mentioned in
the famous passage in Isaiah 11:1–3, a passage that was equally
important for early Christians, although the Messiah expected
by the Community does not share the characteristics attributed
to Yeshua.

Another small fragment speaks of the Jewish opponents of the Community, here called the "scoffers" and the "seekers after smooth things," while one other fragment seems to identify the Community with Isaiah's vision of a New Jerusalem. One line of this last *pesher* mentions "the twelve," usually understood to refer to the twelve priestly leaders of the congregation of the Community, one to represent or govern each of the tribes of Israel. The parallel with the twelve apostles of Christianity has led some scholars to suggest a direct connection between these two movements.

We know that the Book of Psalms were also an extremely important work in the Community, but this may just reflect its widespread popularity among the Jewish community in general. *Pesher* commentaries have survived on most of Psalm 37 and parts of Psalms 45 and 127. As with the other surviving *pesher* from Qumran, the concern here is with the personal conflict between the Teacher of Righteousness and his opponents, the Wicked Priest and the Liar, as well as the greater struggle between the Community and their enemies. The members of the Community are assured that though their evil enemies, who are here again termed "Ephraim" and "Manasseh," may endeavor to harm them, it is these enemies who will eventually be "cut off and blotted out for ever." The Community, on the other hand, shall "possess the High Mountain of Israel for ever and shall enjoy everlasting delights in His sanctuary."

THE HODAYOT

The *Hodayot*, the final sectarian work, is an important collection of hymns found in one poorly preserved manuscript from Cave 1, with a few further fragments from Cave 4. Because of the condition of the surviving manuscripts, it has not been possible to determine the precise number of hymns that would have been included, although it is generally held to be between 25 and 40. Overall, they are reminiscent in style of the biblical Psalms but are actually prayers of thanksgiving or praise to the Lord.

When they were first published by Sukenik it was thought that
they were all composed by the Teacher of Righteousness himself,
but the general view now is that only about half, if indeed any,
may have been written by him. Those particular hymns allude to
the experiences of a religious teacher who, though on intimate
terms with God, has been persecuted by his enemies and abandoned by his disciples; but there is nothing that would conclusively limit them to the authorship of the Teacher. Vermes and
Callaway tend to believe that such hymns describing a righteous
person in conflict with the wicked need not refer solely to the
experiences of the Teacher of Righteousness. Nevertheless they
are impressive compositions in their power and imagery, as the
following extract illustrates:

Clay and dust that I am,
   what can I devise unless Thou wish it,
   and what contrive unless Thou desire it?
What strength shall I have
   unless Thou keep me upright,
   and how shall I understand
   unless by the spirit Thou has shaped for me?
What can I say unless Thou open my mouth
   and how can I answer unless Thou enlighten me?

Since a number of copies were found at Qumran, we can imagine
that these hymns were used by members of the Community for
both private and group acts of worship. Vermes suggests that they
would have been sung or chanted by the Master of the Community
with the new members during their central festival of the year—
the Festival of the Renewal of the Covenant.

Part IV

Who Wrote the Scrolls?

nine

THE ARCHAEOLOGY OF QUMRAN

The dust had hardly settled in Cave 1 after its excavation by de Vaux and Harding, hot on the trail of Dead Sea Scrolls, when they turned their attention to the cluster of ruins that lay silently in the heat about a mile to the south. Known as Khirbet Qumran by the local Arabs, this lonely ancient site had been visited several times in the past by Western travellers eager to find traces of familiar biblical stories in the land of Palestine. Before the scrolls were discovered among the nearby cliffs, these visitors all remarked on the obvious strategic value of the site and concluded that it must have been some kind of Israelite fortress. They were led to this conclusion both by the location of the settlement and by what they could see of its structure protruding from the sands.

Khirbet Qumran is situated on the northwestern shore of the Dead Sea, some 8 miles (13 km) south of Jericho and about 14 miles (22 km) from Jerusalem, on the edge of the arid Judaean desert. A little further south lie the two smaller sites of Ain Feshkha and Ain el-Ghuweir that are believed by many specialists to be associated with Qumran. The group of buildings at Qumran itself was constructed on a terrace that rises above the sea, near a *wadi*, a dry river course, that cuts its way down from the cliffs behind to the shore. This settlement occupies a key position in the area since it would be capable of guarding cities lying inland from hostile incursions from the south, the north and the east. One could almost believe that it was intended as a pair to a site on the eastern shore of the Dead Sea, Machaerus, which is

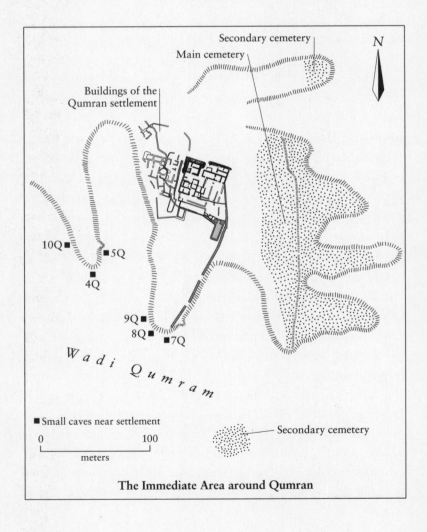

The Immediate Area around Qumran

definitely known to have been a fortress in the Hasmonean period. Some seven years before the discovery of the Dead Sea Scrolls Qumran had just been surveyed and mapped by Michael Avi-Yonah, who also considered it to be a military site—one of many such sites known to exist in the Judaean desert and dating back to the Second Temple period.

It was the discovery of the scroll fragments in the caves above Qumran that led to the first full-scale excavations of the ruins themselves, between 1951 and 1956. Without doubt, the work was carried out carefully and scientifically in accordance with the best archaeological practice of the day. But frustratingly, as is so often the case with archaeologists even today, de Vaux seems to have put aside the tedious though essential work of writing up and publishing the details of the excavations and the finds in favor of attending to the apparently more glamorous work concerning the scroll material from the caves. This makes an objective analysis of the site difficult, since it is clear that de Vaux not only saw what he wanted to see at times but also played down features that conflicted with his cherished view that Qumran had been home to a Jewish monastic community. But since all we have at present is a summary of his findings in *The Archaeology of Qumran* we must largely rely upon his description of what was found, though recently a growing number of specialists have begun to question his conclusions.

ARCHAEOLOGICAL PERIODS AT QUMRAN ACCORDING TO DE VAUX

PERIOD	STRATUM	DATE
Israelite		8th–7th century B.C.E.
Hellenistic	Ia	pre c.134 B.C.E.
	Ib	c.134 B.C.E.–31 B.C.E.
Herodian	II	c.31 B.C.E.–68 C.E.
Roman	III	post 68 C.E.–c.73 C.E.
Bar Kokhba		c.132 C.E.–135 C.E.

In essence, what de Vaux found was evidence of periodic ancient occupation of the Qumran site going back at least to the First Temple Israelite times. The earliest remains from this period were incorporated into or overlaid by a later Hellenistic stratum that de Vaux subdivided into two layers. This in turn gave way to another period of occupation, termed Herodian by de Vaux, followed by a third stratum that he associated with a brief Roman occupation of the site in the immediate aftermath of the Jewish Revolt and the destruction of Jerusalem. However, as we shall find later, some doubt has been cast on the validity of drawing a sharp distinction between the Hellenistic period Ib and the Herodian period of stratum II, and even the idea of a Roman occupation can be called into question. Traces were also found, based largely on the evidence from coins found there, of occasional use of the site still later, up to the time of the Bar-Kokhba Revolt and down into medieval Byzantine times.

In the absence of inscriptions, and apart from pottery styles, the historical distribution of any coins found on a site are the best evidence for dating any particular level. As elsewhere in the world, once monetary economies had been introduced in the Middle East each kingdom produced its own coins, often with new issues appearing during the reigns of successive rulers. Sometimes these coins are dated, giving archaeologists a rough means of dating the level in which they have been found. For example, if one is excavating a site and goes down beyond the modern surface layer, one can expect to find older rather than more recent coins. On a British site the absence of coins from the reign of Queen Elizabeth II in any stratum will suggest that this level is likely to correspond to a period before 1952. If, furthermore, many coins from the reign of Queen Victoria are found, with a few from earlier monarchs but none from later ones, we can assume that this stratum was occupied at least down to the latest dated coin of Victoria's reign but not much beyond that date. We can also assume that the earliest dated coin might mark the beginning of occupation of that level, although we must bear in mind that coins often remain in circulation for some time after their issue.

Let us now take a careful look at what de Vaux reports about the archaeology of the Qumran complex and its associated sites, because, though it may be a little dry, a clear understanding and interpretation of the finds made here are essential if we are to determine the origin of the scroll fragments found in the caves nearby.

The remains of the earliest site dating from the Israelite period were probably rather simple, as they now comprise little more than some walls and a large round water cistern. Though no coins were found that might have helped with a more accurate dating, de Vaux decided that this stratum corresponded to the well-known local Iron Age II period because he found pottery remains characteristic of that time. As far as this level is concerned, de Vaux was happy to concede that it was probably an outpost con-

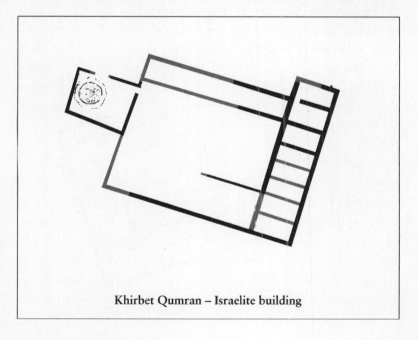

Khirbet Qumran – Israelite building

structed to shelter Israelite military forces patrolling the Judaean desert and Dead Sea region, but he formed definite ideas about the nature of the later occupation of Qumran.

We shall return to this problem later, but for the time being we must bear in mind that de Vaux believed, perhaps correctly, that there was a strong connection between the scroll fragments and the settlement at Qumran. In fact, he maintained that the scrolls had originally been written at Qumran and had formed the library of an ascetic Jewish sect known as the Essenes who lived there throughout the Hellenistic and Herodian periods. Though this interpretation is still held unquestioningly by many, its validity has been attacked by a small group of vocal scholars who challenge the so-called consensus view in the light of new facts that have emerged at the Qumran site.

The key period for the occupation and development of the cluster of buildings at Qumran was appropriately termed Hel-

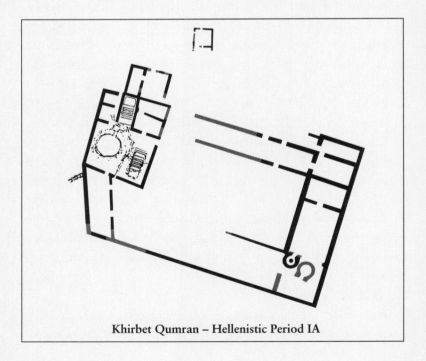

Khirbet Qumran – Hellenistic Period IA

lenistic by de Vaux. He believed he could discern two phases of occupation during this period, which he termed Ia and Ib. Although Ia shares many features with the overlying Ib, a number of elements clearly indicate that they represent two distinct phases in the development of the site.

It would seem from the archaeological evidence that the Qumran site had been abandoned for centuries before it was reoccupied. The Iron Age II layer corresponds, of course, to the pre-exile First Temple period. The Babylonian invasion of Judaea that culminated in the destruction of Jerusalem in 587 B.C.E., followed by the inhabitants' exile in Babylon, would have left much of the country depopulated and in a state of desolation. Small military outposts like that at Qumran would undoubtedly have been abandoned to nature until reoccupied several centuries later. Regardless of the identity and purpose of those who returned to Qumran, we are unfortunately unable to date this phase with any certainty since no coins were found here.

It is quite possible that some elements of the earlier Iron Age II settlement were still usable, even though probably derelict. De Vaux assumes that people returned to the site at least before 134 B.C.E. and possibly as early as 168 B.C.E. It was then that remnants of the Iron Age buildings would have been refurbished, with the addition of extra rooms and enclosing walls. The occupants also constructed at this time a water channel running into the old Iron Age round cistern, as well as two additional rectangular cisterns and a decantation basin to improve their water supply. These two facts lead one to believe that the site was now occupied by a larger number of individuals than during the earlier Iron Age II Israelite period. As indicated above, the precise reason for their occupancy of the Qumran site is one of the greatest points of controversy because it directly relates to the origins or provenance of the Dead Sea Scrolls themselves.

The settlement then saw a period of considerable expansion. Many new features were added to the small original core of buildings, resulting in the elaborate "definitive" structure of Qumran as we see it today. The presence of coins enabled de Vaux to determine in general terms the beginning and end of this phase.

The earliest ones he found were a collection of 15 bronze and silver coins that had been issued by the Syrian-based Seleucid Empire, which at various times ruled over much of Palestine including Judaea. The oldest of these coins were a bronze one from the reign of Antiochus III (223 B.C.E.–187 B.C.E.) and another from the reign of Antiochus IV (175 B.C.E.–163 B.C.E.). Since the bulk of these Seleucid coins date from the 130s B.C.E., the site was probably already in use during that time.

However, caution must be exercised when interpreting this kind of data. Many countries in modern times have changed their currency, so when we look at the contents of our pockets or purses we no longer find significantly earlier coins. In the United Kingdom, new coinage was issued in the early 1970s at the introduction of decimalization and all older coins immediately became obsolete. Until that time it was not unusual to find pennies dating from the 1830s rubbing alongside coins from the 1960s. Just because de Vaux's team happened to find early Seleucid coins at Qumran does not, therefore, automatically mean that the Hellenistic Ib phase of the settlement should be dated to the 130s B.C.E.— it could well date from a few decades later. We are on firmer ground, however, when we try to determine the end of Ib, since the latest coins found at this level are four issued by Antigonus Mattathias some time between 40 B.C.E. and 37 B.C.E. Antigonus Mattathias was, of course, the last Hasmonean ruler of Judaea before Herod the Great took control.

COIN DATA FROM QUMRAN

Level of Hellenistic Period Ia
No coins found at this level

Level of Hellenistic Period Ib
Seleucid Coins
223–130 B.C.E.:   8 bronze coins
145–125 B.C.E.:   11 silver coins

Jewish Coins
134–104 B.C.E.:	1	(reign of John Hyrcanus)
104–103 B.C.E.:	1	(reign of Aristobulus I)
103–76 B.C.E.:	162	(reign of Alexander Jannaeus)
76–67 B.C.E.:	1	(reign of Salome Alexandra)
c.63–40 B.C.E.:	2	(reign of Hyrcanus II)
c.40–37 B.C.E.:	4	(Parthian period, reign of Antigonus)

Levels of Herodian and Roman Period
103–76 B.C.E.:	12	(reign of Alexander Jannaeus)
c.40–37 B.C.E.:	1	(reign of Antigonus)
37–4 B.C.E.:	11	(reign of Herod the Great)
?–8 B.C.E.:	561	Late Seleucid silver coins, mostly from the autonomous city of Tyre, found in three batches in the "Trading Room"
4 B.C.E.–6 C.E.:	18	(reign of Herod Archelaus)
6–41 C.E.:	92	(period of Roman procurators)
37–44 C.E.	78	(reign of Agrippa I)
54–58 C.E.	33	(reign of Nero)
67 C.E.:	94	bronze Jewish coins (1st year of Jewish Revolt)
68 C.E.	5	bronze Jewish coins (1st year of Jewish Revolt)
+67 C.E.:	6	bronze Jewish coins of 1st Revolt (date illegible)
67–68 C.E.:	13	Roman
69–79 C.E.:	1	Roman
72–73 C.E.:	2	Roman
72–81 C.E.:	4	Roman

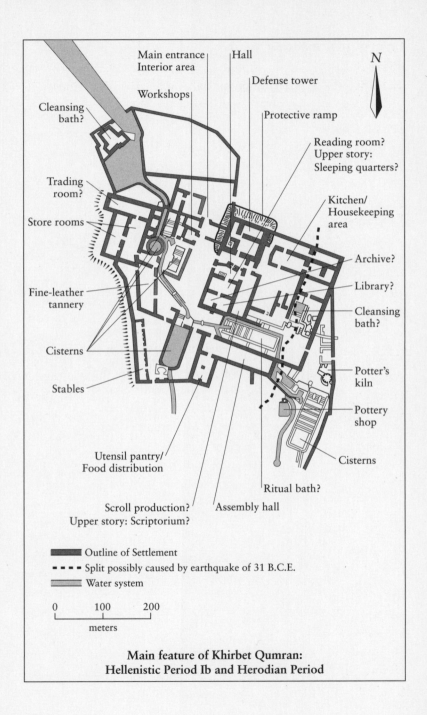

Main entrance
Interior area

Hall

Defense tower

N

Workshops

Protective ramp

Cleansing
bath?

Reading room?
Upper story:
Sleeping quarters?

Trading
room?

Kitchen/
Housekeeping
area

Store rooms

Archive?

Library?

Fine-leather
tannery

Cleansing
bath?

Cisterns

Potter's
kiln

Stables

Pottery
shop

Utensil pantry/
Food distribution

Cisterns

Ritual bath?

Scroll production?
Upper story: Scriptorium?

Assembly hall

████ Outline of Settlement
- - - - Split possibly caused by earthquake of 31 B.C.E.
▓▓▓▓ Water system

0   100   200
|__|__|__|
   meters

**Main feature of Khirbet Qumran:
Hellenistic Period Ib and Herodian Period**

87 C.E.:	1	Roman
98–117 C.E.:	3	Roman
132–6 C.E.:	6	Roman (Bar-Kokhba Revolt period)

The distribution of coin finds indicates that the two periods of greatest activity at Qumran are 103–76 B.C.E, during the reign of Alexander Jannaeus and Heroidan-Roman period, post-8 B.C.E. –67 C E.

So what did the influx of occupants add to the settlement at Qumran during period Ib? Apart from entrances to the east and the northwest, the main gateway into the entire complex lies on the northern side of the settlement and it was here that a sturdy three-story tower was erected. Even today its remains form a substantial feature and, though de Vaux was never prepared to consider that the Qumran settlement had been used for military purposes during the Hellenistic and Herodian periods, even he could not fail to note its strategic advantage: "from the plateau of Qumran, the view extends over the whole of the western shore from the mouth of the Jordan to Ras Feshkha and over the entire northern half of the Dead Sea." In fact, when the tower was still intact the view from the top would have extended even further.

Apart from this tower, many other buildings and features were added. Sometimes using supposition rather than hard evidence, de Vaux identified a number of storage areas, a laundry, a kitchen, a pantry that still contained more than a thousand eating bowls in tumbled stacks, jars, jugs, dishes neatly arranged into sets of a dozen, a large hall that may have served as a refectory or meeting place, and another room with a low built-in bench running around the walls. In addition, elsewhere there were several workshops, a pottery with associated kilns and what may be stables. The entire complex was surrounded by once-sturdy limestone-faced walls, although not much of these remains today.

Clearly the Qumran settlement was now a thriving home to a considerable number of people, so extra water storage facilities had to be constructed. These included several new cisterns, cold-water baths and water channels to link them. The total volume of water available on site at this time would have been sufficient to support several hundred people throughout the eight dry months of the year. Indeed, it has recently been estimated that this volume of water would have been approximately 247,940 gallons (1,127,000 liters), sufficient for the needs of 750 people. This figure is significant, and will be explained later.

Due to the fact that Qumran seems to have been heavily damaged by the Romans some time during the Jewish War (66–72 C.E.), much valuable evidence has been lost. In particular, it is believed that most of the buildings in the main complex were two-story structures which collapsed at that time. Just south of the great tower were found remnants of what would have been a second-floor hall that had fallen through to the debris on the ground floor.

At this point we should remember that de Vaux believed the Qumran site functioned as a kind of Jewish "monastery." Since he directly linked the manuscript finds from the nearby caves with the Qumran site, he assumed that there would have been some kind of library and, more importantly, a place where these manuscripts were copied, rather like the *scriptorium* found in medieval Christian monasteries. Finding several pieces of odd stone table-like items and three inkwells among the rubble in this area, he took them to be part of the furnishings of a *scriptorium* that had occupied the now lost second floor.

Although many still accept elements of this interpretation, there is a growing body of younger scholars who have challenged it. Most recently, the Belgian historian Pauline Donceel, who has been involved with her husband in preparing parts of the final Qumran site report for the École Biblique, announced her findings in 1992. After re-examining all the available elements linked to the so-called *scriptorium*, and drawing on data from other sites of the period, she has claimed that the *scriptorium* was in fact a kind of luxury private dining room common in the ancient world known as a *triclinium*. What de Vaux had interpreted as the remnants of writing tables may actually be portions of benches that were attached to the walls upon which diners reclined while they ate.

Despite all the signs that Qumran was a thriving settlement at this time, with its own industrial activities that would have included pottery making, leather tanning and the production of date syrup, and despite the considerable quantity of animal bones discarded from meals and the many finds of coins at this level, there is no area on the site that obviously functioned as the living or sleeping quarters of its many inhabitants. This strange anomaly has been explained in several ways.

As we have seen, many of the buildings originally had two stories, and since these have now collapsed no definite traces remain of the specific use of each area of the upper story—the living and sleeping quarters could well have been located there. On the other hand, some authorities think that the nearby caves, in some of which the scroll fragments were found, would originally have been used as dwelling areas. There is some merit to this solution since we know from the finds in a number of the caves—pottery fragments, food remains, scraps of leather, cloth and mats—that they had indeed been occupied by people around this time, but whether they slept there or just used them as workshops and the like is difficult to determine. One final possibility is that the occupants of Qumran spent their rest time in a camp of tents pitched in the area, but of all the alternatives this is naturally the most difficult to substantiate.

In his summary report, de Vaux separates his Hellenistic period Ib from the Herodian period on the ground of a major geological fault-line with considerable associated damage that he believed the site sustained in the last half of the first century B.C.E. This fault-line runs from north to south at the eastern end of the main building complex. Being a well-read historian, de Vaux immediately concluded that this damage had been caused by the major earthquake reported by the Jewish historian Josephus that had occurred in the region in 31 B.C.E. There was another earthquake in 24 B.C.E., but de Vaux did not take this one into consideration.

Associated with this damage are traces of a major fire at the site, but it is debatable whether this happened at the same time as the fault-line damage since the extent of the conflagration suggests that it was intentional rather than accidental. The fault-line damage affected several water channels and a reservoir in that area of the site, and the overflow of water caused a layer of sediment to build up, which led de Vaux to estimate that the site was abandoned for up to 30 years from between 31 B.C.E. and 4 B.C.E., though even his colleague Milik later distanced himself from this view. One important point is that the traces of fire damage lie beneath this layer of sediment, so although we cannot say whether the fire occurred at the same time as the fault-line damage or before it, it could not have happened afterwards. Be that as it may, de Vaux maintained that this damage marks the end of his Hellenistic period Ib and that the Qumran site was left abandoned for several decades until reoccupied and repaired at the beginning of his Herodian period.

Although de Vaux seems convinced that the structural damage associated with this fault-line was caused by the earthquake of 31 B.C.E., this is not the only possible explanation. Recently, Karcz and Kafri have cast doubt on the earthquake theory and consequently call into question the date of the supposed boundary between the Hellenistic period Ib and the Herodian period. They point out that the whole area is built on unstable marl which may well have slipped down towards the Dead Sea through the action of water, resulting in heaving, seepage and percolation, which would have destabilized the buildings. If that is the case, it could have happened at any time and not necessarily in 31 B.C.E.

Additionally, since the evidence of fires around this time lie beneath the sediment that built up after the structural damage had occurred, they, too, can be easily explained in other ways. As we saw in Chapter 4, the whole of this border region was frequently under attack from hostile neighbors. During the early Hasmonean period the Seleucids often invaded Judaea and left considerable destruction in their wake. Even more likely candidates for invaders who could have attacked and burnt Qumran were the Parthians who came from the east and ravaged the area around 40 B.C.E., or it could have been destroyed by Herod the Great in 37 B.C.E. as he made his way to secure Jerusalem for himself.

Although on archaeological grounds one can distinguish between de Vaux's Hellenistic period Ib and his Herodian period, there are no strong grounds for considering that there was a long hiatus between these two periods from the point of view of the occupants. The evidence supplied by coins is ambivalent and need not necessarily lead us to believe that decades passed before anybody returned to the site—it could have been just a matter of months or a year at the most, since the deposit of sediment found at the eastern end of the site could have built up in a relatively short time. Indeed, apart from the repair work that was carried out after the damage associated with the fault-line there is no strong evidence that there was a break in the habitation of Qumran at this time.

It is, however, probable that there were fewer inhabitants after this incident, for no wholesale attempt was made to clear away all the debris or to rebuild the site as it had been formerly. Certain areas were abandoned, while other buildings had their walls buttressed or doubled in thickness; a few new buildings, including a workshop with a forge or furnace and an area with millstones, were also constructed at this time. One important structure was given particular attention: the tower by the main gateway. Huge stone buttresses were constructed around its base on all sides, reaching up to the top of the ground floor. These buttresses are more like ramps, with surfaces at a 45 degree angle. Whoever was living at Qumran at this time obviously attached great importance to this particular structure.

THE DESTRUCTION OF QUMRAN

It is commonly believed that the occupation of Qumran came to an abrupt end some time during or after 68 C.E. This view is based on coin evidence and on signs of destruction through warfare, such as Roman arrowheads and a layer of black ash. Moreover, it is universally agreed that this event must have occurred as the Romans were moving through the country crushing resistance during the Jewish Revolt. But to know the precise year when this happened is crucial for our understanding of the nature of the complex of buildings at Qumran.

For many years the majority of scholars have suggested that it must have occurred in the early summer of 68 C.E. But it could also be argued that the date may be slightly later, after the fall of Jerusalem in 70 C.E., during the mopping-up operations. It is well known that Titus and his legions did not immediately deal with a number of fortresses in this region, such as Herodium, Machaerus and Masada, only crushing them once Jerusalem had been destroyed. Given the location of Qumran in relationship to these fortresses, it seems more likely that this settlement, whatever its function might have been, was also attacked and destroyed by the Romans only after 70 C.E.

After it had been cleared of its Jewish inhabitants Qumran was occupied for a brief period, according to de Vaux, by Roman soldiers who were presumably guarding the area against attacks from

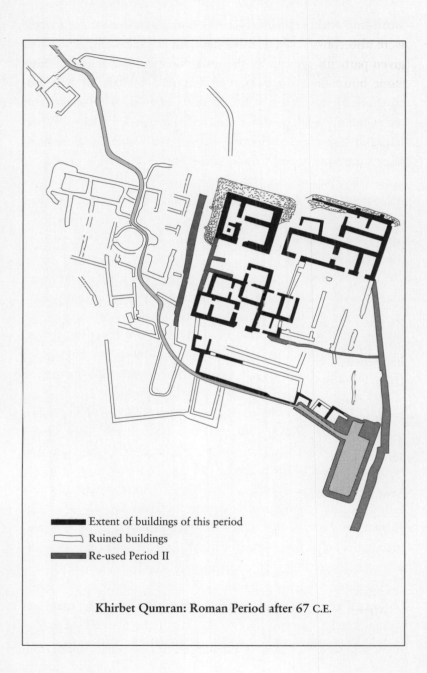

Extent of buildings of this period
Ruined buildings
Re-used Period II

Khirbet Qumran: Roman Period after 67 C.E.

small Jewish guerrilla bands that continued to operate for a while in the region. During their stay at Qumran the Romans seem to have cleared up only a small area of the settlement and to have made a minimum of repairs or alterations to the site. In the main, all they did was simplify the structure of existing buildings and water supply and reinforce the walls in certain places. When Jewish resistance had been quashed, the Roman legionnaires were no doubt happy to pack their bags and leave a couple of years later, perhaps around 74 C.E. based on the coin evidence. After the Romans had left, the site seems to have been abandoned for around 60 years (if we are to believe de Vaux's interpretation), until the time of the Bar-Kokhba Revolt of 132–135 C.E., when it was again briefly occupied.

There is, however, at least one scholar, Robert Eisenman, who disagrees entirely with this reconstruction of events that culminated in the undisputed damage to the Qumran complex. Since he has urged a reconsideration of the coin evidence, let us first quickly review de Vaux's grounds for assuming that the settlement at Qumran was largely destroyed by the Romans during the Jewish Revolt—around 68–69 C.E., in his opinion.

Once the Zealots who instigated the Jewish Revolt had made a *de facto* declaration of independence from Rome, they issued their own Jewish coinage. Considerable numbers of coins minted in the third year of the rebellion (68 C.E.) were found at Qumran, but none from the fourth or final years. The next type of coins found there are all Roman in origin. As far as de Vaux was concerned, this meant that Qumran was destroyed in 68 C.E. and then reoccupied by a detachment of Roman soldiers—the consensus scenario that I have followed above.

Eisenman points out that there are several obstacles to accepting this theory. If Jewish coins of the third year of the rebellion were minted in the spring of 68 C.E., it is rather surprising that so many had already found their way to Qumran by June of that year, when de Vaux claims it was attacked. As we have seen above, there is also good evidence that the Romans were not even active in the Qumran area until the fall of Jerusalem. Moreover, although none was found by de Vaux at Qumran, a Jewish coin from the fourth year of the rebellion (69–70 C.E.) was discovered at nearby Ain Feshkha, a site that de Vaux and many others link to the main Qumran settlement. Eisenman also points out that Roman coins found on the site are only mute witnesses and do not tell us who dropped them—after the collapse of the rebellion Roman coins would have been in common circulation and used by everybody, Jew or Roman.

For his own reasons, which will be discussed later, Eisenman concludes that all we can say with certainty is that Qumran was occupied by Jews at least until mid-68 C.E., but this does not preclude the possibility that the site was occupied by Jews down to 136 C.E. at the end of the Bar-Kokhba Revolt. He suggests that the fire at Qumran may well have been caused by the Romans as they passed through, but this does not necessarily mean that any Roman soldiers even garrisoned the settlement during the last phase of the rebellion. Eisenman postulates that the inhabitants, who he does not believe were Jewish military personnel, could have hidden until the Romans had marched on, then returned to the site and refurbished it along the lines described in de Vaux's published preliminary report.

The only problem with this theory derives from an additional piece of information unmentioned by de Vaux but provided later by Frank Cross, who also worked on the site. Some of the outer walls of the complex have collapsed after being mined. It was a common Roman military tactic, also used in the siege of Jerusalem, to tunnel under impregnable walls, propping up the ever-lengthening tunnel with timber supports. These were then set on fire and the whole tunnel would collapse, causing the walls above to crash down.

Before we leave Qumran one important feature remains: the cemeteries that lie to the east of the main building complex. There are three—a large one with around 1100 graves some 30 yards (27 meters) to the east of the settlement, and two smaller ones situated to the north and the south of the central cemetery containing 12 and 30 graves respectively. All the graves are laid out neatly in regular rows, marked with piled-up stones and with a north–south orientation. This arrangement is not unique to Qumran—a similar alignment has also been found at Jericho and in southern Jerusalem, among other places.

Some of these graves had already been excavated in the 1870s, more were excavated by de Vaux's team and yet others have been investigated more recently. Although nothing has come to light from the graves that might help date the cemetery more precisely, the style of the potsherds found in them would put the cemetery in de Vaux's Hellenistic period Ib and Herodian period. In the 43 graves that de Vaux's team excavated, the remains of 30 men, 7 women and 4 children were found. If the ratio of male to female bodies found so far is representative of the whole cemetery, we would expect about 20 percent of the adult graves to be burials of women. This point creates difficulties for the consensus view, which de Vaux initiated, that Qumran was occupied by members of a celibate monastic sect.

De Vaux also believed that the cemetery functioned as the last resting-place of members of this community throughout the 200-odd years that the Qumran complex is thought to have been occupied. Here again a problem arises. Any graveyard that has been in use for that length of time displays some degree of stratification. That is to say, the tops of some graves will have gradually sunk below the surrounding surface and even become obscured by the soil and debris from later graves as they were dug. But this is not the case at Qumran—the tops of all the graves lie at the same level, clearly visible on the surface. This suggests that this cemetery is not an accumulation of several generations of graves but that all are, for some reason, virtually contemporaneous.

Recent excavations carried out in the cemetery throw new light on this problem. Dr. Z. Kapera, a Polish scholar, has publicized the work of H. Steckoll, who has carried out a detailed examination of human remains from other graves at Qumran. What he reveals is very dramatic. A number of the skeletons he examined showed signs of having been burned, though not through intentional cremation, and an additional 10 percent had broken bones. In sum, the neat rows of graves—the majority of which were dug around the same time—the mixture of sexes and the signs of violent death all suggest that we are dealing not with a peaceful monastic graveyard but the mass burial of massacre or war victims. If this is the case, who were these people and when did they die?

First, the number of bodies suggests that almost the entire population was slaughtered—after all, we know from the water-storage facilities that Qumran could have supported over 750 people for eight months, so there would have been no problem housing a larger number of people there for a shorter span of time. We might first think that the graves contain the bodies of people killed by the Romans when they attacked and torched Qumran during the Jewish Revolt, but this seems unlikely. Whatever the victorious Romans normally did with the bodies of their vanquished enemies, it is unlikely they would have gone to the trouble of placing each body in its own well-constructed grave, laid out in neat rows, all aligned with the heads to the north. Given the consensus view that Roman forces remained for several years at Qumran to guard it, it is also unlikely that any pious Jews would have been able to get anywhere near the place to give the dead a decent burial. My guess is that the majority of these people were killed earlier, and their deaths may well be linked to the signs of burning that de Vaux found in association with, or just below, what he thought was earthquake damage. As we saw above, this area was ravaged by invading Parthian forces around 40 B.C.E. Either they, or the soldiers of Herod the Great a decade later, seem most likely to have been responsible for this slaughter.

QUMRAN'S ENVIRONS

Of the two small settlements sometimes linked to Qumran, Ain Feshkha lies about 2 miles (3 km) south and takes its name from a nearby freshwater spring. Judging from the archaeological remains, it seems to have been a small industrial outpost associated with local agriculture. Looking at the pottery evidence, de Vaux thought it had been occupied by the same people who lived at Qumran during his Hellenistic period I and Herodian period. The structures found there consist of a large building 72 by 54 feet (24 by 18m) that once had two stories, an enclosure with possible stables or storage sheds to the south, and a courtyard to the north with basins that are thought to have been used as a tannery. There is no sign of any "earthquake" damage such as was found at Qumran and which de Vaux used to demarcate his period Ib and period II, although he claims that habitation came to an abrupt end at the same time as at Qumran, around 68 C.E. No graves have been found at Ain Feshkha, so if there were ever war victims here their bodies may have been carried the short distance up to Qumran and buried with the others.

Also a farm-like settlement, Ain el-Ghuweir lies 15 miles (24 km) south of Qumran near another spring. This site is smaller than Ain Feshkha and merely consists of a walled courtyard, a four-roomed building, a hall, a large kitchen and two further rooms to the east. Archaeologists have distinguished two periods of occupation that, based on pottery evidence, correspond to Qumran Ib and II. No coins later than 43 C.E. have been found on the site, so this settlement had probably been abandoned some time before the Jewish Revolt and was probably derelict by the time the Romans passed through here on their way to Masada. Signs of a conflagration occur between levels that correspond to Qumran Ib and II, which also have signs of fire damage. These events would therefore appear to be linked.

Unlike Ain Feshkha, Ain el-Ghuweir has a small cemetery of its own half a mile (800m) to the north. Just as at Qumran, the graves are laid out in neat rows with a north–south alignment. The 20 graves excavated were found to contain the remains of twelve men, seven women and one boy. We might speculate that these, too, could be the bodies of people slaughtered when the settlement was attacked and burned, but no corroborating studies have as yet been carried out on the skeletons.

Nevertheless, since the graves at Ain el-Ghuweir have the same alignment as those at Qumran, and because pottery found here seemed identical to that from Qumran, de Vaux was initially happy to link the two sites, suggesting that Ain el-Ghuweir was one of several outlying secondary Essene settlements. This view was still supported by others as late as the 1980s until the pottery from Ain el-Ghuweir was subjected to neutron-activation tests, which conclusively showed that it had a different origin from that at Qumran. The desire to link this site to Qumran on the basis of the graves, if not the pottery, has been further undermined by the discovery of still more burials in the same style and alignment at numerous small sites all along the Dead Sea shore, as well as those mentioned earlier that were found at Jericho and elsewhere.

As archaeological exploration of the western shores of the Dead Sea has progressed in recent years, we now know that the whole area was once far more densely populated than we might imagine from visiting it today. Numerous small settlements have now been found dotted along the narrow belt of land between the shore and the Judaean desert. Although life would not have been easy by modern standards, the skilled use of local resources would have made life reasonably comfortable—enough to permit the construction of a number of substantial farmsteads and industrial outposts such as Ain Feshkha and Ain el-Ghuweir.

The key to survival in this region would have been water. Apart from the occasional freshwater springs that run down into the Dead Sea, rainfall running down the *wadis* during the few wet months of the year was carefully channelled into reservoirs for storage, as at Qumran. Judging from the remains found at the sites so far excavated, the inhabitants of the region were engaged in several types of agriculture. First, they probably grew some barley since large grindstones for milling were found at Qumran. They would have raised flocks of sheep and goats, as people there still do to this very day. Not only would these animals have provided meat, milk and wool, but their hides would have been tanned and made into leather.

The discovery of pottery kilns at Qumran indicates that further income would have been generated by the manufacture of ceramics, typified by the elegant jars found in the caves above Qumran. The region is also dotted with groves of date-palms that must have provided several important resources apart from the dates themselves: thatching material, wood for fuel and date-syrup. Even the Dead Sea with its salty sterile water provided useful materials. Rushes growing along its shores were used to make baskets, matting and probably additional material for thatching. The sea itself was famous in ancient times for the valuable asphalt and lumps of bitumen that float on its surface, which was collected and sold to the towns inland. So, despite the apparently hostile nature of this region, we can see all the signs of a thriving if small-scale economy that supported relatively large numbers of people.

WHO LIVED AT QUMRAN?

So now we come to the crux of the problem: Based on the archaeological evidence, who lived at Khirbet Qumran? De Vaux was certain that this settlement was the home of the mysterious ascetic

Jewish sect known as the Essenes. His reasons were fairly straight-forward, even though we might say in hindsight that though basically sound they are a little simplistic and he sometimes seems to have tailored the archaeological evidence to suit his presupposition. After the scroll fragments had been discovered in the near-by caves, de Vaux concluded that they must have been linked intimately with the ruins. Before the scrolls were examined in detail, this might have seemed reasonable. De Vaux associated Qumran with the Essenes because of some words written by the Roman author Pliny who visited Palestine around 75 C.E., shortly after the end of the Jewish Revolt:

> To the west [of the Dead Sea], the Essenes have put the necessary distance between themselves and the insalu-brious shore. They are a people unique of its kind and admirable beyond all others in the whole world, with-out women and renouncing love entirely, without money, and having only the palm trees for company. Owing to the throng of newcomers, this people is daily reborn in equal numbers; indeed, those whom wearied by the fluctuations of fortune, life leads to adopt their customs, stream in great numbers. Thus, unbelievable though this may seem, for thousands of centuries a people has existed which is eternal yet into which no one is born: so fruitful for them is the repentance which others feel for their past lives! Below the Essenes was the town Engedi, which yielded only to Jerusalem in fertility and palm groves but today is become another ash-heap.

The decisive statement for de Vaux was "below the Essenes was the town Engedi"—in other words, the Essenes lived some-where to the north of Engedi on the western shore of the Dead Sea. A quick look at a map of the region shows that Engedi was located about midway down the western coast of the Dead Sea and, since there does not seem to be any other suitable site in the area, de Vaux immediately thought of Qumran and decided that this must the place Pliny was talking about. This identification with the Essenes was further strengthened by certain aspects of the Dead Sea Scrolls that he had read, which suggested that they were produced by a strict Jewish separatist sect. Yet if we look more carefully at Pliny's statement and compare what he says with the known facts concerning Qumran, we begin to encounter anomalies that some believe cast doubts on this early and still popular identification.

First, Pliny talks about the Essenes using the present tense, suggesting that they were *currently* living somewhere in the region at the time he was writing, which was after the Jewish Revolt. This is corroborated by his statement that Engedi was then a heap of ashes like Jerusalem (or Jericho as some scholars read the text)— though whether he intended to refer to Jericho or Jerusalem is irrelevant, since both were destroyed by the Romans. We also know from the archaeological evidence that Qumran itself was captured, destroyed and possibly garrisoned by the Romans some time during the Jewish Revolt. We might simply conclude on this basis that Pliny's Essenes were not at Qumran after all, but must have been living somewhere else as yet unknown.

Of course, de Vaux and his successors eventually had to address this problem and, by way of a solution, they rationalized Pliny to fit their conclusions about the Essenes and Qumran. It was suggested that Pliny's report had been editorially amended, with the statement about the destruction of Engedi being inserted at a later date, while his account of the Essenes who lived on the shores of the Dead Sea had been derived from earlier secondary sources, which made Pliny's words unreliable as a historically accurate statement.

To me this response seems evasive, both when we consider that elsewhere in his description of Palestine Pliny clearly describes the situation he found there *after* the destruction wrought in the course of the Jewish Revolt, and when we compare further statements about the Essenes made by Pliny and other ancient authors with what has been found at Qumran. On the other hand, Robert Eisenman's theory that the Romans merely passed through Qumran, burned it and then moved on southwards could explain why Jewish inhabitants had already returned by the time Pliny was writing. Overall, the problem with the earlier form of the consensus view was that it enthusiastically and rather simplistically tried to identify the Essenes, as they were described by Josephus and Pliny, with possible inhabitants of the Khirbet Qumran settlement, when in fact the evidence is not so unequivocal.

Further features of the Qumran site also clash with Pliny's report. He and other ancient writers all concur that the Essenes were basically a celibate group who disdained the company of women; yet, as we have seen, a number of female skeletons have been found in the Qumran cemetery, indicating that there were women living at Qumran at some time. Moreover, everything we read about the Essenes stresses that they were poor and lived without money, yet considerable hoards of coins, many silver, were found by de Vaux and his team at Qumran. Other ancient writers on the Essenes, such as Josephus and Philo of Alexandria, give the impression that they were pacifists and possibly vegetarian. But this does not square with what we know about the people who lived at Qumran, who obviously put up a fight when besieged by the Romans and who left large quantities of discarded animal bones from their meals.

So there are numerous features associated with Qumran that indicate that the inhabitants were not a celibate, ascetic Jewish group like the Essenes as we know them from classical sources. Dr. Norman Golb in particular advocates the theory that the settlement was never home to any religious group but had always functioned as a Jewish military outpost.

First, the once sturdy walls encircling the entire settlement, the massive reinforced tower and the complex water storage system capable of supporting over 700 people do not suggest that Qumran was inhabited by pacifist recluses engaged in prayer and meditation, but have all the hallmarks of military defenses. The much-vaunted *scriptorium* has now been shown to have more probably been a *triclinium*, the kind of private dining room found only in luxury homes in Roman times—hardly the kind of facility one would associate with ascetics. The probability that Qumran was the scene of major scribal activity is also undermined by the total absence of any finds, apart from the three inkwells, associated with writing activities such as pens or parchment fragments: these could have survived if they had been there to begin with.

Finally, a major difficulty connected with the cemetery, apart from the fact that it contains the skeletal remains of women, is its location. The sectarian people with whom some of the scrolls are linked were ultra-orthodox Jews who separated themselves from their fellows because of the strictness with which they observed Jewish ritual law. The nearest edge of the cemetery is just over 30 yards (27 meters) from the eastern flank of the Qumran buildings, while Jewish law stipulates that graves should be no nearer than 50 cubits (25 yards/23 meters) from human habitation. Given the ultra-zealous nature of the Essenes this would have been just too near for comfort—in fact it would have been quite in character for them to have laid out their graves at an even greater distance. But as we have already seen, there is nothing about this cemetery that suggests it was used over several generations by devout monk-like ascetics. Rather, it seems more likely that most of the bodies in the graves were the victims of a mass slaughter and buried around the same time.

An alternative theory has recently been proposed about the function of the Qumran complex during the Hellenistic and Herodian periods by the Belgian husband and wife team, Robert and

Pauline Donceel. Presumably, unlike the majority of scholars, they have had privileged access to Roland de Vaux's excavation notes and associated material. Apart from de Vaux's *scriptorium* (Donceel's *triclinium*) other elements from the site suggest that it was not the home of an ascetic group. The artifacts found include fragments of glass, a valuable commodity in ancient times, as well as shards of luxury high-status pottery. Coupled with the large caches of coins found hidden on the site, these items, the Donceels suggest, seem out of place if Qumran had been a semi-monastic community but would be exactly the kind of thing to be expected in a villa belonging to some well-to-do member of the Jerusalem aristocracy.

Any archaeological evidence of a Roman attack during the time of the Jewish Revolt can also be explained relatively simply. What escalated into a revolt against Rome started out as a bitter conflict between the Zealots and the rich aristocratic families of Jerusalem. As they gained the upper hand, it is known from the account of Josephus that many aristocrats were murdered and their homes looted. If Qumran had originally been a luxury villa, it could well have been appropriated and occupied by Zealot fighters in view of its strategic location, and would eventually have merited Roman attention.

CONCLUSION

We have seen that there are three current hypotheses concerning the original function of the complex of buildings at Qumran. Roland de Vaux believed that it was the monastery-like home of an ascetic Jewish group and interpreted everything his team found on the site as corroboration of this theory. Anything that seemed to contradict this interpretation was either ignored or quietly relegated to the footnotes. Despite the fact that de Vaux himself later had doubts about certain aspects of his theory, it still remains the predominant explanation for the use of the site even among scholars who in other respects hold controversial views about the nature of the scrolls found in the caves and their ultimate connection with the Qumran settlement.

Despite the close proximity of the caves, nothing had been found until recently that could definitively link the scrolls with the Qumran site. The fact that a number of pottery jars found in the caves seemed identical to those found on the site does not in itself prove a link—whoever lived at Qumran could have easily provided the jars as a kindness to the visiting owners of the scrolls. However, in 1996 several ostraca were found at the base of the eastern wall that separates the buildings from the cemetery. An ostracon is a broken piece of pottery with something jotted on it, usually something ephemeral like a short letter or a receipt—a kind of ancient substitute for notepaper. Thus it was with the two pieces found at Qumran. One of them records the gift of a certain estate with its grounds in fulfillment of some oath and was dated "in year two of . . .." The missing part of the date is easy to restore, as it clearly refers to Year Two of the Jewish Revolt—68 C.E.

This particular ostracon has attracted huge interest since the deciphered inscription includes the Hebrew word *yahad*, or community, who seem to be the beneficiary of the gift. This word is widely used in the sectarian portions of the Dead Sea Scrolls by their authors to denote their group: the Community. However, not all scholars agree with this reading and claim that the evidence is being manipulated to fit the hypothesis. Again, even if this ostracon was connected with a sectarian community, it still does not follow that the inhabitants of Qumran were a sectarian group, given the late date of the piece and the fact that it was found outside the site proper.

We have seen that there is a strong second hypothesis for the original use of the Qumran complex as a military stronghold. Though this view has come under fierce attack by those who accept the consensus view based on de Vaux's findings, it has attracted a

THE ARCHAEOLOGY OF QUMRAN

good degree of support in recent years. There are clear signs of military use of the site, in particular the vast water storage facilities and the fortified tower, as well as the mined outer walls that suggest a prolonged siege. I find this hypothesis more persuasive than the popular monastic scenario, although the ostracon mentioned above calls for some explanation if it indeed includes the word for "community."

Perhaps in recognition of this problem, Jean-Baptiste Humbert of the École Biblique tries to have the best of both worlds and suggests that Qumran was first a Maccabean outpost that was later occupied by the Essenes. Alternatively, if we are to retain the idea that the site was occupied by a religious group, perhaps we should not expect them to have been quite the pacifists that classical writers would have us believe. This may turn out to be the best solution, and is fairly plausible in the light of the bellicose contents of many of the writings found in the nearby caves, such as the *War Scroll*.

The third hypothesis, that the Qumran complex was a country villa, also has some merit and is not entirely at odds with the fortress theory. Living in turbulent times, many of the last rulers of Judaea and their scions were constantly under threat from various disaffected sections of the populace as well as from foreign invaders. We know that it was quite common in these circumstances for a small palace to be combined with elements of a fortress, as can be seen at Masada, Herodion and Machaerus. The same situation is found in most European countries.

Yet ultimately all these attempts to determine the true function of the complex of buildings at Qumran are still hampered by Roland de Vaux's dilettante approach to archaeology, just as the study of the scroll fragments themselves was hindered for decades by his disastrous stewardship of them. Until everybody gets full access to all the excavation records, it will remain impossible to arrive at any definitive solution. Even then this may not be possible, since in the course of any excavation vital evidence is lost or destroyed and we know from de Vaux's published preliminary report that much of the data seems muddled and confused. For example, not only does the coin evidence seem open to several interpretations, but the coins he found have been securely locked away in the École Biblique and have not been seen, let alone re-evaluated, by anybody, to my knowledge. Again, a number of coins that may clinch the argument for the date when the site is thought to have been abandoned by its Jewish inhabitants are badly corroded and illegible. Modern techniques might yield some traces of useful inscriptions, but use of such methods has not yet been permitted.

ten

THE IDENTITY OF THE COMMUNITY

N ow that we have considered the archaeology of the Khirbet Qumran settlement and the contents of the scrolls
found in the nearby caves, we can turn to the vexed
question of the identity of the sectarian group associated with a
substantial portion of the manuscript fragments. It has generated
a very large number of books, both popular and learned, and academic papers—perhaps more has been written on this topic than
on any other aspect of the Dead Sea Scrolls. It is regrettable that
the sectarian group do not identify themselves anywhere in the
scrolls with a name that would clearly and definitively link them
with known Jewish groups active in Judaea during the Second
Temple period. Often they merely refer to themselves as the Community (*yahad*), although they also liked to use a wide range of
epithets such as the Poor (*ebionim*), the Meek (*'anayyim*), the Sons
of Zadok, the Sons of Light and the Saints (*kedoshim*). Drawing on
the sparse internal evidence of the writings of this Community,
scholars have attempted, with varying degrees of credibility, to
identify them with this or that Jewish group known from other
sources. To understand the reasoning behind these attempts to

place the Community in a Judaean religious and social context we must first look at the variety of religious groups that are known to have existed during the period in question.

The Babylonian conquest of the kingdom of Judah, the destruction of the Solomonic Temple and the deportation of tens of thousands to Mesopotamia marked a watershed in the religious history of Israel. Prior to this, the Israelites believed that they had a unique relationship with God by virtue of the Covenant with Abraham and that God was not only present among the people but took special care of them. To be sure, there had been times when their enemies had briefly gained the upper hand, but eventually they had always been overcome and the status quo restored.

This confidence was struck a blow by the Assyrian destruction and depopulation of the Northern Kingdom in the 720s B.C.E. and then another even more severe with the Babylonian invasion just over a hundred years later. These events must have provided much food for thought among the religious leaders of the exiles, who seem to have endeavored to ensure that the Judaean exiles retained their distinct ethnic and religious identity. It would seem that these leaders for the most part still interpreted the calamitous events in terms that would have been familiar to the earlier prophets. That is to say, the people had sinned and turned from God, who then inflicted the punishment of the exile as a punishment to make them repent. If they would only turn from sin and repent, the suffering would end and the Judaean people would be restored to their lands with peace and prosperity.

When the Babylonian Empire was overthrown by the Persians, Cyrus the Great declared that exiles were free to return to their ancestral lands. God had been appeased and the future looked rosy, even though the land of Judah was now a Persian province. Led by Zerubbabel, the first wave of exiles made their way back to Jerusalem.

Almost the first task to be undertaken was the rebuilding of the Temple, which was completed in 515 B.C.E. Over the next hundred years further streams of exiles began making their way back to Judah although many were probably reluctant to leave the relative comforts of Babylon for uncertainties that faced them amid the ruins of Jerusalem. Nevertheless, sufficient numbers returned and, under the leadership of two prophets Ezra and Nehemiah, a wide range of measures were taken to safeguard them from a repetition of divine wrath. Walls were thrown up around Jerusalem. Priests whose credentials were deemed suspect were barred from officiating at the Temple worship and sacrifices. Those Jews who had remained in Judah and not gone into exile, and who had intermarried with non-Jews and adopted pagan customs, were subjected to stringent penalties and censure.

Most importantly for our discussion, Ezra and his followers prepared a definitive version of the Torah and other scriptural works. Great attention was paid to the observance of the Torah, especially in respect of its practical application to the rituals enacted in the Jerusalem Temple. Ezra is said to have assembled all the inhabitants, read the Torah out to them and asked if they would accept it as perpetually binding—which they did.

Since pious observance of the Law had become so important, it is hardly surprising that a new and independent group of religious specialists, the scribes (*soferim*), emerged alongside the Temple priesthood—though many of the priests were themselves scribes. These scribes were, despite their name, actually scholars whose task was to interpret the often abstruse or contradictory rules laid down in the Torah. Since correct observance of the religious rules was of vital importance for the welfare of both individual and nation, these scribes played a key role in Jewish life and were themselves held in great respect—the term "rabbi" is first used around this time to address them, although still in its literal sense of "my lord."

It fell to these scribes to develop and establish the scriptures by studying and resolving potential problems in its explanation and application. This process resulted in two categories of interpretation: *halakhah* and *haggadah*. *Halakhah* was focused on orthopraxis—what should one do to be a good Jew—and encompassed matters concerning sacrifice in the Temple, the celebration of festivals, calendrical problems, the tithes and dues to be presented to the Temple and its priesthood, and the large volume of rules concerning religious purity and impurity. *Haggadah* concerned the interpretation of historical and religious doctrines. Judaism is primarily a religion of orthopraxis, which, beyond a small core of basic beliefs, allows a surprisingly wide range of views on doctrinal matters. It is thought that the noticable duplication or supplementation of accounts of historical events through biblical and para-biblical works such as Chronicles, the Book of Jubilees, Enoch and so forth originated from the hands of the specialist *haggadah* scribes. As readers will recollect, many such books were found among the scroll fragments found at Qumran, which testifies to the prolific output of these scholars. We shall also see in Chapter 11 that an accompanying and ever-intensifying interest in eschatological and apocalyptic writings, culminating in full-blown messianic theories, is characteristic of the Second Temple period.

During the early years of the Second Temple period, then, two groups of religious specialists existed side by side—the priesthood and the scribes. Over the years a number of competing Jewish groups arose, many of which had their origins in one or other of these two early groups. Unfortunately, our knowledge of these groups is extremely scanty and for the most part we must rely on the Jewish historian Josephus and passing references in Maccabees I and II. As far as we know, it would not be accurate to call these groups "sects," since that term usually applies to those with differing doctrinal views. The main features that distinguished these groups concerned interpretation of religious law as codified in the Torah, although a few doctrinal matters were also included.

A major factor in the development of these rival Jewish groups began to be felt after the conquest of Palestine by Alexander the Great in 332 B.C.E. As he moved throughout the Middle East on his long campaign of conquest that led him to the borders of India, Alexander encouraged Greek settlers to follow his army and establish cities throughout the region, bestowing what was in their eyes the benign civilizing influence of Hellenism upon the local inhabitants. Palestine did not escape this process, and within a few decades of Alexander's death in 323 B.C.E. there were numerous thriving conurbations built and governed along Hellenistic lines, such as the famous string of ten cities known as the Decapolis northeast of Judah. The closeness of these cosmopolitan Hellenistic cities, with all their innovations and ideas, had a profound influence upon Jews living in Judah. Educated and wealthy Jews were thus exposed to a range of influences hitherto unknown in the Middle East, and the charisma of Greek culture was extremely attractive to this social class.

Yet inevitably there were tensions that grew as time went by. As we have seen, the earlier successors of Alexander who ruled Judah adopted a policy of non-interference in Jewish religious matters, but many Jews must have voluntarily adopted a number of aspects of the Hellenistic lifestyle. Though there is little documentary evidence, the question of Hellenism must have been a topic of fierce debate even at this stage. Given that the continuing welfare of Jews was believed to depend upon a scrupulous observance of God's commandments as laid down in the Torah, many must have wrestled with the problem of how far it was possible to assimilate and adopt Greek culture.

It is in the Seleucid period that we first hear of distinct religious parties and groups in Judah. By this time, we can surmise, the earlier simple categories of priests and scribes would have further evolved and subdivided into two wings: the Hellenized Jews and the pious traditionalists, each drawing some supporters from the priesthood and the scribes. In general terms, cultural affiliation seemed to be a matter of class—the upper class tending to welcome Hellenism and the lower class remaining loyal to traditional values.

One of these groups, the Hasidim, which was to play an important role in later developments in Jewish history, must have already been in existence some time before we read of them in Maccabees I and II. We do not have a clear picture of these pious observant Jews, so it may be a mistake to think of them as a homogeneous group. Rather, the epithet *hasidim*—the righteous or pious ones—was probably attached to people whose only common characteristic was their opposition to the adoption of Hellenistic customs inasmuch as they compromised a traditional understanding of Jewish duties. For example, we know that members of the Hasidim flocked to the assistance of Judas Maccabee when he began his revolt against Antiochus IV in 166 B.C.E., but there is contradictory evidence about the extent and manner of their participation.

According to Maccabees I, they tended to be pacifistic and only supported the Maccabean Revolt in its initial years, withdrawing from active involvement when its religious aims had been achieved. On the other hand, it seems from Maccabees II that the Hasidim were far more martial in their outlook and formed the main body of the Maccabean forces right up to the founding of the Hasmonean dynasty. It is likely that at least two distinct parties of Hasidim are involved here—something we should remember, too, when considering other Jewish groups.

Apart from what can be gleaned from the two books of the Maccabees, the various works by Josephus are our sole source of detailed information about the religious groups during the latter years of the Second Temple period. Valuable though Josephus is, we should be mindful that he was writing not for a Jewish audience but for a Roman one in his attempt to present Judaism. He therefore describes the various Jewish groups in terms that would have made sense to Gentiles. For this reason, we must be on our guard and not assume that Josephus presents an entirely accurate picture of the doctrines and customs of each of these groups. Nevertheless, Josephus and other sources such as the biblical and para-biblical writings, provide some idea of the core issues that separated these groups.

Given the paramount importance attached to observance of the Torah and the role of the Temple, we can readily understand that most disagreements were based on matters related to Temple worship and sacrifice together with the activities of the priesthood, especially those of the High Priest. The question of free will, and theories about reward and punishment and the corollary problem of resurrection, formed another cluster of potentially divisive topics. Other debates are known to have focused on the nature of revelation and the existence of angels.

Each of the four Jewish groups that Josephus mentions in detail had its own views about these matters, so we should look at each in turn to see if any are identical or similar to those held by the Qumran sectarians. The four groups are the Sadducees, the Pharisees, the Zealots and the Essenes. Though some early proto-Christians would have been active by the time Josephus wrote, they were either numerically insignificant or else subsumed into one of the above groups.

For reasons that will become obvious, the Sadducees may well have been the earliest of these four to emerge as a distinct group, though Josephus' first mention of their presence as a separate group in Judaea is in connection with events around the late date of 150 B.C.E. Although the name is familiar from the Christian Gospels, we know surprisingly few details about the beliefs and attitudes of the Sadducees. Indeed, what we do know derives largely from sources that were hostile to them for various reasons —Josephus because he was a member of the opposing Pharisees, the Talmud since it was compiled by the rabbinical successors of the Pharisees, and the Christians because they do not have a good word to say for any Jewish group.

However, one thing is very obvious: for the most part the Sadducees were priests, though not all priests were Sadducees. The name itself derives from Zadok, the High Priest appointed by Solomon to officiate in his Temple and who was said to be descended from the priestly line of Aaron. Zadok's own descendants acted as High Priests throughout the First Temple period and later during the Second Temple period, until their power was usurped by the Maccabees. The higher ranks of the priesthood which eventually formed the Sadducees were therefore primarily members of upper-class families that traced their ancestry back to Zadok, though the descendants of other priestly families and their supporters would also have been included.

By late Second Temple times, just before the Maccabean uprising, the Sadducees seem to have been generally pro-Hellenic and cooperative with the Seleucid rulers. Josephus tells us that there were no more than a few thousand Sadducees, but their influence greatly outweighed their numbers. To understand why, we must remember that only one legitimate Temple existed in the entire Jewish world. Moreover, compulsory sacrifices had to be performed on a daily, monthly and annual basis for the benefit of the nation and individuals in order to fulfill the conditions of the Covenant with God, and these sacrifices were only valid if carried out at the Jerusalem Temple. In other words, to be a pious observant Jew one had to rely exclusively on the services of the Temple priests.

This central role of the predominantly Sadducean priesthood in Jewish life was further compounded by their involvement in secular affairs, since they also controlled the tribunal or council known as the Gerousia, the forerunner of the Sanhedrin. Nevertheless, despite their importance in all aspects of Judaean life, the

Sadducees enjoyed little popularity or support among ordinary people.

As a privileged group within society the Sadducees were fairly conservative in their approach, for they granted the Torah primacy in their affairs and, although not strict literalists, they did not accept the interpretative Oral Law that the Pharisees developed. This differing attitude to religious laws generated sharp disagreements between the Sadducees and the Pharisees. For example, in contrast to the Pharisees they asserted that the stringent purity laws only applied to the Temple and its priests and were not applicable to most aspects of daily life. Another bone of contention was the Sadducean adoption of a solar calendar in opposition to the Pharisaic use of the ancient lunar calendar.

Since the Sadducees were mainly priests concerned with the correct performance of the Temple rituals based on the stipulations of the Torah, their doctrinal views were relatively simple—if we can trust Josephus' late account of their beliefs. He tells us that they believed God did not have any direct control over human affairs, but that people themselves had been endowed with absolute free will. Additionally, and most strangely from our modern perspective, they did not believe there were any rewards or punishments awaiting people after death—they rejected both the idea of the immortality of the soul and the concomitant belief in a future resurrection of the body after death. In fact, they seem to have been reluctant to accept other aspects of a spiritual dimension to the world for, unlike many other Jews, they were also said to have generally rejected the idea of the existence of angels as supernatural beings acting in the world.

But this description of the Sadducees depends primarily upon Josephus, who wrote over 200 years after they emerged as an identifiable group in Jerusalem. His account may therefore not convey all the nuances and trends that must have developed during that period. It is quite possible that there were factions within the Sadducean party, for some would have been more pro-Hellenic than others. Indeed, there are some indications that there was a smaller pious group of Sadducees, perhaps drawing from members of the lower priesthood, which was unhappy with the more Hellenized priests.

This rift within the priesthood would have become more pronounced after the Maccabees usurped the office of High Priest, for though there was at first a degree of antagonism towards the Hellenizers under the Hasmonean dynasty, the aristocratic Sadducees lent their legitimizing support to those rulers and thus maintained their own status in society. Indeed, the main group of Sadducees retained much considerable religious and secular power in Jerusalem up to the eve of the Jewish Revolt, apart from a brief setback in the reign of Salome Alexandra who favored the Pharisees. Yet it was also this close identification with the Temple that sealed the long-term fate of the Sadducees: when the Romans destroyed the Temple that was their power base, the Sadducean *raison d'être* also ceased and they soon disappeared from Jewish life.

The Pharisees were another Jewish group familiar to many from the Christian Gospels, but the negative manner in which they are portrayed there does not do justice to their importance and popularity in Judaea. Though they too are first mentioned by name in connection with the reign of Jonathan Maccabee around 150 B.C.E., it is likely that their roots go back some time earlier. Several possible groups that existed in the earlier Second Temple period may have been their ancestors. Given the developments in religious law for which the Pharisees were responsible, some scholars believe their origins lie among the scribes of the Persian and early Hellenistic period; others link them to the Hasidim, who were mentioned as supporters of Maccabean Revolt.

Their name derives from the Hebrew word *perushim*, which means something like "the separated." Many scholars believe that this name was originally applied to the group as a pejorative term, but was adopted by them since it highlights their distinctive features. In contrast to the Sadducees, the Pharisees demanded a very strict interpretation and observance of the Torah, which they thought should be applicable to Jews from all walks of life. In a sense, it was their objective to raise the status of ordinary Jews to that of the priesthood and, in order to guarantee the necessary purity, the Pharisees developed a secondary set of rules, the Oral Law, which they derived from their interpretation of the Torah as a protective bulwark around the written Torah. In their zeal for maintaining all aspects of the Law as they understood it, the Pharisees scrupulously avoided or "separated" themselves from contact with the ritually unclean common people and Gentiles, and from all other sources of impurity such as foodstuffs that had not been handled properly according to the purity laws.

It is during this period that we also find mention of small close-knit associations or fellowships of like-minded people known as *havurah* that are often assumed to have been Pharisaic in their practices. Whether all such fellowships were an exclusively Pharisaic phenomenon is unclear but, since this type of organization was popular not only in Jewish circles but also in the wider ancient world, it is not unreasonable to suppose that there would have been considerable differences between some of these associations.

It is important to note here that several of the rule books found at Qumran, such as the *Community Rule*, could easily be viewed as compositions written in the milieu of such small, zealous fellowships for their guidance. This would suggest that we should look for the origins of the Qumran Community, whoever they were, among some of these *havurah* groups.

In virtually every aspect of their lives, the Pharisees stood at the opposite pole to the Sadducees. Though numerically not great—Josephus states that there were around 6,000 in his time—they were popular and highly respected among the ordinary people, for the Pharisees themselves belonged to the middle and lower classes of society. This popularity often seems to have been used to force Sadducee compliance to their demands for a stricter observance of various aspects of religious laws.

The Pharisees were not hostile to the priesthood as such because some of the priests, especially among the lower ranks, were Pharisees themselves. But unlike the Sadducees, the Pharisees were either minimally Hellenized or not at all and thus would have been viewed as the true protectors of Jewish national identity that was so closely linked to matters of religious law.

While some Pharisees accepted a degree of Hellenization provided the essentials of the Jewish religion remained uncompromised, others wanted no government unless it was run on Pharisaic lines. These two positions regarding the alien culture depended on how one viewed the rule of their country by Gentiles. On the one hand, there were scriptural grounds for believing that this foreign rule was desired by God as a chastisement for their transgressions, so the Jews would be obliged to accept the situation in submission to God's will. Other people argued that, if the Israelite nation was the elect or chosen people of God, any foreign Gentile domination was intolerable and should be resisted because Israel should acknowledge no other ruler but God.

It is difficult to determine which of these positions would have been dominant among the Pharisees over the centuries, but in 6 C.E. a breakaway group eventually split off from the main party and advocated open rebellion against the Romans. Prior to this event the Pharisees had become increasingly politicized during the Hasmonean dynasty, in opposition to the apparent laxity and illegitimacy of the rulers who combined the offices of High Priest and king. Growing hostility to the Hasmoneans and their supporters can be detected by the time of John Hyrcanus I, which ultimately erupted in open conflict for six years during the reign of Alexander Jannaeus, whom they almost succeeded in deposing. However, in the long term it was the Pharisees who were the victors in the religious and political disputes that were a feature of Jewish life during the Second Temple period. As we have seen, their Sadducean rivals ceased to exist as a group after the destruction of the Temple, while the Pharisees went on to evolve into the later rabbinical school of Judaism that has been largely standard ever since then.

Not only did the Pharisees accept the "traditions of the fathers," which they maintained should supplement or even supersede the written Torah, but their doctrinal and theological views differed from those of the Sadducees in almost every respect. Although they accepted the notion of human free will and moral responsibility, they also thought that God sometimes predetermined events in the world. In other words, the Pharisees maintained that some things were brought about by destiny or divine intervention and others solely through human free will.

Reflecting later post-exile developments in Judaism, they also believed in the immortality of the soul and in a life after death that would see some form of reward or punishment by God for deeds done during one's earthly lifetime. The righteous would be rewarded with eternal life through bodily resurrection in the future messianic kingdom, or even in heaven in the presence of God, while the wicked would be punished with eternal torment in fire. The Pharisaic belief that God sometimes intervened directly in human affairs also led them to accept, unlike the Sadducees, the existence of angels as supernatural beings who also occasionally interacted with humans in this world.

As we saw above, there were tensions within the Pharisee party over the question of cooperation with foreign rulers who had dominion over the Israelite nation. As the situation deteriorated in Judaea under the Herodians and their Roman masters, one group broke away from the Pharisees around 6 C.E. to form what Josephus terms the "Fourth Philosophy" under the leadership of

Judas of Gamala and Zaddok the Pharisee. The supporters of this movement were none other than the Zealots, whom Josephus disingenuously tells us differed from the other three religious groups he mentions except that they agreed with the Pharisees in everything and "they have a passion for liberty." We cannot expect a sympathetic evaluation of the Zealots from the collaborationist Josephus, who was totally pro-Roman by the time by wrote his historical works: he blames the Zealots for the Jewish Revolt and all that befell Judaea subsequently.

The initial cause of the emergence of the Zealots was the census of Quirinius, the Roman governor of Syria who was also responsible for the province of Judaea, which they viewed as a measure designed to reduce the Jewish population to slavery though their lord was God alone. Certainly this census was a prelude to taxation of the population by the Romans—with taxes to be paid in Roman coins bearing the image of Caesar. This matter continued to vex Jews for years to come, for the Gospels tell us that Yeshua was challenged with just this point—though he skillfully avoided a position which would have undermined his standing in Jewish society.

Many of the Zealots were less subtle: they incited the Jews to rebel against Rome in protest against the census and, though they failed to prevent the implementation of Roman taxation, they gathered increasing numbers of supporters, some of whom were even found among the disciples of Yeshua, and eventually rebelled against Rome in 66 C.E. in open warfare. Yet here again we must exercise caution, for not all those labelled Zealots may have belonged to the same homogeneous group as we are led to believe. Since the Hasidim who supported the Maccabees in the struggle for liberation from the Seleucids would have been classed as Zealots by later writers such as Josephus if they had been contemporaries, we can well imagine that not all, if any, of the Zealots were the barbarous brigands that Josephus and others describe.

In Roman times, rather as today, rebels were often classed as brigands or terrorists—especially when on the losing side. So Josephus usually refers to various bands within the Zealot movement as *lestes*, or brigands, while, according to the Gospels, Yeshua was crucified with two such brigands. On the other hand, it is true that some members of the Zealot movement the *sicarii*, or daggermen did engage in a form of urban terrorism. This faction was named after the short curved dagger known as the *sica* that they carried concealed under their robes and used to assassinate perceived collaborators when the chance presented itself.

Like the Maccabean rebels, the Zealots undertook a brave though ultimately futile attempt to establish the idealized dominion of God on earth—the same Kingdom of God of which Yeshua often spoke. Since we do not possess a sympathetic account of the Zealots, we cannot tell to what extent they believed they would have to fight the Romans for their freedom and how far they expected God to intervene and assist them. The *War Scroll* and the *Congregational Rule* found among the manuscripts at Qumran provide documentary evidence that some Jews sincerely thought that they were living in the End Times, the period of turmoil that would precede the inevitable victory of the Messiah and the forces of righteousness. It is not unlikely that many of the Zealots held similar views, as did followers of Yeshua, for the notion of the imminent arrival of the Messiah reached fever pitch in the decades prior to the First Jewish Revolt. Indeed, so strong was this belief that many Zealots still believed that redemption and deliverance were at hand even after the destruction of the Temple, as we can discern from the Second Jewish Revolt led in 132 C.E. by Simeon bar-Kokhba. Following the failure of this second attempt to force the hand of God, the Zealots faded away as a significant force within Judaism.

The last of the known Jewish groups that would have been in existence when the sectarian literature among Qumran finds was written were the enigmatic Essenes. We must look carefully at them because many scholars have linked the Essenes with the sectarian Community and this is still the mainstream consensus view.

Josephus provides us with much information, but we also have a description of the group from the hand of the Hellenized Jewish philosopher Philo of Alexandria, as well as the Roman writer Pliny and several other later Christian authors. But once again we should remember that both Josephus and Philo had their own agendas when writing about the Essenes. There are also some fundamental contradictions between the accounts of Josephus and Philo, though that of Josephus is normally regarded as more reliable since he relates that, though a Pharisee, he had toyed with the idea of joining the Essenes in his youth and had some direct contact with them. Philo, in contrast, may only have known of them by repute.

Although we have a degree of useful information about the Essenes, we know little about their history and even the origin of their name is uncertain. Unless they are to be identified as the Qumran sectarians, they have left us no literature of their own that would enlighten us about these matters. It is widely agreed that the name "Essene" is a Greek form of some Semitic word, but there is no consensus about which word. Most commonly, it is suggested that the name derives from either the Syriac *hase'*, meaning "pious," or the Aramaic *assayya*, "healers." If the former is correct there is a possible link with the earlier Hasidim since their name derives from a Hebrew word with the same meaning. On the other hand, since the Essenes were reputed to be experts in healing body and spirit, it is also possible that their name comes from the Aramaic source.

Another solution has been provided by Robert Eisenman, who maintains it derives from *osim ha-Torah*, the "Doers of the Law," a term which he points out was often used by the Qumran Community. Though he has undoubtedly used earlier sources, the

Christian writer Epiphanius mentions a heretical Jewish sect called the Ossenes that once lived around the Dead Sea. The Greek form of the name he uses is closer to the singular form of the noun for Eisenman's "Doers," which is *ose*, than the other suggested terms. It could well provide a link between the "Essenes" and the Qumran settlement, and consequently with the sectarian writings found nearby.

As with the Sadducees and the Pharisees, the existence of the Essenes is first mentioned by Josephus during the reign of Jonathan Maccabaeus around 150 B.C.E. As with them, it seems probable that there were a number of groups with various shades of beliefs and practices who were conveniently lumped together under one blanket name. In his *Refutation of All Heresies*, the early Church Father Hippolytus (c.170–c.236 C.E.) repeats views partially based on Josephus. But he also recounts from an unknown source that the Zealots and the Sicarii were simply more extreme, nationalistic Essene groups, and tells us that there were four types of Essenes in all. If we consider the question of Essene origins from the accounts given by Josephus and Philo, we can see that they occupy a complex position in doctrinal and practical matters with respect to the Sadducees and the Pharisees because they combine certain features from both these groups.

One persuasive theory suggests that the early group of pious Jews known as the Hasidim had their origins in the scribes who emerged during the early decades of the Second Temple period, as described above. As we saw, the scribes were initially closely linked with the Temple priesthood but functioned as specialists in the exegesis and interpretation of the Torah. As the scribes became more independent from, and perhaps at times opposed to, the Temple priests, we can hypothesize that many of their members came to be regarded as Hasidim on account of their zeal and piety. Subsequent to this development, it is thought that one group of Hasidim evolved into Pharisees while another more hard-line group became the Essenes during the Hasmonean period. This lineage seems possible for the Essenes when we realize that they combined Sadducean ideas about the supremacy of the Temple priesthood with the Pharisaic emphasis on doctrinal and legal innovations and adaptations through biblical exegesis. These features can also be detected in the sectarian writings found at Qumran.

According to Josephus, the numbers of Essenes were second only to the Pharisees, with a membership of around 4,000. Though they were supposed to have lived only in Palestine, the Essenes are said to have been found in many places throughout the land. That we may be dealing with several groups with the same general name is further suggested by the information given us by the ancient writers about where exactly they lived. While Josephus says they could be found in every town in Judaea, Philo tells us that they mostly lived in villages and chose to avoid the towns because of the immorality of their inhabitants. Writing after the First Jewish Revolt, Pliny says they only lived near Engedi by the Dead Sea. But regardless of whether the Essenes lived in towns or villages, it is curious that no such group is ever mentioned by name in the Christian Gospels or Epistles, espe- cially given the presence of a relatively large number of Essenes in Palestine as well as the high regard in which both Josephus and Philo held them. Of course, as we shall see later in this chapter, this presents no problem for Robert Eisenman, for whom the Essenes were the early Jewish Christians.

If we summarize the details provided by Josephus and Philo we can form some idea of the structure and lifestyle of the Essenes, though we should continue to bear in mind that such characteristics may not have been shared by all of them. It seems that they lived in small local congregations in communal dwellings under the leadership of a superior to whom they were bound in obedience. Full membership of these congregations was not granted immediately but was attained by going through four stages or grades. Only adult men were apparently admitted as full members into the group, though some aspects of Philo's and Josephus' accounts seem to indicate that women were included among the Essenes.

Those wishing to join were accepted with a one-year period of probation before they were admitted to ritual ablutions that formed a key element of Essene practice. Candidates were given a white robe, a small pick and an apron—the robe to wear, and the apron and pick to be used when defecating. If the probationary year was passed satisfactorily, a further two years of initiation followed, culminating in a ceremony in which an oath of fidelity was taken. The initiate was finally allowed to participate in the fellowship that ate meals together after swearing an oath of fidelity. These virtually sacramental common meals, only open to initiates, were prepared by priests following strict purity laws and were eaten twice daily, preceded and followed by prayer. After the oath of fidelity to the Essene ideals and leadership had been accepted, any serious transgressions of the rules resulted in permanent expulsion after judgement by a court comprising a hundred judges.

One unique feature of the Essenes lay in their holding all property communally, for new members were required to hand over all their property and earnings to the superiors. To provide for their daily needs, a steward issued food and clothing as required as well as organized the care of the sick and the elderly. From what we can glean from the ancient writers, we also know that the Essenes were extremely frugal or even ascetic in their daily lifestyle—their diet was quite spartan and they did not wear new clothes until the old ones had worn out. Possibly because of the inherent dangers of ritual impurity associated with many trades, the main occupation of the Essenes seems to have been agriculture, while commerce and the manufacture of weapons were strictly forbidden.

A number of special, curious characteristics are known about their lifestyle, which have elements in common with the rules laid down for the Qumran Community. Being of an ascetic bent, the Essenes did not use oil on their bodies but preferred a rough appearance; they always wore white robes to emphasize their purity; they took purificatory baths in cold water before meals and after excreting; they completely avoided excretion on the Sabbath; they were not to spit towards the middle or to the right, they held no slaves in their community; they did not swear oaths to verify a statement; and they were believed to reject marriage, although Josephus mentions that one branch of the Essenes allowed marriage and sexual intercourse for the purpose of reproduction only. Apart from these traits, something of the origin of the Essenes may be guessed from the fact that they kept away from the Temple and did not carry out animal sacrifices, though they did send votive offerings. This hints at some kind of serious break with the Temple priesthood, most likely on the grounds that during the Hasmonean and Herodian dynasties it was corrupt, illegitimate and impure.

We can conclude this survey of the Essenes by looking briefly at the beliefs ascribed to them by Josephus and Philo. Unlike the Sadducees or even the Pharisees, the Essenes believed that people did not have free will but that God had completely preordained the moral nature of each individual and that people were predestined for salvation or damnation. This belief in predestination, reminiscent of the Calvinist Christian position, also required a belief in some form of survival after death when the righteous would enjoy eternal bliss and the wicked would endure eternal torment. It is not clear whether they also thought that this postmortem survival would involve a physical resurrection of the body, but on balance it seems they assumed this was a spiritual affair involving only the soul.

As is obvious from their practices, the Essenes held the ancestral laws of the Torah in high regard, but Philo also relates that they engaged in allegorical interpretation of the Torah, though he does not give any details of what this involved. In common with the Pharisees, the Essenes accepted the existence of angels and were said to possess arcane doctrines in secret books that included the names of angels. Knowledge of the names of angels, both good and evil, was commonly thought to be the means by which one gained power over them. By means of this power, the Essenes were able to study and practice the healing of body and spirit, for many ordinary Jewish people thought that diseases were caused by some form of demonic possession. One final characteristic that might be linked to the secret teachings guarded by the Essenes was their reputation for making accurate prophecies.

We know nothing of the fate of the Essenes following the destruction of Jerusalem and the Temple at the time of the First Jewish Revolt. Pliny seems to imply that they were still in existence after those events, but they are not mentioned in any of the later rabbinical literature such as the Talmud. If we put aside for the moment those theories that link some wings of the Essene movement to the early Jewish Christians, there remains the possibility that there is a tenuous connection between some of the Essenes and the medieval Jewish Karaite sect which, as we saw in Chapter 5, may have come into possession of the *Damascus Document* and other writings in early medieval times around the time that scrolls were reported to have been found near the Dead Sea.

THE COMMUNITY

As we have seen above, there were several Jewish groups known to have been active in Judaea around the time that the so-called Community is thought to have written or copied the sectarian elements of the Dead Sea Scrolls. There was, of course, one other Jewish group that merged during this period: Yeshua and his followers, from whose ranks Christianity soon evolved.

Let us look at the main features of the Community and whatever we can reconstruct of its history from the cryptic hints that can be gleaned from their extant writings—the members of the Community, it will be recalled, never identified who they were in terms that allow us to make an immediate connection with any of the other Jewish groups already considered, but preferred to refer to themselves and their enemies by various epithets and sobriquets.

We have already looked at the key documents that may allow us to reconstruct their ideology and practices—the *Rule of the Community*, the *Manual of Discipline*, the *Congregational Rule* and the *Damascus Document*. Since these documents are composite in nature, it should not surprise us to find disagreements or contradictions when we compare the contents of each of them. If they all originated with the same Community, as might reasonably be assumed, these rule books might represent different stages of development in the history of the Community. Nevertheless, there are sufficient features in common that allow us to outline a general portrait of the Community and its concerns.

The *Damascus Document* is thought by most scholars to be the oldest rule book used by the Community and was intended for use by members dwelling as small groups in towns and cities, while the later *Rule of the Community* seems designed for a monastic type of society. It is possible that these rule books were used by two distinct but related wings of the Community, or else they may hint at an evolution from a urban-based organization to a cenobitic group dwelling in the desert. Both of these alternatives have some merit. As we saw earlier, none of the other Jewish groups was entirely homogeneous, while at the same time the profoundly eschatological beliefs of the Community led its members to think that they were living in the Last Days before the advent of the Messiah, which necessitated a single-minded devotion to "righteousness" that probably rejected marriage and other forms of conventional social behavior. This latter viewpoint may have been prevalent in the late years of the Second Temple period because similar sentiments are expressed in parts of the Christian Gospels and the Pauline letters.

The main characteristic of the Community was that it saw itself as an elite; its members referred to themselves as the Elect and implicitly claimed to be the true Israel, the genuine tradition of Judaism. Overall, the Community was grouped into twelve "tribes" and hierarchically divided into two kinds of participants: the priests and Levites, and the initiated laity. Undoubtedly this represents a conscious parallel with ancient Israelite society, to which the Community thought it was heir. Within the Community, the supreme authority for both religious and secular matters—the distinction may not have existed for them—lay in the hands of the priests, although it was governed by a Council. Yet even within the Council the priests, known in the documents as the Sons of Zadok or the Sons of Aaron, seem to have had the final say in all things. The overall management of the Community's affairs in each place where its members lived was stated to be entrusted to an individual known as the Master or Overseer (*mevaqqer*) both in the *Damascus Document* and in the *Rule of the Community*. This particular office may have been instituted to take over the role of the founding Teacher of Righteousness after his death, for part of the Master's responsibilities was to deal with the admission and instruction of candidates seeking initiation into the Community.

According to the *Rule of the Community*, the first stage of admission began with a solemn oath to obey all the laws of Moses according to the interpretation of the Community's priestly hierarchy. In this way, candidates became "members of the Covenant." This first contact with the Community was followed by an unspecified period of instruction given by the Master after which the candidate was required to appear before the congregation who either accepted him as a novice or rejected him. A further two years of training followed, with a test during the festival of the Renewal of the Covenant. The second year decided whether the person would be permitted to become a full member and participate in communal activities such as meals, worship and study.

We have already seen that the various rule books laid down various degrees of penance or even expulsion for transgressions, which were dealt with by a tribunal composed of ten judges. The *Damascus Document* goes so far as to mention imprisonment or even execution as penalties, although it seems improbable that the Community could actually have meted out these punishments.

The question of property ownership is dealt with differently in the *Damascus Document* and the *Rule of the Community*, perhaps because one legislated for the urban-dwelling members while the other for the monastic members. The *Damascus Document* allows the ownership of private possessions, although strict rules are laid down for the guidance of the members regarding any aspects of property that might involve matters of ritual purity and impurity. The *Rule of the Community,* on the other hand, stipulates that all private property was to be made over to the Community upon entry and was to be administered by a bursar who allocated food, clothing and other items to members according to their needs. The different circumstances of members, according to whether they lived in urban-based groups or monastic groups in the desert, reflected in these two rule books can also be seen in their attitude to marriage. Predictably, the *Damascus Document* allows for the presence of women, married and single, as well as children, while the *Rule of the Community* is concerned with an all-male celibate organization.

As will by now be well known, the members of the Community believed fervently, one might almost say fanatically, that they were an elect group chosen by God for salvation at the end of time when the Messiah was to appear and destroy all evil forces in the world. By entering the Community, members regarded themselves as belonging to a new Covenant, one based on the teachings of Moses and the prophets but as understood by the Teacher of Righteousness and the additional exegesis given by the Sons of Zadok. As with orthodox Judaism, the Community regarded the *halakhic* rules governing purity as central to their lives, as testified by many of their documents such as the *Rule of the Community*, the *Damascus Rule* and the *War Scroll*. However, it is also evident from these documents that the Community had withdrawn from any form of participation in worship and sacrifice in the Temple, which they regarded as a place of abomination polluted by the immorality and wickedness of its priests.

For the Community, the validity of the key festivals throughout the year was also called into question because in their eyes the wrong calendar was in use—the Community insisted on the use of the solar calendar to fix the dates of these festivals. Since it did not participate in the religious lives of other Jews, whom it regarded as all but lost, the Community decided to carry on with their own spiritual sacrifice and worship until the Temple was finally cleansed and restored to purity in the seventh year of the eschatological war described in the *War Scroll*. To this end, the members of the Community devoted their lives to continuous worship of God in which they, the Sons of Light on earth, were joined by the angels in the heavens above. The daily sacred communal meal, which was only open to full initiates, is thought by many scholars to have been instituted as a substitute for the sacrifices that were carried out every day in the Jerusalem Temple.

Some of the Community's documents from Qumran suggest that its members also engaged in certain secret forms of mystical practice. Their confident belief in themselves as the preordained elect of God also led them to realize that their very salvation was a gift from God. One aspect of this gift included a special knowledge of good and evil, which was revealed to them alone through the Teacher of Righteousness and his successors. Further, since they were God's chosen people He had also given them the special ability to embrace what is true and to practice righteousness almost instinctively.

This arrogant and intolerant certitude that they alone as members of the elect Community were destined for salvation pervades much of the Community's writings, and could not have endeared them to other less fanatical Jews. Moreover, just as with the Gnostics, this idea that they were endowed with a special form of knowledge unavailable to others also led them to believe that its use would reveal all the secrets of the heavens to them, even a vision of the divine throne described in various canonical and extra-canonical scriptures.

The problem concerning the identity of the Community involves two aspects: who were they, and did they actually live at Qumran? The so-called consensus answer to these questions inherited from the early days of Dead Sea Scroll studies is quite simple: the Community were the Essenes as described by Josephus and Philo, and they lived at Qumran. Not everybody agreed with this view even in the 1950s, but more voices of dissent have emerged in recent years. Even these, however, are far from unanimous about the provenance of the Scrolls, their authors and the inhabitants of the Khirbet Qumran settlement. Nevertheless, the Essenes as far as we know them from ancient sources seem to be closest in many aspects to what we know of the Community in its beliefs and practices.

We know that both groups believed in predestination, were organized hierarchically, restricted full membership to those who had been initiated, and allowed only their initiates to participate in the sacred communal meals. One strand of thought within the Community, as attested by the *Rule of the Community*, advocated common ownership of property and celibacy, as did the Essenes. Other common features include a developed belief in angels, a strict observance of religious laws governing purity and impurity, an interest in healing, and finally a reluctance to take part in the various activities of worship and sacrifice carried out in the Temple.

There are also points of difference between the Essenes and the Community or parts of it which opponents of the Essene hypothesis have seized upon as proof that the two groups cannot be related. For example, the presence of female skeletons in the cemetery at Qumran seems to contradict the idea that the Community, if they were the inhabitants of the settlement, were celibate. This argument may be valid if the burials at Qumran can be shown to be distributed over a long period of time but, as we saw in Chapter 9, most of the burials seem to have been made at the same time and moreover some of the skeletons show signs of violent death. So even if a celibate group had lived at Qumran we might have here the remains of war victims, perhaps of a massacre, who were slaughtered during any one of the bloody incidents that regularly punctuated life during the later Second Temple period. One can well imagine refugees fleeing to the safety of Qumran only to be trapped and killed there.

Other objections are arguments from silence, though this is never a very strong basis for rejecting a theory. It is claimed, for instance, that the name "Essene" is never used in the scrolls, while the key question of the solar calendar is never mentioned by ancient authors. In answer to these objections one might point out that both Josephus and Philo, our main sources, were writing for a Gentile audience and may have considered the solar calendar too arcane or irrelevant for their intended readers. One could also challenge the idea that the name "Essene" is never found in the scrolls. For one thing, one would not expect it to be found precisely in that form since it represents a disputed term from Hebrew or Aramaic in a Greek guise. Moreover, as we saw above, Dr. Robert Eisenman suggests a possible origin for the name "Essene" in the Hebrew *osim ha-Torah*, a hypothesis that receives some corroboration from the name "Ossenes" used by Epiphanius.

Another potentially grave objection lies in the apparent contrast between the pacifism of the Essenes and the military features exhibited by the Qumran settlement, coupled with the bellicose instructions contained in the *War Scroll*. One solution to this problem quickly springs to mind: the name "Essene" may not have referred to a homogeneous group but been applied to a range of related groups that shared many core beliefs but differed in other aspects. We have already seen that Hippolytus tells us that there were four groups of Essenes, of which the Zealots were merely a more extreme wing. Though Josephus, for his own reasons, prefers to describe the pacifist face of the Essenes, some of them were warriors—he also mentions one John the Essene, who fought and died as a revolutionary commander during the First Jewish Revolt.

There is one final valuable piece of information that may serve both to identify the Community and to link it to the settlement at Qumran. Many documents have been found in the Judaean desert close to Qumran that unequivocally date from the Second Jewish Revolt, including a number in the hand of their leader, Simeon bar-Kokhba. One of these pieces of correspondence speaks of a "fortress of the Hasidaeans" (*mezad ha-hassidim*) located somewhere in the Dead Sea region. Khirbet Qumran is the best if not the only likely candidate for this fortress. Linked in one phrase here we have a fortress and the Hasidim, an epithet used for self-reference with great frequency by the members of the Community because it simply means the "Righteous Ones." We also know from Pliny, as we saw in Chapter 9, that he had heard of a group of "Essenes" living north of Engedi, which would seem to suggest he was thinking of Khirbet Qumran. If he had not, as seems likely, encountered these Essenes first hand, perhaps his informant had slanted or idealized his account of the Essenes for the ears of his Roman interlocutor.

All these facts suggest that we may safely link the Community both with the Essenes and with the Khirbet Qumran settlement, although on this basis we may have to revise our ideas about the Essenes radically. So if we allow that not all the Essenes were as pacifist in their ideology as previously thought, the above evidence points, on balance, to an identification between the Community and some more extremist wings of the Essenes.

The existence of religious warriors is well attested throughout history. Not only is there the obvious example of the Hasidim, possible ancestors of the Community, who supported the Maccabean Revolt, but in more recent times we have witnessed similar groups such as the Islamic revolutionary followers of Ayatollah Khomeini in Iran. A close parallel might be found in the medieval religious orders of Christian knights such as the Knights Templars, who were ascetic and celibate, lived as a community and took up arms to defend their faith. I would also suggest that the evidence indicates that the settlement at Qumran was occupied by some, though clearly not all, members of this organization.

Dr. Norman Golb objects to locating any members of a pacifist group like the Essenes at Qumran because of the military features of the place, but perhaps my scenario may satisfy his objections. He also rejects the idea that the scrolls were written at Qumran for another reason often passed over by those who would simplistically identify the Essenes of the ancient authors with a small ascetic Community living and copying scrolls at Qumran. Golb draws our attention to the fact that the range and variety of handwriting used in the entire body of scroll fragments shows definite evidence of the work of at least 500 scribes. As he says, it is difficult to imagine that number of scribes having lived and worked at Qumran throughout the relatively brief period it was occupied. He hypothesizes that the scrolls have no connection with the Qumran settlement, which was for him a Zealot fortress at the time of the Jewish Revolt.

He believes instead that the scrolls originated in Jerusalem, possibly even having formed a part of the Temple library, and were smuggled out of Jerusalem through secret underground passages during the early years of Titus' siege of Jerusalem. His contention that the scrolls did not originate at Qumran seems quite reasonable, but if we allow that the occupants of the Qumran complex were just a fraction of the total membership of the Community who lived throughout Judaea, we might view the scrolls as the precious holdings of the wider Community brought to a place of safety during the Jewish War. Moreover, if the members of the Community at Qumran were, in later years at least, a group of religious warriors affiliated to or at least sympathetic to the Zealots holding out in Jerusalem, even the baffling presence of the *Copper Scroll* at Qumran can be easily explained.

We may also consider here one other variant theory concerning the identity of the Community associated with Qumran that has recently been proposed by Dr. Lawrence Schiffman. In contrast to Dr. Golb, Schiffman has no objections to locating a religious group at Qumran and ascribing the scroll findings to them, but he rejects the traditional consensus that associates the Community with the Essenes. Basing his argument primarily upon the legal arguments that feature in the now famous 4QMMT text, generally known as *Some Legal Rulings Pertaining to the Torah*, he maintains that the Community were either Sadducean in origin or else that "the Essene movement must be totally redefined as having emerged out of Sadducean beginnings." That 4QMMT does display overall Sadducean tendencies has been accepted by many scholars including the consensus stalwart Dr. Geza Vermes, though he believes that it should be linked to an early breakaway group of lesser Sadducean priests in Jerusalem. Again, I think the problem here arises from viewing the various religious parties active in Judaea at that time as monolithic groups, whereas a whole spectrum of variant ideologies and practices seems historically more probable. If we do indeed need to revise our assessment of the Essene movement in the light of my earlier suggestions, Dr. Schiffman's hypothesis seems less controversial than many have deemed it to be.

Despite a number of legalistic points of similarity between the Community and the Sadducees, certain views prominent in the sectarian writings of the Community do stand in complete contrast to what we know of the Sadducees, such as the belief in predestination and angels, so I think we can safely reject a simplistic identification between the Community and the Sadducees. We shall shortly be considering various aspects of the history of the Community, but we can say here that the second of Schiffman's alternative theories for the origins of the Community, coupled with Vermes' evaluation of 4QMMT, actually point us in the right direction.

I would place the origins of the Community among the alliance of zealous Jews known in Maccabees I and II as the Hasidim. As the Hasmonean dynasty established itself, this motley alliance of fervent Jews fractured and various distinct groups emerged from them. As for the Qumran Community, we know that they must have had some kind of relationship at one time with the Temple since their leadership were priests who called themselves the "Sons of Zadok." Indeed, the title by which the Sadducees called themselves is also related to the name Zadok. We should also remember that not all the priests at the Temple were Sadducees in a formal sense, and other shades of doctrinal opinion must have been represented among its members. This suggests that a group of dissident priests broke away from the Temple priesthood and, while maintaining certain traits in common with those who went on to become the Sadducees proper, formed what became the Community with their own characteristic tenets.

Finally, we can look at the scrolls to see if they shed any further light on the history and development of the Community. Before we go into detail, the short answer is that, regrettably, very little historical data can be derived from the scrolls—though this has not prevented many scholars from presenting a considerable range of theories ranging from the plausible to the fantastic. The sources commonly used to reconstruct a history of the Community are quite small in number—the *Damascus Document* and some of the *pesharim*—but even these yield very little hard evidence. Part of the reason lies in the fact that it was not the intention of the authors to write systematic history textbooks but to link supposedly prophetic passages in earlier biblical works with contemporary events. Additionally, this was not done in a transparent manner that would be comprehensible to all but in a veiled or coded manner that would have been readily understood by initiated members of the Community but by few others— much of what they wrote would have been considered treason by their opponents.

With these caveats in mind, let us look first at one of the oldest texts associated with the Community, the *Damascus Document*, and see what we can learn from it. Apart from detailing how the Community was to be organized and governed, this work seeks to contextualize its more theological message with references to certain individuals and events. It opens with a passage that seems to allude to the origins of the Community:

> For when they were unfaithful and forsook Him, He hid
> His face from Israel and His Sanctuary and delivered
> them up to the sword. But remembering the Covenant
> of the forefathers, He left a remnant to Israel and did not
> deliver it up to be destroyed. And in the age of wrath,
> three hundred and ninety years after he had given them
> into the hands of King Nebuchadnezzar of Babylon, He
> visited them and caused a plant-root to spring from
> Israel and Aaron to inherit His land and prosper on the
> good things of His earth. And they perceived their iniq-
> uity and recognized that they were guilty men, yet for
> 20 years they were like blind men groping for the way.
> And God observed their deeds, that they sought Him
> with a whole heart, and He raised for them a Teacher of
> Righteousness to guide them in the way of His heart.

The first lines of this passage obviously refer to the depredations and destruction wrought upon the inhabitants of Israel and Judah by the Assyrians and Babylonians respectively. It alludes to the pious survivors of the exile upon whom God had taken pity, but it is not clear from the statement whether they were included among the initial waves of returnees—though we should note that, by mentioning Israel and Aaron, the author is implying that they included both priests and lay persons.

Jerome Murphy-O'Connor, in his detailed analysis of the *Damascus Document*, suggests that the Community actually originated in Babylon and returned to Judah considerably later than the others. The text goes on to give an approximate date for the emergence of the forerunners of the Community when it mentions the 390 years that had elapsed since the time of Nebuchadnezzar and the exile. Scholars have hotly debated whether this figure is meant literally or as a symbolic reference to the end of time as mentioned in Ezekiel 4:5. However, if we take it literally, 390 years after the beginning of the exile in 586 B.C.E. brings us down to 196 B.C.E., when we are told the founding members of the Community appeared. After a further confused period of 20 years had elapsed, a Teacher of Righteousness emerged around 176 B.C.E. as a leader who would guide them.

The historical information given by the *Damascus Document* reveals that later there was a serious difference of opinion over religious duties between the Teacher and certain other members of his group, who are referred to variously as the "Seekers after Smooth Things," the "Builders of the Wall" or the "Removers of the Bounds." They were led by somebody younger than the Teacher, known as the "Liar" or at other times as the "Scoffer" or the "Spouter of Lies." These dissenters are accused of ritual impurity, of following the wrong calendar for the festivals and of being lovers of money and conflict, and we know from other sectarian texts that the Liar himself was accused of teaching false doctrines and misleading the faithful. Led by the Teacher of Righteousness, those still faithful to his interpretation of God's intentions went into exile into the "land of Damascus," where they entered into a new Covenant.

Here again, much controversy has surrounded the question of the "Damascus" mentioned here. Some take it literally as the city with that name, while others regard it as a symbolic reference to the place of their refuge, assumed by many to be the settlement at Qumran. The Teacher of Righteousness died there after 40 years had elapsed—around 136 B.C.E., if the figures given can be taken literally. The *Damascus Document* also tells us that, during this period, the wicked ones continued to hold sway over the Temple and Jerusalem, although they were punished on occasion by the "Chief King of the Greeks"—a term that must refer to one of the Hellenic Seleucid kings, possibly Antiochus IV Epiphanes or his successor Demetrius I. Finally, the author of these quasi-historical passages mentions that the Community would need to wait a further 40 years after the death of the Teacher for the End of Days to commence with the arrival of the Messiah.

Though they give us some idea of the main events in the formation of the Community, these sparse snippets of information should be read with caution because they do not provide us with anything that would allow us to pinpoint more specifically the events and *dramatis personae* they mention. All that we can really glean from them is that the Community was founded some considerable time after the return from the Babylonian exile, during the period of Seleucid rule before the Maccabean Revolt, and that they were led by a Teacher of Righteousness whose title seems to imply that he may even have been one of the High Priests. A schism occurred within the Community and, as a result, the Community left Jerusalem and went into exile somewhere. The reference to the Chief King of the Greeks implies that these events took place while the Seleucids were still posing a threat to Judaea, either before or after the Maccabean Revolt.

Beyond this outline history, we know nothing from other historical sources outside the Dead Sea Scrolls that would allow us to identify with certainty either the Teacher of Righteousness or the Liar, although there is one clue to the affiliation of the group led by the Liar. Drawing on allusions to these "Seekers after Smooth Ways" found in other sectarian scrolls, most scholars are content to identify them with the Pharisees—although it would be better to think of them as proto-Pharisees given the period that the *Damascus Document* deals with.

This scenario would fit neatly with our earlier discussion of the disintegration of the loose amalgam of zealous Jews known as the Hasidim, who would have comprised priests, scholarly scribes and lay people, into the later Essenes and the Pharisees. At the time under consideration, when the Community first emerged, it is probable that neither the Essenes nor the Pharisees existed as distinct parties but were merely points on a spectrum, each holding a concern with the correct application of religious law as their core ideology. The *Damascus Document* seems to allude to a further breakdown in the former Hasidic alliance, when proto-Pharisees split off from others who evolved into the various Essene groups.

After the death of the Teacher, his followers continued to follow his instructions and lived in expectation of the imminent arrival of the Messiah. Further literature reflecting their world view was produced by the Community, including the writings with a unique approach to interpreting the scriptures known as the *pesher* Several of these also contain references to events in the history of the Community and its leader, most importantly the *pesher* on Habakkuk, the Psalms and Nahum. Yet once again we are faced with considerable difficulties since virtually none of the key players is mentioned by his true name, merely with a range of imaginative sobriquets. In addition to the Teacher of Righteousness, the Liar and the Seekers after Smooth Things, we now encounter many others. These can be grouped according to whether they were used to denote the Community and its leaders or their opponents. We have the Priest, the Men of Truth, the Doers of Torah, the Poor, and the Returnees from the Wilderness representing the Community. Their opponents can be divided into two groups: fellow Jews deemed to be apostates, and Gentiles. The former include the Wicked Priest, the Traitors, Those Violent to the Covenant, the Last Priests of Jerusalem, the Evil Ones of Ephraim and Manasseh, and the Evil Ones of Israel. A few Gentile enemies are mentioned, such as the Kings of Yavan, the Kittim and the Rulers of the Kittim, though these are the easiest to identify—the Kings of Yavan are the Seleucids, while the Kittim and their rulers are the Romans. This mention of the Romans points to a late date of composition, when the Romans had begun to enter the Judaean socio-political arena following the conquest of Palestine by Pompey in 63 B.C.E.

In recent years there has been a marked trend away from treating the *pesher* as historical documents and a number of scholars, such as Phillip Davies, have cast doubts upon their historical value. Nevertheless, it is worth having a look at some of their more striking passages to see if anything can be retrieved from them. As with the *Damascus Document*, the schismatic group led by the Liar is mentioned and here, too, they are termed the Seekers after Smooth Things. In the Habakkuk *pesher* two groups of Traitors are mentioned, an earlier group and a later one active during the last days. The earlier group may be identified with the apostate Liar and his group, since the *pesher* implies that this group of Traitors rejected the Teacher and broke away from his leadership, while the second group seems to allude to those led by the Wicked Priest who were opposed to the entire Community and their Teacher. So although the Wicked Priest was a contemporary of the Teacher of Righteousness, his hostile activities postdate the Liar's schism.

A number of potentially useful pieces of information can be gathered from the *pesher* concerning the Wicked Priest, which may help us identify him. Let us begin by noting that the phrase "Wicked Priest" (*ha-kohen ha-raša'*) was coined as a pun on the Hebrew title of the High Priest (*hakohen ha-ro 'š*), so this individual was likely to have been one of the Jerusalem High Priests. However, we should note that some scholars believe that the sobriquet was used generically for all the illegitimate High Priests of the Hasmonean period. The Habakkuk and Psalms *pesher* give us some biographical details about this Wicked Priest:

The Wicked Priest was called by the name of truth
when he first arose. But when he ruled over Israel his
heart became proud, and he forsook God and betrayed
the precepts for the sake of riches of the men of violence who rebelled against God, and he took the wealth
of the peoples, heaping sinful iniquity upon himself.
And he lived in the ways of abomination amidst every
unclean defilement.

The Priest who rebelled [and violated] the precepts
of God . . . his chastisement by means of judgements of
wickedness. And they afflicted horrors of evil diseases
and took vengeance upon his body of flesh.

The Wicked Priest whom God delivered into the
hands of his enemies because of the iniquity committed
against the Teacher of Righteousness and the men of his
Council, that he might be humbled by means of a
destroying scourge, in bitterness of soul, because he had
done wickedly to His elect.

The Wicked Priest who pursued the Teacher of
Righteousness to the house of his exile that he might
confuse him with his venomous fury. And at the time
appointed for rest, for the day of Atonement, he appeared
before them to confuse them and to cause them to
stumble on the Day of fasting, the Sabbath of repose.

> And God will pay him his reward by delivering him
> into the hand of the violent of the nations, that they
> may execute [judgement] upon him.

Assembling the above data, we learn that the Wicked Priest was somebody, most likely a High Priest, who began his career reasonably well but soon became corrupt and wicked. He persecuted the Teacher of Righteousness and his Community and possibly sought to destroy them, but was himself killed outside Judaea by Gentiles as a divine punishment for his sins. Less obviously, he was deemed to be an illegitimate High Priest since this is implied by a secondary meaning of the term "wicked." Moreover, as High Priest he acted as a ruler over Judaea but not as a king, for the terms in Hebrew are distinct.

Given the approximate dates we established earlier for the Teacher of Righteousness' activities, the Wicked Priest should have ruled up to and possibly beyond 136 B.C.E., placing him some time before 134 B.C.E. when John Hyrcanus became High Priest and ethnarch of Judaea. These facts allow us to narrow down possible candidates for the role of the Wicked Priest. First, we should note that all the High Priests during the Maccabean and Hasmonean period would have been regarded by many, including the Community, as illegitimate since they were not descendants of the Solomonic High Priest Zadok. The title "king" was not used until the accession of Aristobulus I in 104 B.C.E., and the previous Hasmoneans were merely rulers by virtue of their being High Priests. There are five High Priests who fall within the time frame for the formation of the Community and the activities of the Teacher of Righteousness: Jason (175–172 B.C.E.), Menelaus (171–162 B.C.E.), Alcimus (162–160 B.C.E.), Jonathan (152–142 B.C.E.) and Simon (140–135 B.C.E.). If we apply the criteria we can derive from the *pesher* we can eliminate Jason and Simon because they both died within the borders of Judaea, while Alcimus died of a stroke. As regards the remaining two, Menelaus and Jonathan, who were both murdered outside of Judaea, many scholars such as Stegemann put their money on Jonathan since he was noted for his rapaciousness and his love of drink—drunkenness being another characteristic of the Wicked Priest mentioned elsewhere.

As for the Teacher of Righteousness, apart from fringe scholars like Eisenman and Thiering the majority recognize that the information given within the Community's literature and what can be gleaned from other historical writings such as the works of Josephus do not allow us to identify this man with certainty. Stegemann does, however, make some useful suggestions that, though they cannot help us name the individual concerned, can at least pinpoint his period of activity. He observes that the sobriquet itself, the "Teacher of Righteousness" (*more hats-tseddek*) was a traditional title applied only to the Temple High Priest. Other epithets used to describe the Teacher of Righteousness, such as the "Unique Teacher" (*moreh hay-yahid*), the "Interpreter of the Torah" (*doresh hat-torah*), or even just the "Priest" (*ha-kohen*), were all likewise used by the High Priest. He argues that it is reasonable to assume in the context of the Qumran scrolls that the Teacher of Righteousness would not have laid claim to these titles if he had not indeed been the High Priest at one time, even if he had been removed from office.

Looking once again at the short list of High Priests for the period in question, we can see that there is a curious hiatus between Alcimus and Jonathan. Since it is virtually inconceivable that the Temple could have functioned for eight years without an incumbent High Priest, Stegemann maintains that this anonymous individual was none other than the Teacher of Righteousness. He also points out that a similar situation arose with Onias IV, who briefly held the post around 170 B.C.E. after the murder of his father Onias III, before being expelled by Menelaus. While this expelled High Priest fled with his followers to Egypt, where he set up a rival "orthodox" Temple at Leontopolis, the Teacher of Righteous-ness chose a different path and went into the Judaean desert to set up the Qumran Community.

CONFLICTING THEORIES

Let us now look at two idiosyncratic theories concerning the identity of the Community and the persons connected with it that have recently attracted considerable popular interest but have at the same time completely failed to convince the overwhelming majority of Qumranologists and biblical scholars. The first of these has been put forward by Dr. Robert Eisenman of California State University. He disagrees with the conventional dates derived from archaeology, coin finds and carbon-14 dating that are widely accepted for the approximate period of the Community's emer-gence and activities. Instead, he brings the date forward by at least 100 years and places the Community in the late Herodian and Roman period, from around the death of Herod the Great (4 B.C.E.) until the destruction of the Temple in 70 C.E. He entirely bypasses any question of the involvement of Yeshua—whose very existence, he implies, is a fiction—and maintains that the Teacher of Righteousness was James the Just, the supposed brother of Yeshua and, according to the New Testament, the leader of the Jerusalem Church. Since James was executed by the High Priest Ananus in 62 C.E., this individual must consequently have been the Wicked Priest while the Spouter of Lies was the apostle Paul.

Eisenman argues at considerable length in his most recent book, *The Brother of Jesus*, that the sectarian writings from Qumran and the New Testament writings as a whole represent two sides of the same story written by the supporters of James and Paul respec-tively—the Qumran material representing an accurate account of events, and the New Testament writings being a deliberate falsifi-cation and malicious pastiche of it. Though Eisenman presents an overwhelming volume of data that he claims supports his hypothesis (too much to summarize with any fairness here), the main criticism of his work lies in his over-free interpretation of certain passages in the Qumran scrolls and the New Testament, or worse still in his use of dubious translations.

For example, one small but key problem can be seen in his treatment of the important passage found in the fragmentary *Rule of War* that speaks of a messianic figure. At one point this passage reads, according to Eisenman, "They will enter into judgement with . . . and they will put to death the Leader of the Community, the Branch of David . . . and with woundings," but virtually all other scholars are now unanimous in accepting the more coherent Vermes version: "They will enter into judgement with . . . the Prince of the Congregation, the Branch of David, will kill him . . . by strokes and by wounds." While Eisenman sees this passage as a reference to the murder of James, his Teacher of Righteousness, the general context, coupled with Vermes' more convincing translation, suggests that these words are actually describing the actions of the messianic leader who will kill, rather than be killed by, some unspecified person, probably the leader of the Sons of Darkness. Though I am not inclined to accept Eisenman's hypothesis, it should be stressed that his many papers on various aspects of the Dead Sea Scrolls have made important contributions to our understanding of certain aspects of the Community, especially concerning their use of language.

Though Eisenman's hypothesis has been largely rejected within the academic community, his arguments are at least plausible. This cannot, in my opinion, be said of Dr. Barbara Thiering of the University of Sydney, who proposes another startling solution in her recent publications. Indeed, so bizarre are her ideas that when I first read her book *Jesus the Man: A New Interpretation from the Dead Sea Scrolls*, I seriously wondered whether it was an elaborate academic hoax. Sadly, this is not the case: Thiering's interpretation is intended to be taken at face value.

Like Eisenman, she rejects the consensus view that the scrolls date from the mid-Second Temple period and places them in the middle of the first century C.E. She maintains that it was John the Baptist who was the Teacher of Righteousness at Qumran, while the Wicked Priest was Yeshua! Uniquely among biblical scholars, she "decodes" both the Qumranic corpus and the New Testament through her own personal *pesher* style of interpretation. Proceeding in this manner, she reconstructs the history of the Community and its key players in surprising detail.

To summarize, she proposes that John the Baptist was the leader of an Essene movement that comprised two factions: one orthodox or conservative and the other liberal and innovative. These two factions existed in a state of tension under John's leadership until Yeshua, an illegitimate descendant of King David, presented a challenge to John's authority when he attempted to usurp the office of High Priest. Judas Iscariot, a loyal follower of John the Baptist, eventually betrayed Yeshua to Pontius Pilate who rode out to Qumran, became a nominal member of the Community and ordered the crucifixion of Yeshua just beyond the limits of the settlement. For good measure, Thiering also claims that Yeshua was married to Mary Magdalene, that he survived the crucifixion ordeal and later went with Paul to Rome where he lived to a ripe old age. One is left speechless by this uncorroborated nonsense!

A POSSIBLE SOLUTION?

I would like to conclude this chapter with one final hypothesis I found buried in a footnote to an article by Igor Tantleveskij published in the scholarly *Qumran Chronicle* journal in 1995. He makes some interesting proposals concerning the origins of the Community. As a starting point, he draws our attention to the fact that the Community called themselves "the Doers of the Law in the house of Judah" and "the house of Judah." He believes that the name "Judah" is intended as a *double entendre* that denotes both the leader of the Community and the Community as a whole. According to Tantleveskij's reading, this Judah was not the Teacher of Righteousness but his immediate successor, who should be identified as the "Priest." He further suggests that this Judah the Priest may be the same person whom Josephus mentions in several of his works as an Essene leader who was active during the reigns of Aristobulus I and Alexander Jannaeus, who had the power of interpreting future events—a characteristic attributed to the "Priest" in the Qumran corpus—and was persecuted by Alexander Jannaeus.

Tantleveskij also proposes a hypothesis concerning the identity of the Teacher of Righteousness; he notes that the Temple Scroll indicates that the Teacher of Righteousness' personal name was Zadok and thus his followers were consequently termed the "Sons of Zadok." This Zadok, he believes, is the same person mentioned in the *Aboth de-Rabbi Nathan* and by other Jewish writers such as Jakob al-Qiriqisani, Saadia Gaon and Judah Hadassi. According to these sources, this Zadok was a disciple of the well-known Antigonus of Socho, whose attested beliefs correspond to a large degree with those found in the Community's own writings. Thus, if Tantleveskij is correct, the Teacher of Righteousness himself (Zadok?) was not the founder of the Community and that honor goes to his teacher, Antigonus.

Apart from this Zadok, we know that Antigonus had another famous disciple known as Boethus. According to Qiriqisani, both Zadok and Boethus were leaders of the Zadokites and, more interestingly, these same Zadokites became known as "cave men" since their sacred texts had been discovered in caves. As we saw earlier, a schism occurred within the Community with a dissident faction led by the Spouter of Lies who accordingly would have been Boethus—who, we know from other sources, was the leader of a sect named after him.

It has already been noted that there are certain discrepancies in detail, despite overall similarities, between the account given by Josephus about the Essenes and what we know about the Qumran Community. Tantleveskij offers a solution to this conundrum; he believes that we can identify the Essenes of Josephus with the breakaway group of Boethusians who were a more liberal wing of the Essene movement. Moreover, should one not accept the conventional derivation of the term "Boethusian," it has recently been suggested that the underlying Hebrew term *bytwsyn* or *bytysyn*, traditionally rendered as "Boethusian," is actually a slightly altered form of *byt 'ysin*, which means "House [school or community] of Essenes."

Either way, there does seem to be a plausible link between these Boethusians and a wing of the Essenes. Intriguingly, we also know that the Boethusians continued to exist for some time after the destruction of the Jerusalem Temple because they are mentioned in later rabbinical writings and are even claimed by the Kairites to be their own spiritual ancestors. Have we finally unraveled the mystery of the identity of the Community thanks to a modest footnote buried in a small academic journal?

eleven

THE END OF DAYS AND MESSIANISM

The radically altered religious and social landscape of the exile and Second Temple periods presented Jews with a variety of difficult situations that at times threatened to extinguish their unique identity as an ethnic group. New answers were now needed to restore the earlier Israelite confidence in the nation's destiny that had been shattered by a series of conquests by the Assyrians, the Babylonians, the Greeks and finally the Romans. A totally new way of viewing God and the world gradually emerged, in which many Persian religious concepts were merged with traditional Jewish beliefs. To be sure, the Jews still thought of themselves as a special people bound to God by the Abrahamic Covenant, but by the Seleucid period the last hope for devout Jews was the end of the world. This is reflected in the wide range of eschatological and apocalyptic literature produced in the wider Jewish world and among sectarian groups like that associated with the Qumran scrolls.

The basic question facing conservative Jews in Judaea who rejected the more optimistic Hellenizing solution was simple: Why do the chosen people of God suffer so much? Prior to the exile, a simple answer was provided by many of the prophets: God was punishing his people for their transgressions in order to make them repent and mend their ways. But no matter how dutifully Jews carried out their religious obligations, the expected personal and national rewards did not materialize. Rather, the sufferings continued unabated, especially during the oppressive rule of the Seleucids.

APOCALYPTICISM

As the implications of this situation increasingly impinged upon the minds of devout Jews, their attention increasingly turned away from the present to a future time, perhaps not far distant, when they would eventually be vindicated. This idea was not completely without precedent in the writings of the earlier prophets, but the appearance of new religious concepts is a feature of this period of Jewish life. Late Second Temple period apocalyptic writings, like those of Daniel and Enoch, now suggested that the blame lay elsewhere, with evil forces at work in the world that had been allowed temporary freedom by God to inflict harm as part of a mysterious divine plan.

Before the exile the prophets taught that such suffering could be simply ended by sincere repentance and a return to full observance of God's laws as embodied in the Torah, but now this alone was not enough—God himself must intervene to bring about the destruction of the evil ones and inaugurate the "dominion of God." Such concepts were cherished both by the Qumran sect, as we can see from much of their literature, and by the Jewish group that eventually evolved into Christianity. In the meantime, all righteous Jews were expected to remain faithful, obey the Law and wait for God to intervene, in the hope that they might share in the future ideal world.

Initially, with the success of the Maccabean uprising and the liberation of the country from foreign domination, the Judaeans probably thought that matters were proceeding in accordance with the divine plan described in the Book of Daniel. But once again the hopes of many, such as those who eventually formed the Qumran sect, were dashed by the violence, rapaciousness and apparent impiety of the Hasmonean rulers and later by the continued presence of alien rulers in the guise of the Herodians and the Romans.

As we have seen already, Judaism at that time allowed a considerable degree of freedom in matters of doctrinal speculation so long as they fell within the constraints of normal ritual observance. This freedom allowed quite new or revolutionary ideas to emerge at the fringes of Jewish society. Often these ideas were based on hints gleaned from the older writings such as Exodus or from the ever popular Isaiah.

Many people saw the deliverance of the Israelites from bondage in Egypt, their 40 years of tribulation and wandering in the desert, and their eventual conquest of the land of Canaan as a historical model upon which to base present actions. The desert itself was regarded as a place of purity, far from the temptations and corruption of urban life, by a diverse range of Jewish sages and their followers including John the Baptist and Yeshua. It is clear from the Qumran sectarian writings that this group saw their own retreat into the Judaean desert as a preparatory sojourn that would culminate in their triumphal return to Jerusalem. Moreover, just as the Israelites in the past had had charismatic leaders such as Moses and David at times of crisis, many Jews of the late Second Temple period expected a leader to be sent from God—indeed, the Qumran group's *Damascus Rule* explicitly states that the Teacher of Righteousness was sent in this role.

Surprisingly, this idea of a leader who was to be sent by God was quite late in maturing, since even in the Book of Daniel—which based on internal evidence, could not have been written earlier than 167 B.C.E.—there is no explicit mention of this leader, even though all the other eschatological elements, such as the subjugation or destruction of the wicked nations and the victorious rule of the just, were in place. More definite beliefs associated with this leader began to take clearer shape in the *Psalms of Solomon* (c.50 B.C.E.), following the fall of Jerusalem to Roman rule. After the decline and eventual failure of the Hasmonean dynasty to fulfill their initial promise, there was a fervent longing for God to raise up a king from the royal house of David to rule over Israel and purge the Gentiles from the land. Though various permutations existed, such a leader was primarily expected to be of royal descent and so he came to be termed the "Messiah"—the Anointed One. Needless to say, messianic expectations grew still greater during the reign of Herod the Great, during the lifetime of Yeshua and for some time afterwards until the death of Simeon bar-Kokhba.

The general expectation was that, if God himself was not to intervene directly, he would send his agent in the figure of this Messiah to judge or destroy all wrongdoers, including Gentile nations. Once the dominion of God had been re-established, it was believed that the Messiah would live on as ruler of the transformed world. Obviously not all Jews subscribed to this belief, since the idea of a messianic judgement and a future ideal world implied belief in some kind of physical resurrection. The just among those not alive at the time of the messianic victory over the forces of evil were expected to be resurrected and rewarded, while their wicked counterparts would either remain dead or face their punishment for all eternity. Other variations on this theme supposed that the messianic kingdom itself would not last forever but would come to an end with the final dissolution of the world. In that case, a belief in resurrection implied an initial participation in the messianic kingdom, to be followed by an existence of everlasting bliss in heaven while the wicked would be tormented in hell for all eternity.

THE UNFOLDING OF THE LAST DAYS

It is possible to reconstruct in considerable detail the expected course of events that centered on the Messiah and the Last Days before the destruction of the forces of evil, and we shall look at them here since they largely correspond to the beliefs held by the Qumran group. Though readers may notice many parallels with similar ideas found in early Christian writings, it should be stressed that such concepts were widespread throughout the Judaean world at that time. It is not therefore surprising to find them held by the early Christians, too, since they were originally just another Jewish sect.

The portent for the End of Days, as the time of the final conflict was known, was a period of extreme tribulation and confusion, a time of ordeal that would precede the dawning of deliverance. It was clear to Jews who subscribed to such beliefs, such as the Qumran Community as well as the early Christians, that this time had already begun as Judaea was tossed back and forth between the major Gentile powers such as the Seleucids and the Romans. It was believed that some kind of prophetic figure would soon appear to pave the way for the Messiah himself—perhaps even Elijah himself returning to the world. John the Baptist was believed by the early Christians to be this prophet laying the way for his successor, Yeshua the Messiah, while the Teacher of Righteousness, after his death, seems to have played the same role in the beliefs of the Qumran group. Judging from many of their writings, such as the rule books and the *War Scroll*, the motive behind the spartan life of the Qumran Community may have been a desperate wish to trigger the advent of the Messiah and thereby bring about the end of the world as they knew it.

Though the Messiah figure was later seen by the Christians as a kind of divine emanation from God, for Jews in the time under consideration the Messiah was expected to be a human individual from the royal house of David—despite the fact that some sources attribute superhuman powers to him. Not only would he be a king, he would also be a powerful, righteous, wise and holy man fully equipped to carry out his task. We should note that we can find hints of the later Christian ideas about the divinity of the Messiah in various concepts about the origin of the Messiah. For example, it was sometimes believed, based on Isaiah 53:4, that the Messiah would undergo some kind of suffering but, unlike in Christianity, this suffering was never thought to be expiatory in nature.

Again, though not divine in himself, the Messiah was thought by some, including possibly the Qumran group, to have been preexistent "in a state of concealment in God" and as such to resemble one of the angels. But whatever his precise nature might be, it was believed that there was to be one final assault on the righteous by the wicked, usually typified as the Gentile nations headed by the Romans, though it would end in failure. Once defeated, the wicked would be judged by the Messiah and avenging angels would be unleashed to wreak punishment upon them. Then when all such wicked people, whether apostate Jews or Gentiles, had disappeared from the earth the Messianic Age, also known as the Dominion of God, would begin.

One of the first events to occur in this new world would be a renewal of Jerusalem, in which both the city and the Temple were to be cleansed or even reconstructed as suggested by the *Temple Scroll*. More extravagantly, some messianic Jewish groups went so far as to believe that a pre-existing perfect Jerusalem would miraculously descend from heaven and replace the present city. But all viewpoints envisaged that this new world order would be overseen with justice and righteousness by the Messiah, yet it would also be under the direct dominion of God—the so-called Kingdom of God or Kingdom of Heaven—who would fully exercise His rule.

Though Jerusalem would lie at its temporal and spiritual heart, this kingdom was expected to embrace the entire world for the benefit of both righteous Jews and the surviving Gentiles who feared God and acknowledged his rule. As befits any ideal realm, all physical pain and sickness would be banished and all wars and civil strife would be replaced by universal peace, righteousness and love. This idyllic world would, as we have seen, be enjoyed not only by those alive at the time of its inauguration but also by all the dead righteous people, who would be physically resurrected for this purpose.

The views held by different Jewish groups were not unanimous about what was to happen next. Some thought that this messianic kingdom would be without end, while others held that it would have a limited duration of a thousand years or so, followed by a Final Judgement and renewal of the world. Though no details seem to have survived about the latter view, some groups thought that the old world was to be destroyed by fire—as God promised Noah—which would be followed by the dawn of a new world, often known as the "world to come." This final destruction would also be characterized by a Final Judgement in which the reward of eternal bliss or punishment of eternal damnation was to be confirmed.

QUMRANIC MESSIANISM

The eschatological beliefs of the Qumran Community conform overall to the sequence of events described above but there are a few specific points of difference in their writings. However, there also seems to have been a gradual shift in some aspects of these beliefs as time went by and things did not transpire as they had apparently hoped. As we have seen, many Jewish messianic groups believed in the appearance of an Elijah-like prophet who would herald the arrival of the Messiah. The Qumran Community were no exception. As far as we can tell, they eventually came to regard the Teacher of Righteousness as this prophet, although it is quite likely that the Community initially thought of him as the actual Messiah until his death prevented him from leading them to victory over the Sons of Darkness as expected. Indeed, the possibility that the Community at one time saw the Teacher of Righteousness as the Messiah is strengthened by a possibly unique feature of the Community's messianic concepts.

As far as we know, other Jewish groups only believed in a royal Davidic Messiah, but the Community also supposed there would be a parallel priestly Aaronic Messiah as mentioned in the *Community Rule* 9:11. Such a pairing of Messiahs, one secular and the other priestly, seems to have been based on similar patterns found in the scriptures, as exemplified by Moses and Aaron or Joshua and Zerubbabel. It is noteworthy, however, that this type of partnership can also be seen in the pairing of the early Zealot leaders, Judas and Zadok, and perhaps of John the Baptist and Yeshua at a later date. We should bear in mind that the previous example of Judas and Zadok may hint at some kind of ideological link between the Zealots and the Qumran Community. Be that as it may, for the Qumran Community the priestly Messiah was clearly the more important member of the partnership, a fact which again might corroborate the idea that the Teacher of Righteousness was at one time thought to have been the Messiah.

Regardless of how Qumran physically met its end, the eschatological and messianic beliefs of the Community members can be seen as a sufficient if not necessary cause of its disappearance. It is absolutely clear from their writings that they fervently believed they were living in the Last Times, that the arrival of the Messiah was imminent, and that the destruction of the wicked Sons of Darkness and the salvation of themselves, the Sons of Light, were guaranteed. The problem for any group holding such beliefs is that events often do not turn out as expected.

In the course of the Community's history there must have been a few setbacks, such as the death of the Teacher of Righteousness, that necessitated a re-evaluation of its members' beliefs. Some adjustments could be, and probably were, made. But they would have been totally unprepared for the utter cataclysm that befell the Jewish people during the Jewish Revolt and in its wake, culminating in the destruction of the Temple. It is difficult to see how the members of the Community could have coped with the shock. If their final hope was an eschatological end they certainly got it—but not with the outcome they had expected. Even if its members were not immediately slaughtered or enslaved by the Romans, it is difficult to see how the Community as a whole could have survived for long unless it stripped away or radically modified many of its cherished beliefs that had hitherto set it apart from other contemporary Jewish groups.

There was, however, one other Jewish group that also believed in an imminent eschatological end of the world and yet which managed to survive and indeed flourish when that hope failed to materialize. It went on to become Christianity. Though it is not the purpose of this book to consider how the early Christians managed to transform themselves from a minor Jewish sect into one of the world's great religions, it is worth examining a number of features shared with the Qumran Community. For controversial scholars like Robert Eisenman and Barbara Thiering such features come as no surprise since they claim that the Qumran Community and early Jewish Christianity were in essence identical. There may be some merit to such theories in general if they are stripped of their more sensational aspects, for it seems curious that early Christian writings never mention the Community or any faction of the Essenes—if that is who they were—while there are no allusions to Yeshua and his followers unless we follow Eisenman and Thiering in linking John the Baptist, Yeshua or his brother James and Paul with the Teacher of Righteousness, the Wicked Priest and the Spouter of Lies.

However, the majority of scholars rejects all such hypotheses for the simple reason that they believe the Qumran writings all predate the birth of Yeshua and, had there been any direct links between the Jewish Christians and the Qumran Community, one might reasonably expect some fragments of New Testament writings to have emerged from the caves. It is true that Jose O'Callahan claimed to have identified certain tiny pieces of papyrus manuscripts written in Greek from Cave 7 that contained parts of St. Mark's Gospel and other New Testament writings but, despite the recent efforts of some to resurrect this claim, it has been totally discredited. However, the similarity of some elements of both religious groups is sufficiently striking for us to imagine that there were points of contact between the two at some time.

All scholars agree that the importance of the Dead Sea Scroll material must be acknowledged for the light it casts upon the background matrix of Judaism from which Yeshua and his teachings emerged, since prior to the discoveries at Qumran no other contemporary Jewish religious literature was known to exist. Apart from the ubiquitous Josephus, all that was available were the works of highly Hellenized Jews like Philo of Alexandria or later rabbinical writings that both emerged from very different cultural and social worlds from that of Yeshua and his first followers. For many Christian readers the Qumran scrolls must be somewhat unsettling since, though they contain oddly familiar teachings, at the same time the overall tone of the Community's writings probably seems quite alien. It is easier, perhaps, to account for the differences when we consider the circumstances in which the writings of each group were produced.

According to the conventional view, the Community composed its literature long before the shock of the destruction of the Temple during the Jewish Revolt, while all early Christian literature, with the exception of the genuine Pauline letters, such as his epistles to the Romans, the Corinthians and the Galatians, is generally believed to have been compiled after that event. Another reason for the differences lies in the intended audiences of each collection of writings. The Qumran sectarian material was written by and for an exclusive and elitist group of zealous Jews in Hebrew or Aramaic, while the Christian works were largely aimed at a wide Gentile readership of potential or actual converts, and written for the most part by non-Jews in Greek rather than Hebrew many decades after the events they purport to describe.

There is also the question of the authenticity of many of the sayings attributed to Yeshua in the Gospels, though this is not the place to analyze Christian biblical literature in detail. Yet, without wishing to offend the sensibilities of committed Christians, it should be pointed out that the most recent and exhaustive study of the Gospel material by the 200 biblical scholars who produced the so-called Scholars' Edition of the Gospels in 1993 was unable to consider genuine more than 20 percent of the total sayings attributed to Yeshua. In other words, very considerable amounts of the Gospel literature comprise material, often alien to Jewish ways of thinking, that was invented for later doctrinal reasons and attributed to Yeshua as a way of imposing such new ideas upon the early Church.

These facts make it extremely difficult for scholars when they try to discern what, if any, influence the Qumran Community had upon Yeshua and his early Jewish followers. Nevertheless, there are some doctrinal features that are sufficiently striking to be worth considering as points of contact between these two groups—though we must exercise caution because they may only illustrate just how widespread such shared teachings and ways of expressing them were in Jewish society of the time. For example, the parallel ideas concerning the imminence of the Last Days and the role of the Messiah seem to have been common property among many Jewish groups, including the Community and the Yeshua movement.

Of all the persons mentioned in the Gospels, it is John the Baptist who seems to be the most obvious candidate for some form of involvement in the Community. Like the members of the

Community, John was a very austere ascetic figure who preached the need for righteousness and zeal for the Law. He was born into a priestly family and we are told that his father predicted that he would spend his life preparing for the coming end of the world, while Luke (1:80) tells us that he spent his formative years in the desert. When he began his mission, John preached and baptized on the banks of the Jordan a few miles north of Qumran and, if we accept that the Community was present at Qumran, it seems probable that both parties would have been aware of the other's existence.

Some scholars go so far as to suggest that John was even a member of the Qumran Community for awhile before breaking away and establishing his own independent movement. But even if he had at one time been associated with the Community, there are also clear differences between their respective practices. Most important of these is the attitude that each held towards the Jewish populace, for while the Community was highly elitist John bestowed his baptismal rite and teachings upon people from all walks of life without any distinction—even upon tax-gatherers and soldiers.

Both the sectarian literature and the archaeological evidence indicate that ritual bathing or baptism were central to the life of the Community at Qumran, but the use of such bathing differs from the way in which John the Baptist practiced it. For him, this rite of baptism was a unique and unrepeatable event while we know from the rule books that for the Community members it could be repeated regularly as a prelude to participating in the sacred meal. Yet at the same time there are certain similarities regarding the connection between baptism and purification of sin. In both cases, the purificatory baptism was intended to cleanse the recipient of wickedness or, as the Gospels state, to be a token of "repentance for the forgiveness of sins."

But despite the passing resemblance we can detect between John the Baptist and the Community, there is nothing about these similarities that compels us to link the two unequivocally. Indeed, we still know so little about the various Jewish groups in existence at that time that we cannot even be certain how widespread the idea of a sanctifying baptism in Judaea was—all we can safely say is that this rite was not unique to John the Baptist, as was once thought.

Almost as soon as the scrolls had been discovered at Qumran there were scholars who were prepared to link Yeshua directly with the Community; some, such as John Allegro, even went so far as to identify him with the Teacher of Righteousness. As we saw earlier, Eisenman and Thiering imaginatively associate Yeshua in some way with persons known to us from the sectarian scrolls only by their sobriquets, but these claims have received scant appreciation in the wider world of Qumranology. As with John the Baptist, the grounds for the claims of these writers can partly be found in the widely accepted parallels between the Gospel reports of Yeshua's teachings and activities and what we read in the writings of the Community.

But even more than is the case with John the Baptist, we must exercise great caution in extricating the historical Yeshua from the later theological construct we find overlaying him in the Gospels. If, as we have seen, so little material in the Gospels can be reliably attributed to Yeshua himself, we should realize that every generation creates a Yeshua that suits its needs and aspirations. Stripping away the later overlay, perhaps all we can say of Yeshua the man is that he was at least a kind of devout holy man who would have shared many of the attitudes of the wider Hasidic movement that emerged decades before his birth. But at the same time there are, as we shall see, a number of aspects in which Yeshua seems closer to the Community than with other groups active in Palestine.

To begin with, Yeshua and his immediate successors seem to have had an attitude very similar to the Community as far as the ownership of private property—he frequently warns his followers of the corrupting influence of excessive wealth. Like the Community, Yeshua seems to have set up a system of pooling financial resources for use by his followers, since the Gospels mention that Judas Iscariot held the purse containing their funds. We also find this custom mentioned by Luke in Acts 2:44–45, which says, "All whose faith had drawn them together held everything in common: they would sell their property and possessions and make a general distribution as the need of each required." This exactly parallels the stipulations mentioned in the *Community Rule*, which states concerning a novice member that "his property and earnings shall be handed over to the Bursar of the Congregation who shall register it to his account" (6:19–20) and later upon full admission, "his property shall be merged" (6:22). The eschatological belief held by both groups in the approaching end of the present world is probably connected in part with this custom since it would be natural for such people to scorn private property in the days running up to the advent of the Messiah and the establishment of the Dominion of God when, presumably, money would no longer be used.

Around the time of Yeshua, it was widely thought that diseases were caused by malefic influence or even possession of the victim by evil spirits. Healers needed to possess the spiritual power to cast out or exorcise such spirits in order to heal those afflicted. We know that the Essenes were reputed to be great healers, and this should be linked to reports of their interest in means to gain power over angels and demons. Allusions to this practice of exorcism are found in some of the writings from Qumran, such as the *Genesis Apocryphon*, where it says, "So I prayed [for him] . . . and I laid my hands on his [head]; and the scourge departed from him and the evil spirit was expelled [from him]" (XX 22.29). Perhaps this method of curing sickness was not so unusual after all, but many Christians imagined that only Yeshua was endowed with this ability until the writings of the Community came to light.

The scrolls have also been useful in providing valuable background information for ideas hitherto found only in the Gospels. For many years scholars had been baffled by the ban that Yeshua imposed upon divorce and remarriage because this ruling had not been found in any other Jewish sources. But when works like the *Temple Scroll* and the *Damascus Document* came to light, it was soon noticed that members of the Community were similarly forbidden to divorce. The *Damascus Document* warns people that "they shall be caught in fornication twice by taking a second wife while the first is alive" (CD I:20–21), while the *Temple Scroll* likewise stipulates that the king should "not take another wife in addition to [the first], for she alone shall be with him all the time of her life" (LVII:17–19).

Another puzzle dramatically solved by the scrolls concerns the famous words reported in Matthew 5:43 where Yeshua says, "You have learned that they were told, 'Love your neighbor, hate your enemy.' But what I tell you is this: love your enemies and pray for your persecutors." No Jewish group had been known to teach its followers to hate their enemies, so the origin of this exhortation was mysterious until the writings of the Community were read. There we can see that members of the Community were repeatedly encouraged to hate, curse and pray for the destruction of their enemies. We can now see that Yeshua seems to be referring to the Community, which did have such teachings—here we have a rare allusion to the Qumran Community in the Gospels. This starkly different attitude towards enemies also tends to undermine attempts to link Yeshua directly with the Community, since their views stand in direct opposition.

The shared ritual meal also may be a feature of the Yeshua movement that finds its parallel at Qumran. Unfortunately, the account given by the Gospels of the so-called Last Supper has clearly been modified for the sake of later theological considerations, so it is difficult to unravel what was actually practiced by Yeshua and his followers. However, since the Gospel accounts suggest that participation was limited to Yeshua's immediate circle of chosen disciples, we might suppose that there was some kind of initiatory restriction upon participation just as we find stipulated in the Qumran writings. Also, we can note that Yeshua blesses the bread and wine just as food and drink were blessed by the officiating priest in the Community.

But again we must be cautious in proposing any direct influence from the Community upon the Yeshua movement in connection with shared meals since few details are known of many aspects of Jewish sectarian life at that time. It is believed that other groups, such as the *havurah* fraternities, had such a custom and Yeshua may have been inspired by them rather than by the Qumran Community. Nevertheless, there are certain features that do seem to link the Qumran ritual meals with those of the Christians. We can detect strong eschatological and messianic traits in both cases: according to the *Congregational Rule*, the Messiah was to bless the bread and wine for the meal after his advent just as did Yeshua, who was later viewed as the Messiah by his own followers.

THE BEATITUDES

Even teachings of Yeshua previously thought to be unique, such as the Beatitudes, which he enumerates in the course of the Sermon on the Mount, find a parallel among the writings of the Qumran Community. One such work known as *Beatitudes* (4QBeat) speaks of a number of virtues in a very similar spirit to the way in which the Beatitudes are mentioned in the New Testament. In this text, a series of beatitudes are listed that each begin with the words "Blessed be they who . . .," though, unlike the ones mentioned by Yeshua, they do not speak of any reward for those blessed with such virtues. Another dissimilarity lies in the specific content of each set of beatitudes: while those of Yeshua have a marked eschatological flavor, those from Qumran are more reminiscent of various works known as "wisdom texts" and seem more commonplace in their inspiration. Once again, this is unlikely to be a case of direct influence, despite the stylistic similarity, but merely a reflection of a popular, though now forgotten, literary genre.

As previously noted, this is the idea that humanity is divided into two opposing poles of good and evil, often symbolized by phrases mentioning "light" and "darkness." In the eschatological war that both the Community and the proto-Christians believed was about to be unleashed, these two opposing camps would clash and the forces of evil would be destroyed or subjugated as a result. We have seen how this final conflict is described repeatedly in the Qumran material, where the good are often termed the "Sons of Light" and the wicked the "Sons of Darkness." This dualistic conflict is also envisaged by the writers of the New Testament, especially in the Gospel of John and the Book of Revelation. Though recognized by biblical scholars to be the youngest of the Christian Gospels, and the one most heavily influenced by later theological considerations, it is noteworthy that St. John's Gospel has proved to be rich in parallels with the Qumranic material with its discussion of the opposition between light and darkness such as in 1:4–5, 3:19, 12:35–36 and elsewhere. Even the term "Sons of Light" appears elsewhere in the New Testament, such as in Thessalonians 5:5 and Luke 16:8, although curiously the term "Sons of Darkness" is not used. Since these Christian texts were written after the Jewish Revolt, we might suppose that some refugee members of the Community did join the initially similar proto-Christian movement and brought with them their special terminology and theological concerns that we now see reflected in certain passages of the New Testament.

Whether they are a result of direct influence at some stage or not, we can see other areas where interesting similarities exist between the writings of the Qumran Community and those of the early Christians. For example, we saw in Chapter 8 that writers in the Community used the unique *pesher* method of interpreting older scriptural texts in terms of contemporary events. When doing so, however, they expressed their interpretations in a heavily coded manner. As any student of the New Testament will know, the Christian writers also made liberal use of passages from the Prophets and other biblical books to prove that Yeshua was the Messiah and that everything that befell him was a preordained part of God's plan for the salvation of the world.

Overall, the specific texts and the manner in which they were used by both groups to prove their respective claims are very similar, each having strong predilection for the Book of Isaiah, as can be seen from the table in Chapter 5. Yet there is a significant difference in the way the Christian writers used their scriptural testimonies: as opposed to the secrecy that surrounds the *pesher* interpretations, the New Testament writings use their quotations in an open and transparent manner. This probably reflects the different organizational nature of each group: while membership of the Community was by initiation and constrained by strict secrecy, the Christians wrote their books for a wide audience in the hope of gaining converts and were consequently less secretive.

The Dead Sea Scrolls have also been valuable in establishing the Hebrew or Aramaic origins of certain characteristic terms used in the New Testament that were hitherto known only in their Greek form. As seen previously, the members of the Community liked to refer to themselves by a wide range of descriptive terms, and biblical scholars have now realized that a number of these are the exact equivalent of words used by the New Testament writers to denote the followers of Yeshua.

For example, in each case we have '*ani*, "the Meek," *Ebionim*, "the Poor," or *ha-rabbim*, normally translated as "the congregation" but which is literally equivalent to the Greek expression *ton pleionon*, "the many," which is used frequently by Christian writers. As with the Community, the Yeshua movement soon established an administrative system under a local *episkopos*, often translated as a "bishop" but which is now known to correspond to the Qumranic *mebaqqer*, "Overseer." Likewise, one of the common terms used in the Qumranic writings to denote their wicked opponents is the "Violent Ones" (*'Arizim*), which is the New Testament "men of violence."

A number of key theological terms are also found in both sources. In his letters Paul uses phrases that we now know had a Hebrew origin rather than being inventions of his own. When he speaks of "the righteousness of God" (*dikaiosyne theou*) he no doubt had the equivalent Hebrew phrase *sidqat 'el* in mind; likewise *gehal 'el* for "the church of God" (Greek *he ekklesia tou theou*), *ma'aseh torah* for "works of the Law" (*erga nomou*), or *bene 'or* for the noteworthy "Sons of Light" (*huloi photos*).

Of even greater importance for Christians is the discovery that their epithet "Son of God," applied to Yeshua to stress either his particular ties with God or his own divinity, was also used in Qumran literature. This was thought to have been a non-Semitic Christian innovation; though it is used in the Tanakh, it has a smaller range of meaning: it is applied to angels, Davidic kings, any particularly righteous Israelite or even to the collective Israelite nation, but never has a messianic sense as in the New Testament. Before the discovery of the Dead Sea Scrolls, it was assumed that the Christian understanding of the term as an epithet to describe a divine Messiah figure was influenced by the Roman use of *divi filius* (Greek *theou huios*), as applied to Augustus Caesar and others. Now it can be seen that the short fragment known as the *Aramaic Apocalypse* (4Q246) also apparently uses the "Son of God" (*bereh di 'el*) in reference to a person who clearly seems to be messianic in nature.

CONCLUSION

All biblical scholars agree that, apart from their intrinsic value, the sectarian scrolls are of tremendous importance as background information to the social and religious conditions in Judaea that led to the rise of Christianity. Although there were some sensational claims, both in the early days of Qumranic studies and more recently, that the Dead Sea Scrolls contain material that is potentially explosive in its implications for the emergence of the Yeshua movement, it is probably safe to say that this is not so, no matter how beguiling the arguments of scholars like Robert Eisenman.

Nevertheless, to my mind there are more subtle implications that can be derived from the Qumran texts because they not only provide interesting parallels to Christian concepts and practices but tend to reduce the uniqueness of the Yeshua movement. It is reasonable to assume that there was perhaps not much direct contact between most members of each community, but that there was a pool of religious language and beliefs shared by many other Jewish groups which have long since disappeared.

What we have been left with is an impressive body of material that survived precisely because its users, the Community, did not, yet the writings of the New Testament are still used today throughout the world by one of the most successful religious movements the world has seen. Perhaps the lesson we should learn from this is that any belief system that is tied so closely to specific eschatological or messianic expectations, coupled with an implacable hatred of its enemies, is ultimately doomed to failure. Even in the case of Christianity, which developed from the Palestinian Yeshua movement, there have been examples throughout history of more extreme factions or quasi-heretical groups that have ended in disaster, like the late medieval Anabaptists or most recently the group led by David Koresh at Waco.

JUDAEAN CHRONOLOGY

587 B.C.E.	Destruction of Jerusalem and Temple, beginning of Judaean exile.
	Jeremiah and Ezekiel active in early period. Second Isaiah, Haggai and Zakariah active in late period.
539 B.C.E.	Persian conquest of Babylonia by Cyrus the Great.
530 and 520 B.C.E.	Return of some exiles in two waves.
516 B.C.E.	Rebuilding and dedication of Temple.
?c.458 B.C.E.	Ezra active: led another wave of returnees from Babylon, ? edited Torah.
?c.445 B.C.E.	Nehemiah active: religious reforms, rebuilding Jerusalem walls.
332 B.C.E.	Alexander the Great conquers Palestine including Judaea.
323 B.C.E.	Death of Alexander, division of his empire.

312 B.C.E.	Ptolemy conquers Judaea and takes Jerusalem but grants people religious autonomy.
201–198 B.C.E.	Seleucid conquest of Palestine.
197 B.C.E.	Judaea becomes province of Syrian Seleucid Empire under rule of Antiochus III (223–187 B.C.E.).
187–175 B.C.E.	Beginning of Hellenistic infiltration, resisted by Onias III.
175–164 B.C.E.	Antiochus IV Epiphanes.
175 B.C.E.	Onias III deposed.
175–171 B.C.E.	Jason High Priest.
c.175 B.C.E.	Hellenistic reforms.
172 B.C.E.	Jason expelled from office, his brother Menelaus takes over.
172–162 B.C.E.	Menelaus High Priest.
171 B.C.E.	Onias III murdered at instigation of Menelaus.
169 B.C.E.	Led by Menelaus, Antiochus profanes and plunders Temple.
168 B.C.E.	Antiochus attempts second Egyptian campaign but is blocked by Romans.
167 B.C.E.	Antiochius decrees persecution of Jews who oppose integration of Judaea into unified Seleucid Empire based on Greek religion and culture. Official abolition of Jewish religion and practice. Temple transformed into a sanctuary of Zeus.
166–160 B.C.E.	Judas Maccabee leads rebellion of traditionalists.

164 B.C.E.	Judas Maccabee conquers Jerusalem. Truce and cleansing of Temple still occupied by Menelaus.
162–150 B.C.E.	Demetrius I. Menelaus executed by Syrians. Alcimus appointed High Priest by king.
161 B.C.E.	Judas Maccabee defeated and killed. Jonathan Maccabee becomes leader of rebels (161–152 B.C.E.).
?160 B.C.E.	Alcimus dies of stroke. End of Syrian military intervention.
157 B.C.E.	Jonathan Maccabee enters Jerusalem.
152–145 B.C.E.	Alexander Balas usurps Seleucid throne. Murdered in Arabia by treachery.
152 B C.E.	Jonathan Maccabee establishes independence and is appointed High Priest by Alexander Balas.
145–142 B.C.E.	Antiochus IV enthroned by Tryphon as his ward but later murdered by him. Jonathan Maccabee named governor of Syria and Simon Maccabee made military governor of Palestinian area.
143 B.C.E.	Jonathan Maccabee arrested by Tryphon.
143 or 142 B.C.E.	Jonathan Maccabee murdered in prison.
142 B.C.E.	Simon Maccabee assumes rule.
140 B.C.E.	Simon Maccabee confirmed High Priest/ruler by public assembly, his titles granted hereditarily. Beginning of Hasmonean dynasty.
135 or 134 B.C.E.	Murder of Simon Maccabee.
134 or	John Hyrcanus becomes ethnarch and

135–104 B.C.E.	High Priest. Opposed by Pharisees.
104–103 B.C.E.	Aristobulus I becomes High Priest and king.
103–76 B.C.E.	Alexander Jannaeus High Priest, king and conqueror. Resisted by Pharisees.
76–67 B.C.E.	Salome Alexandra, widow of Alexander Jannaeus, friend of Pharisees. Hyrcanus II becomes High Priest.
67 B.C.E.	Hyrcanus II becomes king and High Priest but deposed by his brother Aristobulus II.
67–63 B.C.E.	Aristobulus II king and High Priest. Taken prisoner by Pompey in 63.
63 B.C.E.	Pompey conquers Palestine. After fall of Jerusalem, Judaea becomes a Roman province.
63–40 B.C.E.	Hyrcanus II reinstated as High Priest but without royal title.
40–37 B.C.E.	Antigonus, son of Aristobulus II, occupies throne and pontificate with Parthian support. Hyrcanus II maimed and exiled (end of Hasmonean dynasty).
37 B.C.E.–4 C.E.	Herod the Great.
30 B.C.E.	Hyrcanus II executed.
27–14 B.C.E.	Augustus emperor.
?6 B.C.E.	Birth of Yeshua.
4 B.C.E.–6 C.E.	Archelaus ethnarch of Judaea and Samaria.
14–37 C.E.	Tiberius emperor.
26–36 C.E.	Pontius Pilate prefect of Judaea.
?30 C.E.	Yeshua crucified.

66–70 C.E.	First Jewish War ending with capture of Jerusalem and destruction of Temple under Titus.
73 or 74 C.E.	Fall of Masada.
132–135 C.E.	2nd Jewish Uprising led by Bar Kokhba. Jerusalem razed and rebuilt as Aelia Capitolina.
170 C.E.	Center of Jewish religious life moves to Galilee.

SUGGESTED FURTHER READING

ENGLISH TRANSLATIONS OF THE DEAD SEA SCROLLS

R. Eisenmann, M. Wise, *The Dead Sea Scrolls Uncovered*, Element Books (1992)

F. Garcia Martinez, *The Dead Sea Scrolls Translated*, Brill (1994)

G. Vermes, *The Complete Dead Sea Scrolls in English*, Penguin Books (1998)

GENERAL SECOND TEMPLE PERIOD BACKGROUND

E. Bickerman, *The Jews in the Greek Age*, Harvard University Press (1988)

S. Cohen, *From the Maccabees to the Mishnah*, Westminster Press (1989)

B. Ehrman, *The New Testament: A Historical Introduction to the Early Christian Writings*, Oxford University Press (2000)

R. Funk, R. Hoover and the Jesus Seminar, *The Five Gospels: What Did Jesus Really Say*, HarperCollins (1997)

Jewish Publication Society, *JPS Hebrew-English Tanakh*, Jewish Publication Society (1999)

E. Schürer, G. Vermes, F. Millar and M. Goodman, *The History of the Jewish People in the Age of Jesus Christ*, 3 Vols., Edinburgh University Press (1986)

T. Thompson, *The Bible in History: How Writers Create a Past,* Jonathan Cape (1999)

G.A. Williamson, trans., *Josephus: The Jewish War,* Penguin Books (1959)

J. Winston, trans., *Philo of Alexandria,* SPCK (1981)

THE SCROLLS AND THE COMMUNITY

M. Baigent and R. Leigh, *The Dead Sea Scrolls Deception,* Jonathan Cape (1991)

J. Campbell, *Deciphering the Dead Sea Scrolls,* Fontana (1996)

J. Collins, *Apocalypticism in the Dead Sea Scrolls,* Sheffield University Press (2000)

P.R. Davies, *Behind the Essenes: History and Ideology in the Dead Sea Scrolls,* Scholars Press (1987)

N. Golb, *Who Wrote the Dead Sea Scrolls?,* Michael O'Mara Books (1995)

J. Lefkovits, *The Copper Scroll: 3Q15 A New Appraisal,* Brill (2000)

F. Martinez and J. Barrera, *The People of the Dead Sea Scrolls: Their Writings, Beliefs and Practices,* Brill (1995)

L. Schiffman, *Reclaiming the Dead Sea Scrolls,* Doubleday (1995)

H. Stegemann, *The Library of Qumran: On the Essenes, Qumran, John the Baptist and Jesus,* Wm. Eerdman (1998)

G. Vermes, *An Introduction to the Complete Dead Sea Scrolls,* Penguin Books (1999)

A. Wilson and L. Wills, "Literary Sources of the Temple Scroll," *Harvard Theological Review,* Vol. 75 pp275–288 (1982)

THE SCROLLS AND CHRISTIANITY

J.H. Charlesworth, *Jesus and the Dead Dead Sea Scrolls,* Doubleday (1992)

R. Eisenman, *The Dead Sea Scrolls and the First Christians,* Element Books (1996)

R. Eisenman, *James, the Brother of Jesus*, Faber & Faber (1997)

J. Murphy-O'Connor, ed., *Paul and Qumran*, Crossroad (1968)

M.E. Stone and C.A. Chazon, eds., *Biblical Perspectives: Interpretation of the Bible in the Light of the Dead Sea Scrolls*, Brill (1998)

G. Vermes, *Jesus and the World of Judaism*, SCM Press (1983)

G. Vermes, *Jesus the Jew*, SCM Press (1983)

GLOSSARY

apocalyptic   a category of texts and their associated beliefs popular during the Second Temple period concerned with hidden truths, often concerning the future fate of the world, revealed to holy men either through visions or ascensions to the heavens.

Apocrypha   a class of scripture, "to be hidden away," not forming part of the accepted canon of the Bible; though mostly of Jewish origin, none are included in the Jewish Bible, but those appended to the various editions of the Christian Old Testament are thought to have been composed between 300 B.C.E. and 100 C.E.

Aramaic   a Semitic language of ancient Syria related to Hebrew; by the 6th century B.C.E., and especially during and after the Persian Empire period, it had been adopted as the lingua franca in much of the Middle East.

B.C.E.   Before Common Era—the non-sectarian way of refer-ring to B.C. dates.

C.E.   Common Era—the non-sectarian way of referring to A.D. dates.

canon   a collection of scriptures widely accepted within a religious group as authoritative and genuine.

concordance   a kind of index that alphabetically lists all the words occurring within a text, together with a citation of the phrase in which they occur.

dendrochronology   a system used by archaeologists for dating material derived from the sequence of annual tree rings from sections of wood with a known age.

eschatological   beliefs and expectations concerning the fate of the world and humanity, often linked with apocalyptic scriptures.

Essenes   an ancient Jewish ascetic movement known from the works of Josephus and Philo of Alexandria, thought by many scholars to have been the authors of the sectarian elements of the Dead Sea Scrolls.

Gentile   a term used in the ancient world by Christian and some Jewish writers to indicate the pagan populace in general.

geniza   a storeroom attached to a synagogue intended for the temporary storage of worn-out and discarded texts, usually of a religious nature, so that they may not be profaned in any way.

Gnosticism   a range of syncretic religious movements that emerged during the 1st–3rd centuries C.E., condemned by Christian orthodoxy as heretical. Their followers shared a common belief that they were an elite who alone had access to special knowledge of God and his intentions, and they often maintained that there were two divine beings, one who was evil and had created all that is material to imprison the pure spirit which had been created by a good and pure God.

havurah   a fellowship of pious Jews during the Second Temple Period who formed associations to aid a strict application of religious law and for mutual support.

Hellenism the eclectic fusion of Greek and Near Eastern culture that emerged following the conquests of Alexander the Greek; its pervasive influence in the ancient world can be seen as akin to the modern process of Americanization.

Hassidim the "Righteous Ones," a loose grouping of extremely pious Jews opposed to the compromises resulting from encroachment of Hellenism upon Jewish religious life. They emerged as a distinct group during the early years of the Maccabean uprising in which they seem to have initially participated although they may have withdrawn from military activities when the main religious objectives of the revolt had been achieved.

Iron Age a chronological division used by archaeologists for general dating purposes based on the introduction and use of iron in any given culture—this obviously varies according to the region but in the case of Palestine this conventionally covers a period beginning around 1000 B.C.E. and ending with the Persian period in 650 B.C.E.

liturgical anything related to the liturgy, the prescribed form and words used in public worship.

Messiah derived from the Hebrew term meaning "anointed one." In Jewish circles a Messiah was originally an anointed king, such as David, but in later times he was thought to be a superhuman agent of God who would appear during the Last Days to lead the righteous to victory over the forces of evil. Contrary to Christian beliefs, the expected Messiah was not considered by Jews to be divine, although some thought of him as a kind of pre-existing angelic being.

messianic any belief that focuses on the imminent arrival of a messiah figure; such beliefs were widespread during the latter years of the Second Temple period, but they died out after destruction of the Temple in Jerusalem and the failed Bar-Kokhba uprising, as no authentic messiah seemed to have appeared.

mysticism   a form of spiritual belief and practice by which a person seeks to achieve union with God or any other exalted state through contemplation and self-surrender, and who maintains that the comprehension of spiritual truths lies beyond normal understanding.

Nestorian   a Christian sect espousing the doctrinal position of Nestorius, a 5th-century Alexandrian patriarch; deemed heretical by Christian orthodoxy but was widespread and influential in the Middle and Far East until the Mongol invasions in medieval times.

ossuary   a receptacle, usually made of stone, used for storing bones; the use of ossuaries was necessitated by the late Second Temple period practice of disinterring and removing the remains of the deceased after they had been buried for a period to allow the flesh to rot away.

paleography   the study of ancient scripts and documents.

Pentateuch   the Greek name used in Christian circles for the Torah, the first five books of the Jewish Bible.

Pharisees   A religious group active in the Second Temple Period, their name derives from the Hebrew *perushim*—"the separated." They advocated a very strict interpretation and observance of the Torah that they thought should be applicable to all Jews from all walks of life, and thus developed a secondary set of religious laws, the Oral Law, as a protective bulwark around the written Torah. Their main religious rivals were the Sadducees with whom they disagreed in their interpretation of many areas of religious law. The Pharisees were the forerunners of the rabbis who eventually became the leaders of the Jewish community after the failed uprising of Simeon bar-Kokhba.

pseudepigrapha   a class of ancient Jewish religious writings whose authorship was ascribed to earlier prophets and patriarchs to lend them an air of authenticity and authority.

Sadducees   a numerically small but powerful religious group active in the mid to late Second Temple Period who functioned as priests in the Jerusalem Temple. Many Sadducees were pro-Hellenic in their outlook and were deemed to be very lax in their observation of religious law by their Pharisee rivals.

Sanhedrin   the highest Jewish council based in Jerusalem during the late Second Temple Period; had responsibility for religious, civil and judicial matters.

Scribes   a group of religious specialists who emerged alongside the Jerusalem temple priesthood during the early Second Temple Period. They were scholars whose task was to interpret the rules laid down in the Torah to which end they also developed and established the scriptures by studying and resolving potential problems in their exegesis and application.

Second Temple period   the period of Jewish history dating from the time of the construction of the second temple in Jerusalem after the return from the Babylonian exile in 516 B.C.E. until its destruction by the Romans during the Jewish Revolt of 66–70 C.E.

Septuagint   the Greek translation of the Jewish Bible, favored by the early Christian Church, produced in Alexandria traditionally by 70 Jewish scholars during the early Ptolomaic Egyptian period.

Talmud   the body of Jewish religious law and history developed and compiled by the early rabbis after the 4th century C.E.

Tanakh   the Hebrew name for the Jewish Bible, derived from the first letter of the three component parts: the *Torah* (Instructions), the *Nevi 'im* (Prophets) and the *Kethuvim* (Writings).

Torah   the Law as revealed by God to Moses; also the first
five books of the Jewish Bible—Genesis, Exodus, Leviticus,
Deuteronomy and Numbers—which contain an account of
these Laws and the events surrounding them.

Zoroastrianism   a Persian monotheistic religion founded by
the prophet Zoroaster in the 6th century B.C.E. which holds that
the supreme God Ahura Mazda created two twin spirits, one
good and one evil, associated with light and darkness respec-
tively. The human world is a battleground where these two
spirits struggle for control throughout the ages, although the
ultimate victory of goodness is assured by the expected intervention of Ahura Mazda. Beliefs of this religion were influential
in the formation of Second Temple Period Judaism and the rise
of Messianism and apocalypticism.

INDEX

Strugnell, John, 21, 23, 24, 25
Sukenik, Eleazar, 3, 4, 5, 19, 131
Syria, 35, 40, 41, 46, 49, 52, 58

Talmud, 120, 187
Tanakh (Jewish Bible), 9, 82–88,
    89, 100, 229
    apocrypha, 81–82
Tantlevskij, Igor, 208–10
Targums, 85
Teacher of Righteousness, xii,
    124–25, 127, 128, 130, 131,
    191, 199, 213, 217–18
    death, 118, 189, 200, 218
    identity, 205–206, 208, 209, 223
Teaching on the Two Spirits, 114–16
Temple of Solomon, 32, 104. See
    also Jerusalem Temple
Temple Scroll, 18, 75, 80, 102–105,
    216 225
Testament of Levi, 75, 99
Testament of Naphtali, 99–100
Testament of Qahar, 75
Testaments of the Twelve
    Patriarchs, 99
Testamonia, 71
Thanksgiving Hymns, 3–4, 75,
    130–31
Thessalonians, 227
Thiering, Barbara, xii, 205,
    207–208, 219, 223
Tiberias, 57
Timotheus I of Seleucia, 11–12, 17
Timotheus I, Patriarch of Baghdad,
    120
Titus, 8, 60, 150
Tobit, Book of, 82, 90
Torah, 34, 38, 82, 97, 102, 103,
    169
Tov, Emmanuel, 24–25
Trachonitis, 57

Tree rings, 73–74
Trever, John, 5
Triclinium, 147, 162
Tryphon, 44–45, 46
Turkey, 35
Twelve Minor Prophets, 88

Vatican, 14, 20–21, 24–25
Vermes, Geza, 76, 114, 117, 122,
    124, 131, 196
Vespasian, 8, 60

Wacholder, Ben Zion, 25
War Rule, 121
War Scroll, 3, 4, 108, 121–23, 181,
    191
Wicked Priest, xii, 107, 125, 127,
    128, 130, 202–205
    identity, 204–205, 206, 208
Wills, Lawrence, 102–103
Wilson, Andrew, 102–103
Wisdom literature, 89
Wisdom of Solomon, 81
Wisdom schools, 89–90
Wright-Baker, Professor, 23

Yadin, Yigael, 6, 18, 99, 102
Yahad, 164, 167. See also The
    Community
Yeshua (Jesus), x, xiii, 4, 123, 129,
    180, 181, 187, 208, 220–21
    and The Community, 206,
    223–29

Zaddok the Pharisee, 180
Zadok, 174, 204, 209, 218
Zadokite Fragments. See Damascus
    Document
Zealots, 59, 60, 152, 180–81, 218
Zerubbabel, 168
Zoroastrian religion, 32, 115

OTHER SEASTONE TITLES

THE GOSPEL OF THOMAS:
UNEARTHING THE LOST WORDS OF JESUS
John Dart & Ray Riegert   Introduction by John Dominic Crossan, $11.95
This accessible translation of The Gospel of Thomas allows readers to find a Jesus unadulterated by 2000 years of myth and interpretation—a strikingly different figure from the portrait in the New Testament.

THE HISTORICAL MARY: REVEALING THE PAGAN IDENTITY
OF THE VIRGIN MOTHER
Michael Jordan, $14.00
Based on fresh research of ancient Near Eastern, Jewish and early Christian texts, this book unravels the mystery of who Mary really was and what role she played in Jesus' life and ancient society.

JESUS AND MOSES: THE PARALLEL SAYINGS
Joey Green   Introduction by Rabbi Stewart Vogel, $19.00
Jesus and Moses presents the sayings of Jesus and the parallel teachings of Judaism found in the Old Testament, Talmud and other Jewish works. Hardback.

JESUS AND MUHAMMAD: THE PARALLEL SAYINGS
Joey Green, Editor   Foreword by Dr. Sayyid M. Syeed
Introduction by Dr. Kenneth Atkinson, $14.00
Jesus and Muhammad presents, for the first time, parables of Jesus and the parallel ethical teachings of Muhammad. This book clearly shows that the core values of Christianity—love, compassion, peace, forgiveness and repentance—match the central tenets of Islam.

THE LOST GOSPEL Q: THE ORIGINAL SAYINGS OF JESUS
Marcus Borg, Editor   Introduction by Thomas Moore, $11.95
The sayings within this book represent the very first Gospel. Here is the original Sermon on the Mount, the Lord's Prayer and Beatitudes. Reconstructed by biblical historians, Q provides a window into the world of ancient Christianity.

THE LOST SUTRAS OF JESUS: UNLOCKING THE ANCIENT WISDOM OF THE XIAN MONKS

Edited by Ray Riegert & Thomas Moore, $18.00

Combining the amazing story of the writing of the sutras, their disappearance and rediscovery and an exploration of their message, *The Lost Sutras of Jesus* is a fascinating historical journey. It is also a unique spiritual quest into the heart of Jesus' teachings and the essence of Eastern religion. Hardback.

MUSIC OF SILENCE: A SACRED JOURNEY THROUGH THE HOURS OF THE DAY

David Steindl-Rast & Sharon Lebell   Introduction by Kathleen Norris, $12.00

A noted Benedictine monk shows us how to incorporate the sacred meaning of monastic life into our everyday world by paying attention to the "seasons of the day" and the enlivening messages to be found in each moment.

12 TRIBES, 10 PLAGUES & THE 2 MEN WHO WERE MOSES: A HISTORICAL JOURNEY INTO BIBLICAL TIMES

Graham Phillips, $14.95

From the Exodus and the ten plagues of Egypt to the conquest of Canaan and the battle between David and Eshbaal at the Pool of Gibeon, this book shows that many fascinating Old Testament stories can in fact be scientifically corroborated.

To order these books call 800-377-2542 or 510-601-8301, fax 510-601-8307, e-mail ulysses@ulyssespress.com, or write to Ulysses Press, P.O. Box 3440, Berkeley, CA 94703. All retail orders are shipped free of charge. California residents must include sales tax. Allow two to three weeks for delivery.

ABOUT THE AUTHOR

Stephen Hodge is a researcher and writer who specializes in ancient and Oriental religions and theology. He graduated from the School of Oriental and African Studies, did M.A. research in Japan and teaches at the University of London. He is the author of *The World of Zen, The Illustrated Tibetan Book of the Dead*, and the *Piatkus Guide to Tibetan Buddhism*. He lives in London.